ANTHONY BURGESS

MODERN LITERATURE SERIES

GENERAL EDITOR: Philip Winsor

In the same series:

(continued on last page of book)

ANTHONY BURGESS

Samuel Coale

FREDERICK UNGAR PUBLISHING CO.
NEW YORK

Copyright © 1981 by Frederick Ungar Publishing Co., Inc.
Printed in the United States of America
Design by Anita Duncan

Library of Congress Cataloging in Publication Data

Coale, Samuel.
    Anthony Burgess.

    (Modern literature series)
    Bibliography: p.
    Includes index.
    1. Burgess, Anthony, 1917- . 2. Authors,
English--20th century--Biography.   I. Title.
II. Series: Modern literature monographs.
PR6052.U638Z57   823'.914 [B]   81-40459
ISBN 0-8044-2124-2   AACR2

Acknowledgments

For their cheerful typing and correcting of this manuscript, I would like to thank the secretaries and computer wizards at Wheaton College: Nancy Shepardson, Alice Peterson, Kathy Francis, and Lynne Damien. I would also like to thank Beverly Clark for proofreading the manuscript so carefully and doggedly. And I remain grateful to Wheaton for assisting me with travel and research grants to get to Monaco to interview Anthony Burgess. And to Philip Winsor for his meticulous attention to details and to the book as a whole. His carefully itemized letters were immensely helpful to me in revising the manuscript and reveal the mark of a dedicated and thorough editor. Of course, none of this would have been possible without Burgess's fine body of fiction. His long and extensive series of interviews with me were splendid, as we gazed from his balconies to cast a sardonic eye on the contemporary world below us. I will treasure—and perform— the pieces for piano that he wrote for me.

*To Emma Gray, of course,
and Samuel Chase Coale, VI*

Contents

Chronology

1917	25 February: John Anthony Burgess Wilson born in Manchester, England, to Joseph and Elizabeth Burgess Wilson.
1918	Mother and only sister die in influenza epidemic.
1923–1940	Attends and is graduated from the Bishop Bilsborrow School and Xaverian College in Manchester. Writes his honors thesis on Christopher Marlowe at Manchester University and is graduated with a B.A. degree in English literature.
1940	October: Joins the Army. First placed in the Army Medical Corps, then shifted to the Army Educational Corps.
1942	Marries Llewela Isherwood Jones, a Welsh student at Manchester University. She is assaulted by American deserters. Her unborn child is killed.
1943–1946	Serves on Gibraltar as a training college lecturer in Speech and Drama. Promoted to Sergeant Major.
1946–1948	Becomes a member of the Central Advisory Council for Adult Education in the Armed Forces. Lectures at Birmingham University.
1948–1950	Serves as a lecturer in phonetics for the Ministry of Education in Preston, Lancashire. Also teaches drama and English literature.
1950–1954	Teaches English literature, phonetics, Spanish, and music at the Banbury Grammar School in Oxfordshire.

1954–1957	Becomes an education officer for the Colonial Service and teaches as the Senior Lecturer in English at the Malayan Teachers Training College in Kahta Baru, Malaya. In 1956 publishes *Time for a Tiger*.
1957–1959	Continues as an education officer for the Colonial Service as an English Language Specialist in Brunei, Borneo. Publishes *The Enemy in the Blanket* in 1958 and *Beds in the East* in 1959.
1959	Is rushed to a neurological institute in London with a possible brain tumor. Moves to an apartment in Hove, near Sussex.
1960	Publishes *The Doctor Is Sick* and *The Right to an Answer*.
1961	Publishes *Devil of a State and* One Hand Clapping, under the pseudonym, Joseph Kell, and *The Worm and the Ring*, which is withdrawn because of a libel suit. Takes a vacation to Leningrad with his wife.
1962	Publishes *A Clockwork Orange* and *The Wanting Seed*.
1963	Publishes *Honey for the Bears* and *Inside Mr. Enderby*, under the pseudonym, Joseph Kell.
1964	August: son Andrew is born to Burgess and Liliana Macellari, a linguist at Cambridge. Publishes *The Eve of St. Venus*, *Language Made Plain*, and *Nothing Like the Sun*.
1965	Publishes *Here Comes Everybody*, *A Vision of Battlements*, *ReJoyce*, and *The Long Day Wanes* (his first three novels published together).
1966	Publishes *Tremor of Intent*.
1967	Publishes *The Novel Now*.
1968	20 March: Llewela Wilson dies of cirrhosis. In October marries Liliana Macellari. Publishes *Urgent Copy*, *Enderby Outside*, and *Enderby* (which contains both *Inside Mr. Enderby* and *Enderby Outside*). Leaves England for good and moves to Malta.
1969–1970	Writer-in-Residence at the University of North Carolina in Chapel Hill. Moves to a house in Bracciano, Italy and an apartment in Rome. Publishes *Shakespeare*.

1970–1971	Teaches creative writing at both Princeton and Columbia. Translation of Rostand's "Cyrano de Bergerac" performed at the Summer Festival of the Tyrone Guthrie Theatre in Minneapolis. Publishes *MF*.
1972–1973	Distinguished Professor of English at City College in New York. Publishes *Joysprick*.
1974	Publishes *Napoleon Symphony*.
1975	October: his third symphony performed in Iowa City. Publishes *The Clockwork Treatment or Enderby's End*. Moves to Monte Carlo, Monaco.
1976	Publishes *Beard's Roman Women* and *Moses: A Narrative*.
1977	Publishes *Abba Abba*.
1978	Publishes *1985* and *Ernest Hemingway and His World*.
1979	Publishes *Man of Nazareth*.
1980	Publishes *Earthly Powers*.

1

••

The Catholic Exile

John Anthony Burgess Wilson was born in Manchester, England, a big cotton-mill city in the British Midlands, on February 25, 1917. He was the son of Joseph and Elizabeth Burgess Wilson. His father was a cinema and pub pianist, perhaps not unlike the father of Richard Ennis in *A Vision of Battlements*, Burgess's first and most autobiographical novel: "He was a very fine pianist. I associate him with big pounding chords on the piano; the piano used to stagger with the force of them . . . he always gave that impression. Massiveness, you know." When Burgess was less than a year old, Burgess's father came home one day and found his mother and sister "dead in the same room and myself on the bed, alive."[1] They were victims of the disastrous influenza epidemic at the end of the war. Since Burgess never knew his mother, he remembers her only as others had described her, the "Beautiful Belle Burgess," a singer and dancer in the music hall in Manchester. Richard Ennis describes his mother as "a very Junoesque woman, though she was billed for a time, in her early days, that is, as The Blonde Venus . . . A fair voice, too, I always thought. We are a very musical family."

Joseph Wilson remarried Maggie Byrnes, an Irish widow. She had married into the Dwyer family in Manchester, whose present claim to fame is the archbishop of Birmingham, George Dwyer. Together the Wilsons ran a large pub, called The Golden Eagle, on Lodge Street. According to Burgess

1

the pub contained three singing rooms with a piano in each, and the Eagle was open from six in the morning until midnight. There was always a "colossal lot to drink."

Burgess's Irish background is formidable. His father's mother, Mary Ann Finnegan, was Irish, and his grandfather was half Irish. His mother had no living relatives. Burgess declared that "I'm probably three-fourths Irish and one-fourth something else, whatever it is." Mary Ann Finnegan was "imported" from Ireland to Manchester, thus participating in the long and troubled process of Irish emigration.

Burgess is very aware of and sensitive about his Irish background, particularly in terms of his relationship with England: "Throughout the history of my family, such as it is, and throughout my own career, I've always been aware of this inability on my own part, and the part of my own people, to come to terms with the Protestant establishment in England." To be "a cradle Catholic with Irish blood" ultimately brands you as "a renegade to the outside." Protestant England comes to represent a certain class, a certain preoccupation with old universities and public schools, and a certain language and attitude from which the Irish Catholic is excluded. Already in his childhood, a sensitive and creative boy like Burgess felt a sense of exile: "That's something I'd still like to work out in fiction, in a piece of autobiographical fiction." The family legend of there being a martyr in the Elizabethan era, "somebody who refused to accept the Protestant establishment and was actually executed," certainly added fuel to Burgess's childhood feelings.

Irish emigration certainly familiarized the Irish with "the exile's road."[2] By 1825 there were already 35,000 Irish in Manchester alone, and a sign in a shop window read succinctly, "No coloured, no Irish." In the 1840s 18,000 Irish were crammed into the cellars and tenements of Manchester's Little Ireland. As late as 1951 large clusters of Irish still remained in separate quarters of the city. By 1891 fourteen percent of the British Army were Irish. Viewed

as outsiders and suspected of everything from the most
drunken indolence to the most incendiary violence, the Irish
clustered around such tenets of faith as the sacred homeland
and the Catholic church. According to one historian, "the
Irish publican provided a haven of refuge and a convivial
Irish atmosphere,"[3] and he or she "became the leaders of
their people . . . gave their parlours for mass and their sons
to the priesthood."[4] Burgess's description of the Dwyer family
seems to fit the historical record:

The Dwyers, a very Irish family, were one of those interesting Irish
families that had settled in Manchester, a lot of them, Catholic, ran
a green grocery business and were determined to shove their kids
into the priesthood. George very quickly became Monsignor and
was in charge of missionary services, and then at length became
Bishop of Leeds and finally the Archbishop, which is what they
wanted, which is what the family was after.

In the nineteenth century, particularly at the height of
England's global power, the 1860s to the 1890s, the racial
mystique of Anglo-Saxonism prospered. Anglo-Saxons were
thought to be extremely self-reliant, self-disciplined, and self-
controlled. At all times and in all things they exhibited
restraint, moderation, balance, and an upright, unquestioned
morality. From the Anglo-Saxon point of view, the Celt, and
particularly the Irish, was the antithesis of this Victorian,
manly ideal. "Wild Paddy" was passionate, dirty, violent,
brutal, indolent and intemperate. Matthew Arnold firmly
believed that "the Celt was a prisoner of his own emotions,"[5]
a sentimental soul clearly at odds with the English and
Germanic qualities of hard work and orderly pursuit. Lord
Macaulay in *The History of England* believed that the Irish
"had the susceptibility, the vivacity, the natural turn for
acting and rhetoric which are indigenous on the shores of the
Mediterranean Sea."[6] It is clear that, in English eyes, the
Irish played Mr. Hyde to their Anglo-Saxon Dr. Jekyll. And
one British Colonial, having served twenty years in India,
defined the English attitude as one similar to Prospero's in
Shakespeare's *The Tempest*. The Prospero complex involved

the Anglo-Saxon ideal of authority, order, and service, which
viewed all others outside the pale as inferiors in both race
and class, children in search of a great white father to guide
and teach them.[7] This northern European "predisposition to
identify darker peoples with their own darker impulses"[8]
extended to the Irish as well, and the English attitude toward
the Irish in general certainly affected the childhood feelings
and attitudes of Anthony Burgess. "You're pretty well formed
by your childhood, aren't you?" Burgess admitted.

From the British perspective, to be Irish was to be a
Catholic; the two were virtually inseparable. Catholicism was
the national religion of Ireland. During his childhood Burgess
remained a devout Catholic. He attended the Bishop Bils-
borrow School and Xaverian College in Manchester. He also
displayed a definite musical and artistic talent in that he took
violin lessons, taught himself how to play the piano at
fourteen, wrote musical compositions, wrote stories, and
painted. Doubts, however, crept in. At fifteen he came upon
The Portrait of the Artist as a Young Man by James Joyce,
and was "so horrified by the sermon on hell" in that book
"that I was scared back into the church." He "almost picked
it up with tongs and shoved it in the fire." In one of his
critical works on Joyce, *ReJoyce* (1968), Burgess still remembered that initial confrontation with his favorite writer:
"I still find it difficult to read the hell-chapter without some
of the sense of suffocation I felt when I first met it . . .
myself a Catholic looking for emancipation. I was hurled
back into conformity by this very sermon and this very
vision."[9] Still, at sixteen he managed to sneak the two-volume
Odyssey Press Edition of *Ulysses* into England, "cut up into
sections and distributed all over the body."[10] When he was
seventeen and in the sixth form at Xaverian College, the
discussion of the Reformation by an Irish Catholic history
master seemed to him very convincing. He read more about
it, wrote a play on Luther, and finally stopped going to church
altogether: "I used to go out in the morning on Sunday
morning and say I was going to mass, but actually sit in the

park or something like that." Yet when Burgess joined the Army in October, 1940, he declared himself a Catholic, and his three years in Gibraltar decided "that whatever I did about it, I was still Catholic."

The influence of Catholicism on Burgess's life, outlook, and fiction remains overwhelming. Burgess declared that "the novels I've written are really medieval Catholic in their thinking,"[11] and that "it is very doubtful whether any novel, however trivial, can possess any vitality without an implied set of values derived from religion."[12] This medieval Catholic set of values remains complicated, confused somewhat by Burgess's declaring himself a lapsed and no longer practicing Catholic, but there are certain beliefs and attitudes that have remained with him since his childhood in Manchester.

Chief among the beliefs from Burgess's Catholic heritage is his belief in the Eucharist, the Mass. For him "this representation of a sacrificial death and the resurrection" remains a "great source of inspiration, of refreshment." It is "the still center" of his faith, around which all else revolves. Other dogmatic tenets of the faith may have slipped away, but "one can't throw away the Eucharist quite so easily. And of course this was Joyce's situation." Burgess abhorred the reformed Mass, relishing instead the traditional Latin Mass: "I was horrified by the turning of the altar around for a start. It was like a butcher's shop; the man was preparing some meat. . . . Once you can allow this, once you can allow your priest to go around in flamboyant neckties, that's the end."

Burgess's love of and respect for the Eucharist revealed his love of structure and form in general. He was attracted to rituals, ceremonies, and myths. These appear constantly in his novels. He once admitted that "a novelist who's brought up as a Catholic is interested in structuralism."[13] As a novelist he would like to be remembered as one "hoping to save some aspects of a literary form which I think is extremely valuable." He admired the ritualistic narratives of fairy tales, the way in which they reveal "a fulfillment of a moral law." Even language partakes of this love of ritual and ceremony:

"It's a ritual-making device. It's a ritual-making process
. . . it is in the ritual that opposites are reconciled . . . In
Joyce it is all ritual. It's a substitute for the Mass all the way
through." Language as a sacrament in its own right both
upholds and creates the fictions and forms with which Burgess
so readily experimented.

Like St. Augustine Burgess believed in the general
depravity of mankind. Original Sin and moral evil are for
him synonymous descriptions of the human condition. He
has declared that English Catholics are "earnest and obsessed
with sin. We really absorbed hell, perhaps a very Nordic
notion."[14] All belief in man's perfectibility, in progress, and
in human rationality suggest the purest heresy. Man is
plagued with guilt for all of his actions and thoughts. For
Burgess "guilt's a good thing . . . It's when you get rid of this
very human quality of guilt that you lose a great deal of
humanity." And yet this sin-stained, guilt-ridden creature is
both blessed and cursed with the free will to act and choose
on his own. "This capacity to choose is the big human
attribute,"[15] Burgess declared. Determinism or behaviorism
in any form is wrong, a dodging of human and personal
responsibilities.

Burgess shared St. Paul's vision of man's life as a
struggle between opposites, the extreme opposites of heaven
and hell, good and evil, spirit and flesh. These opposites
form the moral center of his fiction and his personal vision.
His concept of good and evil is far more morally absolute
than are the common ethical beliefs in right and wrong. What
can be right in terms of a political, legal or social code can
be morally evil in a wider spiritual perspective. Burgess
declared, "There is a good beyond ethical good which is
always existential: there is the essential good, that aspect of
God which we can prefigure more in the taste of an apple or
the sound of music than in mere right action or even
charity."[16] It is man's fate to choose what is good in the
privacy of his conscience rather than to go along merely with
what is ethically right at the moment. And it is the duty of

Burgess's art to reveal and explore that primary conflict, particularly in our materialistic age of conspicuous consumption.

Being a lapsed Catholic was not easy for Burgess: "The position of standing on the periphery is one that I share with many men of good will; the state of being a lapsed Catholic is so painful that it sometimes seems to generate a positive charge, as though it has in itself a certain religious validity."[17] Burgess left the church early in his life, almost as much for aesthetic as for personal and doctrinal reasons. He was, in fact, drawn to the austere and fundamentalist customs of Islam, a far cry from the "debased Baroque, debased Rococo" of the Catholic churches in Manchester, "the small church with its incense, with its horrible little paintings and horrible little statues . . . Then you welcome the congregationalist aspect, the bare church, with a little wind blowing through." The revisions made by the Second Vatican Council in the Catholic form of worship did not bring Burgess any closer to his childhood religion. He felt that the church had shed its universal language, Latin, and its intellectual dignity. "Now the church dithers, becomes liberal." It had had a basic core of faith: "This is what we teach. Take it or leave it. Nobody's forcing you to take it. You can leave it if you like. This is the point about birth control. This is the point about homosexuality." In Burgess's mind the liberal ditherings of the church irredeemably debased its form and content. Burgess still believed that "duality is the ultimate reality,"[18] that the world is in effect a "duoverse," made up of oppositions. Life for him "is binary,"[19] but it is no longer his belief that spirit will necessarily overcome the flesh, good conquer evil, and heaven replace hell. Good and evil, spirit and flesh, have so interpenetrated one another in the modern world that it is no longer possible to separate them. This Manichean outlook, along with the tenets of Burgess's lapsed Catholic faith, we will examine more completely when we discuss the novels.

Attracted by the "Catholic quality" and the "tremendous

flood of guilt" in the life and works of Christopher Marlowe, Burgess wrote his thesis on Marlowe at Manchester University. At that time in 1940, he recalled that "the bombs were dropping. The Nazis were overhead . . . so literature then wasn't a pretty game. You were tied up with the matter of life and death."

Burgess was graduated with honors from the University and in October of that year joined the army. He first was placed in the Army Medical Corps, but then was shifted to the Army Education Corps. His real interest was the Intelligence Corps, and he did manage to do some intelligence work under the banner of the Educational Corps in Spain. That occurred between 1943 and 1946, when he spent three years at Gibraltar as a training college lecturer in Speech and Drama. He was promoted finally to sergeant major, became the musical director of a special services unit, and got involved in the secret exchange of money on mainland Spain, keeping good money out of the hands of the Nazis. He was also assigned for a brief time as a sergeant to the asylum for the General Paralysis of the Insane in Winwick, Warrington, Lancashire. During the war the asylum accommodated Emergency Military Sections (not necessarily mental cases), and he dealt with cases of aphasia, in some instances teaching senior officers to relearn the alphabet and read. In 1942 he married a Welsh fellow student at the University, Llewela Isherwood Jones.

Burgess's induction into the army in 1940 was to lead to nearly twenty years of service as a teacher: in the army, in a grammar school, and in the Colonial Service in Malaya and Borneo. For two years after he left the army (1946–48) he became a member of the Central Advisory Council for Adult Education in the Armed Forces. In the Midlands and at Birmingham University, "they'd started expanding the Royal Army Educational Corps . . . in order to give vocational training and some non-vocational training to soldiers, sailors, and the rest of it whose demobilization was delayed." Burgess helped to run command schools for training instructors: "It was frightening, because the instructors we had were too young. We spent two years trying to equip them with the minimal technique for teaching elementary schools."

From 1948 to 1950 Burgess served as a lecturer in phonetics for the Ministry of Education in Preston, Lancashire. Since there was a severe shortage of teachers at the time, the old army camps were turned into residential training centers for people who wanted to join the teaching profession. "We gave them a compressed thirteen-month course in teaching. I taught speech and drama and English and literature."

The most important event during that time for Burgess was the writing of his first novel, *A Vision of Battlements*. He had been busy composing a piano sonata, a concerto for percussion and two pianos, and orchestral incidental music for *Murder in the Cathedral*, *The Aspect of F6*, and *The Adding Machine*, but during his Easter vacation in 1949, he began to write:

Could I, for good or ill, compose an extended piece of prose without getting bored? There was another, submerged motive for writing, and that was to see if I could clear my head of the dead weight of Gibraltar. I had lived with it so long that it still lay in my skull, a chronic migraine: a work of fiction seemed the best way of breaking it up, pulverising it, sweeping it away . . . the pain and loneliness that refused to be exorcised.[20]

In the novel he used an epic framework, as a tribute to Joyce, in his effort to tame the Rock, "an emblem of waste and loneliness."[21] On his way to the Colonial Office in London, Burgess stopped off at the William Heinemann publishing offices—"who'd expressed a desire to see me"—and showed them his novel: "They said they liked this novel but could not publish it as a first novel. They felt it was a second novel." *A Vision of Battlements* was not published until 1965 as Burgess's fifteenth published work of fiction.

Burgess continued to teach English, literature, phonetics, Spanish and music at the Banbury Grammar School in Oxfordshire from 1950 to 1954. The pay of teachers continued to be very low—"this was the beginning of Socialist England"—and he again attempted a novel. The book, based on his experiences at the school, was called *The Worm and the Ring*. It was eventually published in 1961 but was quickly withdrawn from circulation because of a libel suit from persons connected with the school.

Burgess enjoyed teaching, but he was restless and poor. Finally, he applied for a job on the Isle of Sark, one of the Channel Islands. He didn't realize that, of all the islands in the world, Sark was the one place that would not allow a collie bitch. He and his wife had a collie bitch. Nevertheless, fate had taken a hand, and if Burgess is to be believed, it was quite by accident:

I must have got drunk on Saturday evening and applied for a job in a Malayan School and forgot about it and posted the letter drunk. Then I was summoned to the Colonial Office, and I thought I was being summoned for this job in Sark. They sort of looked at me open-mouthed: "Since when have the Channel Islands been under the Colonial Office?" But then quite accidentally I was given this job in Malaya as an Education Officer.

Burgess and his wife sold everything, and from 1954 to 1957 he taught as the Senior Lecturer in English at the Malayan Teachers Training College in Kahta Baru. "I was associated with the liberation movement\ there, a kind of revolutionary movement." The clash between various cultures and religions, which he had already observed and written about in his unpublished first novel, continued to fascinate him on a grander scale. "It enabled me to write. I got a bit of leisure and a bit of money."

At the age of thirty-nine in 1956 he published his first novel, *Time for a Tiger*, with William Heinemann in London. It was at this time, too, that he chose his two middle names to use as his published name: "The real reason was that I started publishing when I was in the Civil Service overseas, and you were not allowed to use your name if you were writing anything of a frivolous nature, like fiction . . . It was recommended strongly, indeed it was enjoined, that I use

another name." This proved to be the first novel in his trilogy
about Malaya, and the other two novels soon followed : *The
Enemy in the Blanket* in 1958 and *Beds in the East* in 1959.
These were well received in England. The novelist had been
officially born.

Burgess moved on to Brunei in Borneo as an English
Language Specialist in 1957. While there he began two more
novels, *The Right to an Answer*, which he finished in 1960
and published that same year, and *Devil of a State*, which
was published in 1961. And then, apparent disaster struck.
He'd complained of headaches in Brunei, but with no real
worry about them. One day he collapsed in his Brunei
classroom: "I was just finished and I couldn't go on, so fed
up and so bored. They were only too glad to get me onto a
stretcher, show me into hospital, and diagnose a possible
tumor on the brain. God knows how they do that." Burgess
wondered if the diagnosis could have had something to do
with his being friendly with certain revolutionary leaders.

Burgess was immediately recalled to England for a series
of tests at the neurological institute in London.

The first thing they do is give you a spinal tap. It is pretty
unpleasant. You feel the whole vertebrae structure collapsing . . .
They said there's probably a tumor or some kind of growth, which
we can't see, which the instruments themselves aren't able to show
us. It may be masked by living tissue or something. So the thing
to do is to discharge you and give you a year to live.

Discharged from the hospital he and his wife took a flat
in Hove near Sussex on the south coast of England. They had
no furniture and no books; almost everything had been left
in Brunei. They were virtually penniless. Burgess couldn't
teach, especially "if I've got a year to live. So I wrote and
I didn't feel too bad. I couldn't really believe I was going to
die, so I just got down to write with great pleasure." He
wrote, as was his custom, two pages of typescript a day,
rewriting each page until it was exactly what he wanted.
When the book was complete, there was no need to revise

it again. His productivity was prodigious. He completed *The Right to an Answer* and in the latter part of 1959, wrote *The Doctor Is Sick*. *Inside Mr. Enderby* was written between January and April of 1960, *The Wanting Seed* during the same period and into the summer, and *One Hand Clapping* between November and December. It was his intention to get them out and published as soon as possible to leave some money for his ailing wife. The first two were published in 1960; *One Hand Clapping* and *Inside Mr. Enderby*, under the pseudonym, Joseph Kell, were published in 1961 and 1963 respectively; and *The Wanting Seed* came out in 1962.

From 1959 until his wife's death in 1968 Burgess maintained his flat in Hove and acquired a second one in Chiswick in the West End of London. He didn't die after his year to live, and no medical explanation has ever been forthcoming. The diagnosis of a tumor was obviously mistaken. Yet he wrote as if death were imminent. Novels spilled out of him as if he couldn't get them down on paper fast enough. A trip to Leningrad in 1961—"My first wife and I were in the wise habit of taking holidays . . . there she was taken ill . . . she collapsed in the street and was shoved into the hospital"—led directly to *Honey for the Bears*, published in 1963, and indirectly to his most famous work, *A Clockwork Orange*, published in 1962. More novels followed: *Nothing Like the Sun*, his biographical novel about Shakespeare, in 1964; *The Eve of St. Venus*, once the libretto for an opera back in 1953, now published in 1964 as a comic spoof of the elaborately written plays of Christopher Fry; *Tremor of Intent*, his cold-war spy novel, in 1966; and *Enderby Outside*, the last novel written while he was still in England, in 1968. At the same time books of nonfiction appeared, along with reviews, articles, columns, and occasional pieces: *The Novel Now* in 1963, *Language Made Plain* in 1964, *Here Comes Everybody* in 1965, *ReJoyce* in 1968, and *Urgent Copy* in 1968. Thus, by 1968, before he left England for good, Burgess had managed to write twenty-two books, including seventeen novels and five works of literary criticism.

Many basic themes from these years of his life show up again and again in Burgess's novels. For one thing he felt himself to be an exile now even more deeply than he had felt it as a child in Manchester. He believed that because of the empire, "it is usually the fate of Englishmen to be in exile" and that "going into exile . . . is a very easy process." But he felt it more keenly in the years after Malaya and Borneo:

If anybody's been abroad—of course, Kipling must have had this feeling, when Kipling got back to England—these were his kind, but at the same time, they knew nothing of his experiences . . . of what it was like to live in India. And anybody who's been abroad must feel that. What kind of television do you have in the Borneo jungle? This was the kind of question they asked . . . I came back with a university degree in the Malayan language. It's been no use to me since, and who the hell is interested in Malay? . . . It's of no use to me now . . .

Like his hero, Joyce, before him, Burgess transformed his exile's perspective into art: "Exile was the artist's stepping back to see more clearly and so draw more accurately; it was the only means . . ."[22]

Burgess announced the conflict between individual free will and collective forces, such as the state and society, as "the big theme of the future." For him all hierarchies and bureaucracies oppose the essential moral order and truth of the individual man. The enemies in his novels turn out to be bureaucracies of all kinds: the hierarchies of hospitals, armies, universities, and the state. These masked their true intentions of depriving the individual soul of choice and free will with heretical arguments about determinism and duty. Burgess hadn't spent twenty years amid incarnations of the modern state for nothing.

Burgess also opposed the "new values" of the modern world, a world of the culture of consumerism and materialism, most closely allied with Americanization. He railed against the infatuation with technique, the idea and novelty of change as an end in itself, the self-indulgence and immediate gratification of sensual stimulation and consumer events, and

the participatoriness of the media and society.[23] In the East
he could see the decay and dissatisfaction beneath the glitter
and speed of pop culture. He disapproved of the Americanization of British culture as well as the socialized, secular
communization of much of the rest of the world.

On the first day of spring, March 20, 1968, Llewela
Jones Wilson died of cirrhosis of the liver. She had always
been a heavy drinker, had attempted suicide as far back as
1960, and had been an invalid for many years. One of
Burgess's bibliographers discovered that she had been attacked and assaulted by American deserters in 1942, an
assault which killed her unborn child and which "contributed
to her death in 1968."[24] Her death allowed Burgess to marry
Liliana Macellari in October of that same year. She was in
the linguistics department at Cambridge and, among other
things, had translated Thomas Pynchon's *V.* into Italian. She
and Burgess had been together since 1963, and she had
borne him a son, Andrew, in August of 1964. The liaison
filled Burgess with guilt and was "kept absolutely quiet
. . . It was very, very clandestine." They lived openly
together from about April 1968. After their wedding in
October, they left England, for the most part to escape the
increased taxation of the welfare state—"It's terrible to live
nowadays. You cannot live without cheating the state"—and
found a house in Malta.

Since 1968 Burgess and his wife have, more or less,
been on the move. Burgess spoke out against the repressive
regime in Malta, and he and Liliana finally had to leave.
They moved into a house by the lake in Bracciano in Italy
and had an apartment in Rome in the Piazza Santa Cecilia,
"which we gave up because of the massive increase in
violence and robbery." They lived in Siena for a time, in
Montalbuccio, in Eze, in Callian, and finally rented a fourth-
floor apartment overlooking one of the main thoroughfares in
Monaco. During the academic year of 1969–70, Burgess
served as the writer in residence at the University of North
Carolina in Chapel Hill. He went on to teach creative writing

at both Princeton and Columbia in 1970–71 and followed this as a Distinguished Professor of English at City College in New York during 1972–73. In 1971 his adaptation and translation of Rostand's "Cyrano de Bergerac" was performed at the Summer Festival of the Tyrone Guthrie Theatre in Minneapolis, complete with music he had composed for the occasion. In October of 1975 his third symphony was performed in Iowa City by the Iowa University orchestra under the direction of James Dixon. He continued to write at a much slower pace given all the academic and public duties. *MF*, his structuralist novel, written in Malta and Rome between 1969 and 1970, was published in 1971; *Napoleon Symphony*, his lyrical verbal symphony based on Beethoven's Eroica, written in Rome between 1972 and 1974, appeared in print in 1974. These were followed by *The Clockwork Testament or Enderby's End* in 1975, *Beard's Roman Women* in 1976, *Abba Abba* in 1977, *1985* in 1978, *Man of Nazareth* in 1979, and *Earthly Powers* in 1980. Recent literary critical biographies include *Shakespeare* in 1970 and *Ernest Hemingway and His World* in 1978.

At present Burgess's life is filled with writing novels, screenplays, television scripts, film and television musical scores, and an endless stream of reviews and articles and columns. In the hallway of his Monaco "atelier" stands a Xerox machine to keep up with the flow of writing that comes from him daily. He is an enthusiastic, extremely articulate, and knowledgeable man with a swirl of long, bushy, gray-brownish hair like some mad poet. The comic sense of the novels is immediately apparent in the man himself, as he talks joyously and eagerly of future projects, current delights, and past encounters. The rooms are filled with books, tape recorders, tables piled with manuscripts and papers, as if he'd just been interrupted in some massive task of unpacking or rearranging. Above the desk in his small study are a photograph of Stonehenge and an autographed picture of Sophia Loren. He lives as though he's about to move on, caught in midsentence, still an exile above the sparkling

wide windows of Monaco, winking with jewelry and reflecting
the mammoth yachts in the harbor. Liliana is at his side,
buxom and bubbling. She edits, translates, and acts as her
husband's literary agent. They seem dependent upon one
another, close, and dedicated to the literary arts with an
ardent Renaissance fervor.

Monaco is a long way from Manchester, but only the
places have changed. The man's observations on the world
at large and the individual's place in it still partake of that
Catholic upbringing in the industrial Midlands city. The exile
triumphs: "Nobody lives in England. No Englishman lives
in England. We leave that to Americans and other foreigners.
Englishmen go back to England to die."

2

●●●

The Clash of East and West

The experiences of Anthony Burgess when he served in outposts of the declining British empire—Borneo (1957–1960), Malaya (1954–1957), and in particular, Gibraltar (1943–46)—shaped and sharpened his instincts as a budding novelist. From his position within the British colonial hierarchy, he was able to look out upon strange worlds and cultures that conflicted with one another. In both Borneo and Malaya he saw the clash among the British colonial powers, Malays, Chinese, Tamils, Sikhs, Bengalis, and Eurasians. In Gibraltar, which he had called "the prototype"[1] of these cultural clashes, he observed the clash among British rule, Spanish Catholicism, and the remains of Islam. What could be a "stranger mixture," he wrote, than the sight in Gibraltar all at once of "Catholic baroque, the onion domes and the barley-sugar columns of the Moors, the soft and fickle humanism of the British?"[2]

At home in England as a Catholic, Burgess had always felt one step removed from the established order. This sense of being an exile in his own homeland clearly intensified the way in which he viewed the clash of cultures in Gibraltar, Malaya, and Borneo. These cultural clashes obviously reflected the feelings and experiences of his childhood and adolescence in England.

Yet, to Burgess it seemed that out of these divergent cultures and religions, the British had brought a certain amount of stability and order. Out of the clash of cultural

17

opposites was forged a new, if always volatile, confluence of cultures. In Gibraltar amid "the current of opposing traditions" and "the community-forging British," Burgess realized that for him "this colonial image of order [was] itself a kind of work of art."[3]

> I learned from Gibraltar that I would be happiest when writing about fantastically varied communities on which an alien but benign role had been imposed . . . There was conflict turned by the British into confluence. At last I could write . . . At last I had become a novelist.[4]

In six of his earlier novels (counting *The Malayan Trilogy* or *The Long Day Wanes* as three novels, as originally published) Burgess wrote about the clash of Eastern and Western cultures, as seen from the point of view of a major character associated with the British hierarchy. He wrote, "when the resolution of cultural, religious, racial conflict—in real life as opposed to fiction—is achieved through gentle colonialism, then fictions, as opposed to real life, can separate out the elements and allow them to touch in tiny electric shocks which tickle the imagination."[5] These shocks were felt by his four major British characters in these six novels: Richard Ennis, the exiled composer in the British army stationed in Gibraltar in *A Vision of Battlements* (1965); Victor Crabbe, the failed history teacher and education officer in Malaya in *The Long Day Wanes* (1964); Francis Lydgate, the harried and hassled passport officer in Dunia (Borneo) in *Devil of a State* (1961); and J. W. Denham, the traveling businessman returned to England in *The Right to an Answer* (1960). Each of these men represents British stability and order at war with an absurd and rapidly disintegrating world. Each fails to stem the tide of disintegration, but each one represents that prototype of sensitivity and order that Burgess admired in the old colonial structure. Whatever the cold realities of the world around them—the Army hierarchy, the Malayan jungles, the suburban adulteries—Burgess consistently admired these characters for taking a stand and voicing their very real concerns about art, order, and values, however inevitably bound to fail.

Burgess admitted that for him literature "suggests a theology or metaphysic of which the story itself is a kind of allegory."[6] Those early novels can be seen as allegories in which the single character representing order tries to bring stability and understanding to the racially, religiously, and culturally confused world around him. He recognizes values and civilized restraints that the world around him does not. His battle is a losing one, complicated by his own personal weaknesses and uncertainties, but it is a battle Burgess felt necessary to wage. The battle may reveal only a world of intense comic disorder and collapse, but at the heart of this world lie certain moral absolutes that should not be relinquished. Out of the clash between East and West, Burgess hoped to point toward possible reconciliation and resolution, even though the battle between opposites remained unresolved.

A Vision of Battlements: "Sin is Life."

Burgess has described his first novel as "very much a self-portrait . . . . All the material in it is personal. You know, the failed musicianship, the conflict between the cultures, the Protestant wife and the dark-haired, dark-skinned European Catholic."[7] The hero—or antihero in this case, since none of his adventures or life strike the reader as very heroic—is Richard Ennis, a sergeant in the Army Vocational and Cultural Corps. Ennis is a visionary of sorts, a rebel opposed to the forced conformity of army regulations and aspirations, a composer of symphonies and concertos, who sees himself as "building a city of sound, a universe of ultimate meaning." He believes that his music "was stronger than love," that art transcended all the petty, insignificant worries and episodes in everyday life: "Besides, I don't think I approve of this visual bias that's creeping into education.

Our civilization is, surely, based on the ear—the dialectics
of Socrates, Shakespeare, and his illiterate audience, the
peripatetic sermons of Christ." He is Burgess's spokesman
for "the full life, sir, the total sensibility. Values, civilized
living, the contact with the bigger reality." Noble sentiments,
surely, the kind that allows one character in the novel to
refer to him as a "spoilt priest."

Ennis, however, lives in the all-too-real world of wartime
1943, the British occupation of Gibraltar, women, and his
own demanding sexuality and lust. He arrives on Gibraltar
on Christmas Eve after a stormy voyage at sea and a run-in
with a blonde woman in the army on her way to Cyprus. For
no apparent reason she has needled Ennis throughout the
gloomy voyage. It is a prelude to his future run-ins with
women. He is also set upon by his commanding officer, Major
Muir, a badly wounded officer in the Army Educational Corps
on Gibraltar, who suffers from megalomania, rules with an
iron fist, and can put up with neither Ennis's procrastinations
nor his sexual rendezvous with Concepción Gomez. Concepción is Ennis's ideal of sexuality: dark, sensuous, Spanish,
and available. While he is making love to her, his wife,
Laurel, continually writes to him from England, nagging at
him to better himself in the army, to get a good job on the
Rock, and to work his way up into the higher ranks of the
establishment. In Laurel's presence Ennis always felt "clod-
dish, cheap, boorish." "He was aware of his base stock, of
her family's condescension to him, of the aura of success that
hovered like a Bond Street perfume round the circle of
relatives and friends." And yet in comparison to Concepción's
garlic-smelling sensuality, Laurel represents "that cool aseptic English charm which, he always thought, was like a clear
note from which all the harmonics had been eliminated."
Ennis's involvement with Concepción causes him to miss
several of his lectures to the troops, much to Major Muir's
concern. At one point Ennis leads a Docks Operating Group
out to a bar to hear some Spanish songs instead of lecturing
them on the new world order of cooperation and material

success that is to come after the war. Muir angrily upbraids
him. He tells Ennis that he is "not the kind of man we want
in the Corps" and that he will not recommend him for a
commission. Ennis sneaks off to Concepción's house, where
she informs him that she is pregnant and she will marry
Barasi, a fat and very wealthy Spanish merchant. Barasi has
been asking for her hand for years, and he, now pleased and
delighted, asks Ennis to write a wedding march for the great
day. On one day in May, the European War is concluded,
Concepción gets married, and Ennis recalls that it is the
anniversary of his father's death and goes to the Engineer's
Mess to get violently drunk. He joins in a race between taxis
up and down the main street of the town, stumbles and falls
into the water, yells at his roommate in the barracks at the
Moorish Castle, and storms out of the room.

Ennis moves in with Julian Agate, a homosexual ballet
dancer, in an attempt to get away from what he considers to
be the harassment of the army, the faithlessness of women,
and the confusions of life in general. In his new world of
"cool epicene voices," he concentrates on writing music, in
particular a piece he calls the *Passacaglia*. Agate sets up an
appointment for him with Withers, the "queen" of the
Commonwealth Council for the Development of the Appreciation of the Arts in Colonial Territories. Withers might
choose Ennis to be his assistant. The interview goes well,
Ennis begins giving piano recitals, and at last he decides to
put together an orchestra to play his pieces. On the day of
the concert, he skips his afternoon class in Elementary
English for the troops, Muir learns of this transgression and
assigns him to teach three classes in elementary shorthand
that night, and the concert scheduled for that night is
cancelled. Shortly thereafter Withers tells him that the job
cannot be his, because Withers' superiors are looking for
someone with a good school background. Ennis is convinced
his rejection is based upon his unwillingness to respond to
Withers' sexual advances.

Muir announces that the army will expand its vocational

and cultural programs to assist the men in their return to civilian life, although to Ennis's dismay, the emphasis on the vocational aspect of the program is greatly increased at the expense of the cultural. Muir returns to the War Office in England to discuss the new expansion, leaving Captain Appleyard, "a willowy, querulous public-school master of a man," in charge. Appleyard thinks it would be a great idea to paint murals in the army classrooms to make them happier places. Ennis and Agate delight in the new idea: "Ennis covered a whole wall with a crayoned representation of the Rock, above which a large octopus crouched, tentacles extended to every cranny. The face of the beast was recognizably that of Major Muir." In Agate's mural, Muir's face is painted upon the bodies of a swan, a bull, and "glinted through a shower of gold," representing Zeus's love for Leda, Danae, and Europa: "In each case the copulation was presented in frank detail." Appleyard, appalled, destroys the murals.

In London Muir meets Laurel, who is impressed with his appearance and authority. She writes to tell Ennis that it's time for him to knuckle down and get to work. Meanwhile high up on the Rock, Ennis meets Lavinia Grantham, a cool, detached army woman, who reminds him of Laurel. She admires Ennis's music; he reads her poetry; they meet for dinner, but she upbraids him for not being honest with her about what he is seeking from her. In the ensuing cat-and-mouse tête-à-tete, Lavinia remains aloof and detached, making Ennis desire her even more. When he finally does get her into bed, he is unable to complete the sexual act and collapses moodily into his own impotence, while she coldly informs him that a Corporal Coneybeare, a professor of harmony, thinks that Ennis has no ear for music whatsoever.

Meanwhile Lieutenant Colonel Muir has returned to Gibraltar with several "eupeptic athletocrats . . . representing a great augmentation of the original establishment." The leader of these is Regimental Sergeant Major Instructor Turner, "a barrel-chested slim-hipped giant, six foot four in his bare feet," prototype of the new age of athlete managers and professional optimists, complete with "empty eyes and full lips." One day, while Ennis is listening to a piece by Delius on the radio in the recreation room, Turner snaps it off in order to play billiards. Ennis growls; Turner at last apologizes, but Ennis storms out. Turner introduces an entire physical training program—healthy bodies for healthy, happy minds—and lets slip that he has his eye on Lavinia Grantham. After Ennis and Lavinia have failed in bed together and get up and go to a Literary Society meeting, Lavinia stops to talk with Turner, almost as if their meeting together had been prearranged. On Boxing Day, the day after Christmas, Ennis, as the volunteer bartender for an army party, loads up Turner's orange squash with gin, rum, sherry, and whiskey and gets him absolutely drunk. Turner and his cohorts vow revenge.

The plot zips along swiftly from episode to episode, trapping Ennis more deeply in awkward situations and at the same time revealing his indecision, his lackluster attempts at juvenile rebellion, and his continued efforts to paint himself as a man more sinned against than sinning. For a speakers' competition he chooses two Spanish poems, both about fornication and adultery. When this is discovered by Dr. Bradshaw, who had offered Ennis a possible job as an assistant in the Civilian Educational Services, Bradshaw withdraws his offer in a letter to Muir and chastises Ennis's choice of poetry. The competition, it turns out, was for children, which Ennis had not known. When civilians on Gibraltar begin staging riots and demonstrations to get the army off the Rock and when the army itself wishes to leave as soon as possible, Ennis incites an antiaircraft unit with his talk on Beethoven, half unaware of what he is doing, half rebellious in his attitude: "Beethoven was a musician . . . He had absolutely no respect for authority . . . He was independent, fearless, alone, no base crawler." The men rally round and spirit Ennis away to a mob scene in front of the Governor's residence, chanting "We want to go home," joined in by the civilians with their cry of "Go home!"

Fighting follows. Ennis hops onto his motorcycle to escape, only to be followed by Turner and his cronies on their motorcycles. The chase leads higher and higher up the towering cliffs of the Rock, where Turner and his men corner Ennis. Ennis sidesteps Turner's swing, and Turner plummets to the sea below. Muir, enraged, declares the next morning that Ennis must return to England as soon as possible to rid the army organization on Gibraltar of a "bad smell."

Before he leaves Gibraltar, Ennis has his fortune told by Mrs. Carraway, a widow. She reads the Tarot cards, sees only blackness ahead, talks of Ennis's failure to love and of the prospect of death in his future. Her crystal ball reveals a priest with a chalice, who may or may not be Ennis himself, deciding to slip out of life's confusion altogether. Depressed and disspirited, Ennis takes a final trip to the Spanish mainland with Agate. They carouse morosely with two old whores through cheap cafés, barroom brawls, cheap rooms, and the ever-present aroma of sour garlic. Ennis gets drunk, calls Franco a pig, is encircled by the police and is miraculously rescued by Barasi, Concepción's husband, who buys off the corrupt officials. Barasi then informs him sadly that Concepción has died in childbirth. Ennis keeps the secret to himself that it is his child. The next day on board ship for England, Ennis receives a final letter from Laurel, who tells him that she's run off with an American. A second letter informs him that the BBC is not interested in playing his *Passacaglia*. He meets the ornery blonde woman again, this time returning from Cyprus, and the two go to bed together as casually as if shaking hands. The nightmarish Rock recedes across the waves in the distance, and Ennis is left to contemplate the ruins of his life and his past: "It shook impotent fists, trying to assert an old power, but it knew that it was becoming too small to be anything but ridiculous or lovable. . . . The Rock sank, englutted to the fading of slow chords, raising not a bubble."

The title of the novel is taken from the opening epigraph, which Burgess has taken from *The Illustrated Family Doctor:*

"Warning of an attack may be given by tingling sensations in the limbs, impairment of vision, flashing lights, a vision of battlements, noises in the ears, mental depression or other phenomena." This clearly suggests the state of Richard Ennis's soul as it voyages out from comfortable England to experience its own dark night on the rocky slopes of Gibraltar.

Quartermain, an army psychologist, attributes part of Ennis's problem to Ennis's Catholicism: "You Catholics make me sick, saving your own measly little souls at the expense of other people's." Ennis then admits that he is a lapsed Catholic, to which Quartermain declares, "You blasted renegades who don't believe in divorce. Separation, sensual itchings for the once beloved. Why the hell can't you make a clean break?" Ennis's response is to acknowledge the continuing existence of Hell, which Quartermain chalks up to self-interested "Catholic masochism." Ennis feels keenly the modern existential state of loneliness and isolation, wondering if he is "incapable of love." He feels it even more keenly because of his having given up the dogmatic Catholicism of his youth. Outside the traditional church he feels punished and uncertain, a victim of some "gangster-god," rejected by love and art, incapable of human communion.

Ennis's own irresponsible actions suggest that he is seeking to be punished. All his high-level talk of art and music seems suspect when he continuously tumbles into awkward situations, often of his own making. He knows what Muir is like, what Turner is like, and yet he taunts them (even if halfheartedly), playing tricks on them, failing to comply even with the minimal requirements of his job. He is, in many ways, a fool. He is trapped somewhere between his ideal world of music, which he himself cannot compose well, and the sordid, real world of lust, army training, and Spanish garlic. He is the prototype of all of Burgess's heroes, the good-natured, often cuckolded, sensitive, idealistic, ineffectual nonhero in an absurd and disintegrating contemporary world.

Burgess's belief in the moral absolutes of good and evil

and the aesthetic absolutes of love and art make him extremely
wary in *A Vision of Battlements* of the coming era of American
culture and the modern consumer ethic. In 1949 he warned
in the novel of "Aseptic American . . . Man and the icebox,
the colonial church with one bell, the drugstore on the
corner." This new world of "improved industrial techniques,
American aid, [and] plenty of jobs" struck him as an assault
upon traditional culture and art itself. He worried in the
novel about "a cult of young hooliganism. State art. Free ill-
health for all. Lots and lots of forms to fill in . . . bureaucracy
growing like a cancer." To traditionalist Burgess, this new
world was like an ancient heresy, the cult of Pelagius, that
great British heretic who believed that there was no Original
Sin. A Captain Mendoza, who wanders into a bar where Ennis
happens to be drinking, puts the case succinctly:

Pelagius . . . was the father of the two big modern heresies—
material progress as a sacred goal; the state as God Almighty . . .
One has produced Americanism . . . America's not real, it's an
idea, a way of looking at things. And then there's Russia, the end-
product of the Socialist process. We're both the same, in a way. We
both offer supra-regional goods—The icebox and the Chevrolet or
the worker, standardised into an overall abstraction at a standardised
production belt. And you, my friend, are going to suffer.

This standardization Burgess abhorred. It became the villain
of his novels, and any rebellion against it, even as weak-
kneed and self-serving as Ennis's, must in some way be
celebrated.

   Ennis, the lapsed Catholic, declares that he has become
"a manichee, at home in a world of perpetual war." Life has
become a place for "the essential opposition—Wet and Dry,
Left Hand and Right Hand, Yin and Yang, X and Y. Here
was the inevitable impasse, the eternal stalemate." Ennis
feels stalemated between his own artistic, private world and
the world of the Rock, "the vast crouching granite dragon,
the towering sky-high sphinx, its forehead bathed in the mild
sun." He's caught between his dark, sensual goddess,
Concepción, and his high-class, blonde maiden, Laurel-

Lavinia. He's trapped between a love for the Mediteranean
world of sun and wine and Catholic Spain and the northern
world of the "braying Oxford vicars, the cold embraces, the
cold climate" of Protestant England. Even Spain seems
broken in half, the idealized Spain of bullfights and fiestas,
the realistic Spain of decay, beggars, whores, "suppliants at
the Venereal Shrine, each with his heavy bag of seed to
throw on the rotten barren ground." The Catholic Ideal, the
eucharistic vows of communion and resurrection, is shattered
by a soulless, splintered reality of drunken revels and human
loneliness. Nothing coheres; everything separates.

   Despite his pessimism, this first novel turned out, to
Burgess's surprise, to be a comic novel: "I see myself as a
creature of gloom and sobriety, but my books reflect a sort
of clown."[8] The comedy comes from the way in which the
novel is written. First of all, Burgess's tone remains detached
and ironic; his characters are the victims or butts of Burgess's
comic situations, ironic statements, and "mad-dashed" episodes.

   The second device which makes *A Vision of Battlements*
essentially comic—however dark a comedy it certainly is—
is Burgess's use of Vergil's *Aeneid*. He intended to "use an
epic framework, diminished and made comic [as] a tyro's
method of giving his story a backbone; it was also a device—
failed, alas—for taming the Rock by enclosing it in myth
. . . to put the Rock, an emblem of waste and loneliness, in
its place."[9] Burgess intended to write a mock epic, to spoof
his hero's antiheroism by enclosing it in a structure reminiscent of a truly great heroic and epic work. In this way Ennis
becomes Aeneas; Agate is Achates; Turner, Turnus; Lavinia,
the same name; Barasi, Iarbas; Concepciön, Dido. Aeneas's
victory over Turnus in the twelfth book of Vergil's *Aeneid*
parallels Ennis's "victory" over Turner in the novel, when
that unfortunate character slips and falls to his death. The
unheroic nature of Ennis's "victory" clearly inverts the
heroism of Aeneas's victory.[10]

   In both instances, however, *A Vision of Battlements*

remains tepid and thin. Burgess telegraphs his ironies and
reports them as if he were delivering some kind of newspaper
account. The novel relies on statements and declarations
instead of more imaginative suggestions and images. The
distancing effect prevents the reader from sympathizing with
any of the characters and reduces them to pawns in some
black-comic game. The mythic structure remains all but
hidden. It makes no difference if it's there or not, for the
mock-heroic quality doesn't show, and the mythic parallels
lie buried and unrealized. Ennis occupies a kind of no-man's-
land, a character caught in a series of episodes and fragments
too schematically shaped to reflect either one side of the
opposing forces or the other. He's a stick figure sketched in
a blueprint, a puppet pushed through the hoops of the plot.

Burgess's basic themes are all here—the solitary and
sensitive hero, the attack on the Pelagian heresy, the lapsed
Catholicism—as early as 1949, but they remain stated rather
than explored, too carefully set up and explained rather than
lived through and developed. The novel clearly reveals the
focus and shape of the fiction to come, but finally remains
hollow and flat.

The Long Day Wanes: "Tida' apa."

Subtitled "A Malayan Trilogy," *The Long Day Wanes* is
composed of three separate novels, each published separately,
but brought together under the one title. These include *Time
for a Tiger* (1956), *The Enemy in the Blanket* (1958), and
Beds in the East (1959). Burgess clearly intended the three
novels to be taken as a fictional whole. First of all, they all
deal with the rise and demise of the British history teacher,
Victor Crabbe, as underlined by the opening epigraph taken
from Robert Burton's *A Digression on the Air*: "Their coming
and going is sure in the night: in the plains of Asia (saith
he), the storks meet on such a set day, he that comes last
is torn to pieces, and so they get them gone." Secondly, the

structure of *The Long Day Wanes* is symphonic, derived from Burgess's love of and familiarity with musical composition. He described the trilogy's essential structure in *Beds in the East:*

The first movement had seemed to suggest a programme, each instrument presenting in turn a national style—a gurgling Indian cantilena on the cello, a Kampong tune on the viola, a pentatonic song on the second violin and some pure Western atonality on the first. And then a scherzo working all these out stridently, ending with no resolution. A slow movement suggesting a sort of tropical afternoon atmosphere. A brief finale, ironic variations on a somewhat rapid "brotherhood of man" motif.

From a purely structural and formal perspective, the first novel introduces the main characters and various problems of Malaya. The second scrutinizes these more closely. The third concludes with Crabbe's comments upon racial understanding and his death. The second opening epigraph refers to this many-faceted structure: "Allah is great, no doubt, and juxtaposition his prophet." Burgess's themes and characters are carefully juxtaposed to one another in one intricate pattern, which we shall examine.

In his career in Malaya Victor Crabbe rises from being a history teacher at the Mansor School in Kuala Hantu to becoming the headmaster of Haju Ali College in Dahaga and finally the Chief Education Officer of Dahaga. He is referred to as a "crank idealist" and as a romantic, since he claims he wants to help Malaya achieve a solid independence in its own right. He feels that Malaya needs him to show it the way toward modernization, "to prepare [it] for the taking over of the dangerous Western engine." At the same time Crabbe believes that history is "an ineluctable process," that there is a dialectic at work out of which must come the new order of Malayan independence. His early university belief in Communism at one time supported and sustained this belief in history as a living, secular pattern, although "the world of sensory phenomena [meant] less to Crabbe than the world of idea and speculation." Crabbe thinks his presence in

Malaya at this particular postwar moment has been ordained
by the ordered inevitabilities of history: "For the end of the
Western pattern was the conquest of time and space. But out
of time and space came point-instants, and out of point-
instants came a universe." It is, inevitably, the Eastern
universe which is awakening to its own potentiality.

Crabbe's career and character, however, are full of
ironies and anomalies. He rises in his career at a point when
Malaya is falling apart at the seams. He is eager to be
absorbed into the coming Malayan way of life, to be integrated
into the complex convergence of races and cultures in Malaya,
but "it is death to be properly integrated, for then there is
no change and one is independent of change," and he is
literally absorbed by drowning in a jungle river. His sense
of history just will not stand up in the light of the outrageous
realities of the Malayan experience, and he is forced to
declare, "We've got to throw up the past, otherwise we can't
live in the present." He is a white man trying to help in an
era when white skin is seen only as the enemy's color. He
knows that "one must love the living," that "the fact of love
remains," but he loves no one, except the idealistic and
abstract image he cherishes of his dead first wife. His way
of life and his manner reveal an ongoing guilt that he cannot
shake. He was at the wheel of the car in which his first wife,
when it plunged into icy water, was drowned. His unconscious
reason for coming to Malaya in the first place may have been
more a matter of atonement and retreat than the more public
proclamations of assistance and education. Since the night
of his first wife's death, he admits that "he had lost the desire
for more complex and civilized patterns." All these anomalies
come together finally to make Crabbe, aptly named for the
lowly creature that walks sideways, an ineffectual teacher
and an aimless, isolated man. His suicide or accidental death
seems the only alternative at the end.

The Malaya Crabbe confronts is appalling. The country,
a country in name only, exists as a wildly chaotic stewpot of
races and cultures, of Chinese, Tamils, Sikhs, Malays,

Islamic people, white parasites, Hindu cults and animistic jungle cannibals. Magic, mayhem, and murder prevail. Even the Malays themselves, for whom the country is named, are "the end-product of God knows what mingling of Achinese pirates, aboriginal bushmen, Bugis bandits, long-hut head-hunters." Crabbe gasps at the "incredible, head-reeling collocation of cultures: Islamic texts sprawling on the Great Wall, a twelve-legged God looking down in exophthalmic frowning benevolence." The races exist in a perpetual state of prejudice, hatred, and open warfare, paralleled by the persistent Communist assassinations and guerrilla battles in the outlying districts. The only certainty seems to be that "there was nothing to believe in except the jungle . . . one and indivisible, ultimate numen," the scene of Crabbe's death. Throughout the novel the phrase, "Tida' apa," recurs as regularly as a chorus: "It doesn't matter," the ultimate cry of impotence and neglect.

What Malaya, or the East in general, does represent is mythical timelessness, an unchanging repetitive world of custom and routine, clearly at war with Western ideas of progress. The dialectical theories of the West dissolve in the face of the heat, the chaos, the "damned, uncultured emptiness," the indifference, and "that calm face of faint astonishment, unmoved at the anger, not understanding the bitterness." Western ideas of "right and wrong are so terribly mixed up." All programs, structures, political ambitions, and arrangements will leave "the smooth timeless body unchanged . . . The future would be like the past . . . Perpetual Malayan summers . . . No seasons, no change." The East is a place of cults, of myths practiced and celebrated again and again, with no thought of progress or historical inevitabilities. After Crabbe drowns, the natives of the river create a small cult in his name which will last until it is swallowed up by a larger one. Historically minded Crabbe has been absorbed into the mythic consciousness of the unchanging and timeless East.

Against such landscape British dominion hasn't a prayer.

The British can maintain a certain order and stability but without this, Burgess suggests, the community would slide into chaos: "Malay hegemony would mean nothing to the real Malay." The frivolous attitude of the East to the "calm processes of Western law" cannot be changed or overcome. The choice for the British intruder is either to stand up to the sun and the jungle and "invite madness" or to become absorbed, lose one's Western identity, and invite death.

In each of the three novels within the triology, Victor Crabbe is caught up in the outrageous twists of plot and with eccentric characters (including his own). As one careful critic has pointed out, each novel contains a foil for Crabbe, a character whose relationship to the Malayan world in some way reflects or comments upon Crabbe's own character and decisions.[11] In *Time for a Tiger* this character is Nabby Adams, the six-foot, eight-inch, alcoholic, police lieutenant in charge of transport for the Police Circle. He's been in the East so long he's rapidly losing his English vocabulary. He remains at bottom a mystery, a kind of mythic expatriated Englishman, large, lewd, and loud. At one point Fenella Crabbe, Victor's blonde second wife, sees Nabby as Prometheus, an Eveless Adam, a Minotaur, and Burgess described him as "a broken Coriolanus." The nihilism that is slowly engulfing him bodes ill for Crabbe's own actions. In *The Enemy in the Blanket*, Rupert Hardman is a British lawyer who marries a wealthy Islamic widow to further his own ambitions. He must accept Islamic customs, even though he believes in none of them, and eventually escapes back to England. In *Beds in the East* the British are nearly all gone; the Malays are taking over. Rosemary Michaels is a Christian Tamil from Kuala Hantu, a ravishingly beautiful creature who will sleep only with white men, in an effort to marry a European and leave Malaya altogether. Her methods fail, as do the plans of the characters who precede her, and as finally do Crabbe's hopes for assimilation and resolution as well.

The main action in *Time for a Tiger*—Tiger is the name of a popular brand of Malayan beer, and in such degenerate

times, there is always time for one—concerns Crabbe's
difficult relationship with the headmaster, Boothby, and the
possible existence of a Communist cell among the students
at the Mansor School, where Crabbe is a resident master. In
the royal town of Kuala Hantu, where the Mansor School is
located, Boothby is the standard, prejudiced British colonial,
who regards all dark-skinned people as "wogs" and argues
for more punishment and order. Crabbe discovers in his
dormitory that a Chinese student, Shiu Hung, seems to be
the leader of a Communist indoctrination class. Shiu Hung
tries to convince Crabbe that he is only teaching his fellow
students about the wrongs of Communism. In an effort to
draw Hung out in conversation, Crabbe tells him of his own
youthful Communist sympathies, but Hung remains close-
mouthed.

Trouble with Boothby begins when Boothby expels a
student who had been caught kissing a woman in a house-
boy's room. Crabbe learns that this is a frame-up by one of
the student prefects in the dorm and, to his class, refers to
it as "no great crime" anyway. He describes the expulsion
of the student as too harsh a sentence. He goes to see
Boothby, who rages and fumes about wogs and fornication,
of Crabbe's liking Asians too much, and of Crabbe's under-
mining his authority as headmaster. Crabbe accuses him of
being "damned autocratic." Later Crabbe's Malaysian language tutor informs him that there is rebellion brewing at the
school, that students and teachers there are aware of Crabbe's
liaison with Rahimah, a Malay woman and dance hostess at
the local Paradise Cabaret, and of his refusal to obey Boothby.

During these goings-on, Nabby Adams and his Muslim
drinking buddy, Police Transport Corporal Alladad Kahn,
become friends with both Crabbe and his wife, Fenella. They
become a foursome, drinking, riding, eating together and
make a "strange spectacle . . . the huge rumbling man with
the jaundiced complexion, the neat Punjabi fingering his
ample moustache, the pale schoolmaster, the film-star woman
with the honeyed skin and the golden hair."

On a Friday, the Muslim Sabbath, with school closed, Crabbe and Fenella decide to join Adams and Khan on a trip to the jungle village of Gila, where Adams has to inspect police vehicles. Rain slows the trip, and by the time they arrive in Gila, it is too late to inspect the vehicles. Adams decides to spend the night in the local jail. The others decide to return to Kuala Hantu so that Crabbe will be certain not to miss Sports Day, which is on Saturday and is attended by many local officials. On the way back through dense and ominous jungle, the car encounters engine trouble and stops. The three of them spend the night in the car in the rain. Chinese mechanics restore the car in the morning, but the trio is ambushed by Communist guerrillas on the way back, and Alladad is shot in the arm. Crabbe, who has telephoned the school to say he'll be late, grabs the wheel and drives off, his first time at the wheel of a car since his first wife's fatal accident. He feels exhilarated, leaves Alladad at the Sungit Hospital, and speeds back to the Mansor School.

Boothby is furious. As part of the school rebellion, the students have refused to take part in the sports. He accuses Crabbe of being behind the student strike, tells of an anonymous letter which lists Crabbe's "crimes" (the result of his "confession" of Communist leanings to the Chinese student, Shiu Hung), calls Crabbe a "traitor," and orders him to accept a transfer to another school. At the traditional Chinese dinner for department masters of the school, Crabbe learns that Boothby is to be transferred as well. His increasing paranoia suggests, as one of the Malayan masters states, that the time is coming for all the British to leave the East, that to rely on one's will to resist the land of jungle and sun invites madness. Students outside chant that they want Crabbe to stay on as headmaster, at which point Boothby storms from the room.

The novel ends on Christmas Eve in the Crabbes' apartment, where everything has been boxed and packaged, ready for moving. Adams, who's just won a state lottery, decides to return to Bombay, the place in the East he likes the most. The four friends sing Christmas carols, Fenella weeps, the sound of distant Communist gunfire in the jungle can be heard, the weather is unbearably hot, and the river continues to rise.

In *The Enemy in the Blanket*—the title refers to Crabbe's calling Shiu Hung, the Chinese Communist student, "the enemy in the blanket"—Crabbe begins a new affair with the wife of the State Education Officer; Rupert Hardman, a down-and-out British lawyer, strikes up a marital deal with a wealthy Islamic widow; and Fenella becomes involved with the Abang, the old feudal ruler of the territory. The territory is Negeri Dahaga on the China Sea, a place of fishermen and rice planters, far less civilized than Kuala Hantu. It is a place where one can hire men with axes to assassinate one's enemies, a place of magic spells and jungle witchcraft. The chief town, Kenching, is Islamic, "bulbous with mosques and loud with the cries of many muezzins."

Burgess's elaborate plot spins forward. Crabbe is now the headmaster of Haji Ali College, but the benefits of his promotion are undermined by Fenella's knowledge of his affair with Rahimah. She has received an anonymous letter telling her of her husband's infidelity. Nevertheless, he slips off to Kuala Lumpur for a weekend of sexual revels with Anne Talbot, the wife of the State Education Officer. Fenella suspects the worst. On the beach one afternoon with Crabbe, Fenella rushes into the sea and pretends she's drowning. Crabbe, fearful of water since his first wife's death, runs in after her but cannot swim to her. Fenella realizes he has never loved her: "When you thought the bandits had got us you were able to drive the car . . . It's the old instinct of self-preservation. But if my life only is involved . . . " She decides to leave him and work as the Abang's secretary abroad, for the Abang has fled the country in the wake of Malayan independence.

One night, after Fenella has discovered Crabbe's new infidelities, Communists from the jungle, led by Crabbe's former cook, Ah Wing, who fled to the jungle to be with his

son-in-law there, come to his house to surrender. They have
heard that if they give themselves up, the government will
grant them amnesty and pay their fares to China. They want
Crabbe to telephone the government. In doing so, he makes
heroic headlines in the newspapers, having "captured single-
handed thirty dangerous Communist terrorists." Talbot is
impressed with the news and offers Crabbe his position of
Chief Education Officer. Crabbe will be the last Britisher to
occupy the post, and part of his job will be to prepare a
Malayan to take it over. Crabbe accepts and, with Hardman
and Fenella gone, is left friendless and wifeless in a hot and
lonely bar.

        As a counterpoint to the marital troubles of Crabbe and
Fenella, Robert Hardman, the penniless lawyer, weds 'Che
Normah, a wealthy twice-divorced Malayan woman. In order
to marry her, Hardman must give up his Christian friendships
and practice Islamic customs. The first to go is Father
LaForgue, a Catholic missionary, who is eventually thrown
out of Dahaga while giving a dying girl the last rites of the
Catholic Church, a forbidden practice in an Islamic society.
Hardman, sick of 'Che Normah's possessiveness and forced
into joining her in a pilgrimage by ship to Mecca, jumps ship
and flies back to England.

        Beds in the East concludes the Malayan trilogy. When
Hardman was pursuing 'Che Normah, he recalled the line
from "Anthony and Cleopatra," "the beds i' the East are
soft." Rosemary Michaels, the gorgeous Tamil woman, pursues her objective to marry a European with a vengeance and
is pursued in kind by Emir Jalil, a lusty Turk; Vythilingam,
the Tamil State Veterinary officer; and Robert Loo, a
precocious Chinese boy who composes symphonies. Crabbe,
the only Britisher in sight for most of the novel, wants to help
Loo get his music performed, viewing it as a tribute to his
notion of an emerging national Malayan State. Unfortunately,
Rosemay seduces Loo, who then decides to write music
which more romantically expresses his new feelings. Toward
the end of the novel, officers at USIS, invited to listen to

Loo's music, declare it "second-rate cinematic romantic stuff, complete with big Rachmaninoff tunes . . . This Chinese boy has sort of rejected the native stuff."

Crabbe receives a message that the headmaster of the Durian Estate School, deep in jungle territory, has been murdered. He must investigate. Leaving racial and social squabbles behind him in town, he sets out. His journey strikes him as ominous and foreboding. He senses the density of the jungle around him and recalls the prophecy of a friend, who once told him that "the country will absorb you and you will cease to be Victor Crabbe . . . you will lose function and identity." On the train he comes upon a British newspaper in which appears a poem by Fenella. In the town of Mawas he meets an American linguist who has heard Fenella Crabbe, the poet, lecture in London. This only adds to Crabbe's unease: "It was as though the river and the jungle together were singling him out for attention, approaching him in terms of his own post . . . Did this mean he was going to die?"

On the train Crabbe meets Tommy Jones, a "hail-fellow well-met" beer salesman, who used to know the alcoholic Nabby Adams. Next day he meets Moneypenny, an assistant protector of Aborigines, who will give him a ride in his Land Rover to Mawas. There he can catch the river launch for the estate. Moneypenny is crazy, believing in taboos and magic charms, and scolds Crabbe for laughing as a butterfly passes by: that is a terrible omen! In Mawas Crabbe meets Temple Haynes, an American linguist, a clean-cut and good-natured innocent, who's come to Malaya to create an alphabet for the Aborigines. At a native shadow play that evening, Haynes is nearly overcome with the heat and Crabbe is stung by a scorpion in his shoe. The bad omens multiply.

At last Crabbe reaches the Durian Estate, a huge up-river plantation in the middle of nowhere, and meets the new manager, George Costard, a paternalistic British colonial, precisely the kind Crabbe abhors. Costard prattles on, "Some of us must keep the traditions alive . . . the feudal tradition, the enlightened patriarchal principle. You people have been

throwing it all away, educating them to revolt against us
. . . I'm the father of these people." Costard tells Crabbe
that his name means an apple, a name all too similar to
Crabbe's own. In conversation the horrible revelation bursts
upon them: Costard was Crabbe's first wife's lover! If she
hadn't drowned, Costard had planned to run off with her
within a week. Crabbe, of course, is stunned. His entire life
suddenly appears as one of idealized illusions and self-
deception. Costard yells at him to leave immediately. When
Crabbe attempts to board the launch, he suddenly slips, falls
into the water, "and the river settled and the launch moved
in again."

Independence Day comes to Malaya at last. The novel
closes with the still unwed Rosemary at a British Officer's
Mess Dance with a Major Anstruther. She suddenly weeps
remembering Crabbe: "Poor Victor. And then somebody
asked her to dance."

Burgess's Malayan trilogy is crammed with a welter of
information and images about the food, customs, geography,
and culture of Malaya. The book teems with local color,
faces, ceremonies, and landscapes. The symphonic structure
resounds with subplots, tangents, and character sketches.
Essentially Burgess has written a novel of manners, a work
of fiction in which all phases and levels of society are
captured in a vast array of characters. Characters act as
representatives of various classes and races: the happy-go-
lucky Sikhs; the hard-working, crafty Chinese shopkeepers;
the Malay villagers; the bureaucratic Tamils in government
service; the colonial British. The overriding culture of Malaya
is Islam, and Burgess was particularly fascinated by Malayan
Islam, because "it has to stand on its own and jostle up
against other religions. See how it gets on. And it's very
amusing . . . when it becomes monolithic and a genuine state
religion, as in Saudi Arabia, then it's rather repulsive . . .
like Calvinism in Geneva."[12]

Burgess observed his characters from the outside, almost
as pawns in a long saga of collapse and disintegration. With

the exception of Victor Crabbe, the reader never really gets inside the characters' minds. They remain walking examples of manners and morals, instead of well-rounded people in their own right. They are the cardboard caricatures of comedy, the butt of Burgess's satiric and ironic comments on the human condition, rather than the flesh-and-blood, soulful celebrants of tragedy. Listening to a conversation in the book, Crabbe seems to explain exactly the manner in which Burgess had written the trilogy: "They threw the ball of question and answer from hand to hand, watching it change shape and colour, dropping it, losing it, all against a fetid background of preserved lizards, tiger's teeth, and whiskers, ancient eggs, fat cats, a picture of Sun Yat Sen."

Burgess's style is at once satiric and comic, and often repellent. His description of 'Che Normah is an example of this: "The Communist bullets that had rendered her twice a widow had merely anticipated, in a single violent instant, what attrition would more subtly have achieved." There's no sense of the blood, pain, and loss those bullets had created, only of Burgess pinning down his character to a witty line about her sexual ardor and its effects upon her previous husbands. In many instances the style seems more reportorial than evocative, more a flat description of passing events than a precise and comprehensive rendering of those events. Much of the book seems unfelt and emotionally cold.

At the heart of the novel lies Victor Crabbe's unease, the kind of existential loneliness and guilt that bothered Richard Ennis, but for the most part this remains unseen and undescribed. The reader is aware of the whirlwind pace of events, the rough and tumble of episodes and incidents. These tend to drown Crabbe even before his actual drowning. We cannot feel his grief and guilt, and therefore, cannot really share it. His death is more the formal working out of a theme of disintegration and collapse than the actual death of someone we care about. Crabbe has fallen victim to Burgess's pervasive comic detachment.

Because of his detachment, Burgess's plot seems extra-

neous at first. Odd incidents and eccentric episodes occur and
then are tossed off. His manner seems to be very casual and
offhand, touching on the comic quality of some coincidence
or the humorous conversation in some confused mix-up. And
yet, slowly out of the apparent randomness of events, a plot
begins to take shape. Patterns begin to emerge. The lost
British cause in Malaya begins to form. Themes appear at
more regular intervals. One must not "surrender to a culture
[American], however inevitable its global spread . . . It
must for as long as possible meet a show of resistance." What
one critic calls Burgess's "imagination of comic disorder"[13]
constantly threatens to overwhelm any hope of theme or
meaning in the tangle of his Malayan mosaic, and yet out of
chaos does emerge an intricate composite of patterns, themes,
and ideas. As Burgess wrote about Loo's music, "It was a
young work, boyish in many ways, but it held together, it was
coherent, and it showed remarkable technical competence."

Burgess seemed to feel in writing this novel that at
bottom all people are similar. They all share the human
weaknesses of sex, appetite, greed, power. They inhabit a
world of unrelenting depravity. Yet his delightful recreation
of manners and morals and his ribald mélange of characters
and episodes transform that depraved world into a comic
realm. His historical outlook depicted a world of disintegration
and chaos. His mythic sensibilities created a world in which
all is possible, in which despite the appearance of decay and
collapse, the human comedy continues. To the Westerners
the Malayan trilogy records collapse. From the point of view
of the timeless, eternal East, however, the trilogy records the
continuing saga of human frailty, gullibility, and comedy.
East and West can never meet, but the dialectical interchange
between them provided Burgess with cosmic chuckles.

Devil of a State: "The little world of the misled."

Burgess's Borneo novel reads like his Malayan trilogy in
miniature. It is fast, light, extremely comic, almost a gloss

on the much richer and fuller Malayan cycle. For that reason
it is both a "thinner" and a more compact version of *The
Long Way Wanes*. If the trilogy often lumbers, *Devil of a
State* zips along at a breakneck pace. What it sacrifices in
depth, it makes up for in comic zest. What it loses in
richness, it makes up for in a zany, hectic comedy of
manners, or in this case, bad manners.

Dunia is, indeed, a devil of a state. An Islamic Caliph
rules over "a Babel, a confusion of unholy cries, and one of
the richest deposits of uranium in the world." It is a place,
more than a country, where "civilization of a kind had nibbled
at the coastline, leaving tooth-marks of names, but the
hinterland remained uneaten save by rivers." "This is a
heathen land and the law is but a scrawl on old sheepskins,
meet only for derision." Cannibalism and headhunters lurk
just up-river. The Dunian flag reveals "the moon of Islam in
custard, and surrounding it, a symbolic armoury of traditional
weapons, everything of curved, serrated, triple-spiked that
could conceivably sophisticate the boring act of just execution." The town is assailed by droughts, heat, the rainy
season, plagues of green and brown frogs, insects and
creatures of all kinds. The Islamic regime relies upon stark,
repressive customs and routines—celibacy, fasts, no drinking—none of which is really adhered to, all of which are
publicly proclaimed as Allah's duties. The British colonists
move routinely between the Dunia Hotel, the Chin Chin
Cinema, and the Kool Kaffi, a sleazy combination of bar and
restaurant. Perhaps Dunia is best summed up by an anonymous verse in the *Times of Dunia:*

> Dunia, the little world of the misled,
> A deadly living for the living dead.
> All mortal sins are venal here; the least
> Of public works officials is a priest
> Ordained by the traditions of his tribe
> For one sole rite—the blessing of the bribe . . .

The cast of characters reflects the Eastern-Western clash

of cultures. Sebastian Hup is a mixed breed of Filipino, Chinese, and Scottish, who works for the British. Patu, long-haired and self-righteous, constantly upbraids the authorities in his role as the local nationalist leader. A man named Forbes is one of the gang of Australian roadbuilders, and his African wife, Eileen, is both a prostitute and the former lover of Maximilian Hup, Sebastian's brother. She is raising Maximilian's child. Paolo and Nando Tasca are hot-blooded, Italian marble workers in Dunia to help build the Caliph's new mosque in time for his birthday celebration. They are also father and son, lazy and querulously in pursuit of women. Carruthers Chung, who teaches grammar at the English school, is also a Christian fundamentalist, eager to save lost souls at prayer and confession at his house. Add to these a sordid assortment of alcoholics and Syrian gamblers, and the British advisers: Harry Mudd, a retired jockey, who is now chairman of the housing board; James Tomlin, the United Nations Advisor, harried, frustrated in his quarrelsome conversations with the Caliph, and going deaf; and Row-landson, a nervous alcoholic district adviser, who is finally beheaded by the villagers he lives among. The supreme ruler, the Caliph, oversees all, chainsmokes, lives in an Edwardian Mansion called the Astana, comes from a line of Berber pirate kings and claims "to be the only living spiritual successor to the Prophet," with his "sort of arrogance of black flag and cutlass." We are again in Burgess country.

The main character of *Devil of a State* is another of Burgess's antiheroes, Francis Burroughs Lydgate, the pass-port officer in Dunia. He is fifty years old, has not seen England for twenty-four years, and is somewhat of an aimless, irresponsible drifter. His black mistress, Wajak, with whom he's already had two half-breed children, is up-river awaiting a third. His second wife, Lydia, from whom he has fled, still lives in Sydney, Australia. His past includes some time in Madrid, three years in Nairobi importing small machine tools, gold prospecting in Malaya, uncounted episodes in New Guinea, and five years in Australia. In Nairobi he married a Miss Featherstone, who left him after six months. In Malaya there was reportedly a Chinese girl, who mysteriously died.

The title of the novel refers not only to the historical state of Dunia itself but to the state of Lydgate's irresponsible soul. He sees himself as an eternal wanderer, as an Orestes hounded by the Furies, more "sinned against than sinning." He believes in the existence of sin but not in his complicity in it. Egged on by Carruthers Chung, he begins to consider the issue of personal responsibility, whether or not, in fact, he has led a life of selfish irresponsibility. When Lydia reappears and tells him that marriage is, indeed, a sacred state and a very responsible one—"I thought if you got married the idea was to stay married. I thought if something went wrong with a marriage you just had to try and put it right"—Lydgate begins to realize that "taking involves giving, that we are all members of one another."

At the moment of accusation and counteraccusation, Lydgate himself suddenly confesses that he deserted his first wife, Agnes, in England many years ago. She was a fundamentalist Christian, opposed to sex, alcohol, and even meat. He had married her for her money. Agnes, he explains is "from the Latin word for a lamb. A lamb is a symbol of purity."

The revelation of Lydgate's marriage to Agnes is softened by the fact that Lydgate had believed she was dead. But then in "some sort of vegetarian magazine published in Calcutta," he recently learned that she was still alive. With Lydia he, therefore, had been a bigamist, living in sin. Lydia is stunned and returns to Australia. At the conclusion of the novel Agnes Lydgate suddenly appears on the scene, eager to take up where she left off. Lydgate, now stunned, is finally and permanently trapped by the everlasting sacrament of marriage.

As in the Malayan trilogy, Burgess weaves characters and episodes skillfully together in a complicated plot, which once wound up, never falters. The novel begins and ends with a search for a key, a symbolic incident as Carruthers Chung is all too anxious to point out: "Everybody is looking

for the key. That is the history of Western Philosophy . . .
But the key is not there." At the beginning, Lydgate searches
for the key to his new house, traversing the town from the
post office to coffee shops to the Dunia Hotel, to the Public
Works Department, back to the post office. The upshot is
that he needs no key, since the door to his new house has
been open all the time. At the end of the novel, the Caliph
desperately searches for the key to his new mosque, but it
is nowhere to be found.

Devil of a State abounds with interconnected subplots,
mirroring Lydgate's wanderings and irresponsibilities. Chief
among them is the raging battle between Paolo Tasca, the
young, good-looking, hot-blooded Italian marble worker, and
his father, Nando Tasca, the old, weather-beaten, hot-blooded
Italian marble worker. Nando makes Paolo do most of the
work in the mosque, while he hoards his money, drinks beer,
and pursues women.

Paolo's rebellion against his father increases when he
discovers letters from his father, written to some jungle
plantation to send him there. Outraged, he puts on his father's
suit, goes to town, sees his father there, and in panic scurries
up the minaret of the new mosque and locks himself in. The
minaret contains broadcasting equipment and a microphone,
through which Paolo can howl his distress and rebellion
across the entire town.

Paolo in his loud broadcasted tirades becomes a symbol
of unjust victimization for the downtrodden in Dunia. They
climb up the tower with food and drink. At last Nando
retrieves him with promises of a return to Italy. What Paolo
doesn't know, however, is that his father has arranged a
marriage back in Italy for him; that will trim his sails. "It
was just," thinks Nando, "marriage was the answer to all
problems."

The second subplot of the novel centers on Dunia's
political strivings. Patu, the nationalist leader, wants to bring
a noted revolutionary speaker, M. Bastians, into the country
to rouse the faithful. Through Patu's underhanded arrange-

ments, M. Bastians arrives, the police escort him from the
airport, and, needless to say, the meeting at the Chin Chin
Cinema that night, turns into a riot. Even political self-
determination in Dunia seems impossible.

The novel concludes with the Caliph's birthday parade,
the circumcision ceremony of two princes, and the failure to
find the key to open the new mosque. Paolo is off to Italy,
Lydgate is stuck with Agnes, and Nando relaxes. The British
Empire continues to collapse, and the state of Dunia, the
imperturbable East, carries on, "heedless of human time or
of any time but its own."

Devil of a State is a comic novel of bad manners. Its
characters—the amorous Italians, the gambling Syrians, the
hypocritical Muslims, the duty bound but quarrelsome British,
the "macho" Australians—exist more or less as stereotypical
illustrations of manners for each class, each caste. The
British attempt to uphold a code of good manners and civility,
but it is constantly violated. As Tomlin, the U.N. Advisor,
ponders, clearly out of his depth, "Why couldn't people live
normal decent lives—a little tennis, a couple of pink gins
before dinner, a little very mild flirtation? . . . Decent
behavior, a decent life, everything in moderation . . . That's
what we Anglo-Saxons have tried to teach the world." He
rails against the Caliph's actions: "You're only able to indulge
in your beautiful Islamic dream because we do the dirty work
. . . You're a pirate king; ruling retired pirates, intruders
just as much as we are." One can overhear Burgess's own
views in this forthright British sermon.

Rebellion is the underlying theme of the novel. It exists
on all levels of society, in the family, in politics, in social
customs, and in religious matters. Paolo, the son, rebels
against his father. Patu rebels against the state. The Caliph
rails against the British Empire. Lydgate complains about
the married state. And yet Lydgate does give in, reluctantly,
to the sacrament of his first marriage. Nando, the father,
does rescue his son, Paolo, and sends him off to get married,
however calculatedly. Patu's rebellion does founder and

fragment. Even the mighty arrogance of the Caliph is checked by his inability to find the key to the mosque. Burgess seems to imply that however rebellious the modern world is, however dissatisfied, there are the older, traditional values like marriage, family loyalty, and political good manners that still are valid and important. It's as if he acknowledged that marriage may be, in fact, corrupt and hellish, but the sacrament itself, the form of that ancient rite, must be respected and maintained. Form becomes more important than the actual content of experience. It is a theme or belief that Burgess would continue to explore in his novels.

Burgess reveals his love of language and ability to create great comic scenes in this novel. When Paolo and Nando have at one another after one of their many encounters, Burgess relishes the epithets and insults they hurl at each other:

From ancient drains and sewers of the language (maritime inns and brothels, soldiers' tents of the days of the Empire's decline), from scrawls in the catacombs, graffiti dug up from beneath the preservative lava, from parodies of religious ritual, whoremasters' chapbooks, with slang of the craft, low terms of the byre and stable, the vocabulary of tavern brawls, with a richness of precise gesture and rudimentary dance they tore into each other.

When he chastises Lydgate's sins and Paolo's lust, he comically plays the Old Testament prophet and uses a quasi-Biblical language, full of "dost's" and "thou's" and "hath's." The scene at the Tomlins' house with the aggressive Patu, the uneasy Rowlandson, the obsequious and chirpy Nando Tasca, and a surly visiting artist is a sheer delight. It is the state of Dunia in miniature. Burgess records and delivers it with such style and grace, we can't help but laugh out loud as it passes before our eyes.

The language and the comic scenes are interwoven in a swift, joyous manner. There is, indeed, an operatic quality about the novel. Characters sing, hum, and whistle. There are choral summaries, recitatives, and full blown arias.

Paolo, listening to Mr. Bastian's speech, thinks of it as a "one-man opera," a phrase which in many ways epitomizes the shape and tone of the novel.

Burgess dedicated *Devil of a State* to Graham Greene. Certainly, at first glance, Lydgate's soul-searching suggests Green's characters, particularly Scobie in *The Heart of the Matter*. The similarity is only superficial, however, since Greene's outlook is far more serious and tragic than Burgess's. Greene makes Scobie's confused love of God and his terrible sense of responsibility and pity palpable to the reader. We are taken deep within Scobie's personal agony and indecision. His emotional commitment is described precisely and deeply. He is spiritually wise and practically foolish, wondering if indeed "one would have to feel pity even for the planets . . . if one reached what they called the heart of the matter."

Burgess's terrain is superficially similar, but his is the territory of satire and comedy. Lydgate is no terribly responsible Scobie; he is a philosophical "lightweight." Burgess maintained a strict distance between the reader and his characters through his use of language and observation. When Burgess upbraids Lydgate in his rich, Biblical language, it is delightful, but Lydgate's "sin" remains a thing of comedy, a frail human condition dependent more on slapstick circumstance than upon the state of one's soul. It is not the intimate and responsible love of God that motivated Burgess; rather it was his sense of comedy and satire in the clash of Eastern and Western customs and cultures.

Devil of a State may finally be too comic and too shrill, as if Burgess were outgrowing his material and tossing this book off too easily. The satire and comedy are much too obvious. The cheap shots at the characters seem almost a caricature of satire and comedy, a too-easy "put-down" of the "little world of the misled" in Dunia. One is aware that it is time for Burgess to move on, to extend his range and fictional devices. In the shadow of *The Long Day Wanes*, *Devil of a State* seems a playful, bright bauble, but more a piece of costume jewelry than a gem of lasting value.

The Right to an Answer: "This shadow life
of buying and selling."

In *The Right to an Answer*, one of Burgess's most carefully
wrought and brightest novels, Burgess inverts his earlier
portrayal of the clash of Eastern and Western cultures. In
this novel J. W. Denham, conservative, stolid businessman
in export and trading, returns from his business dealings in
the East to visit his aged and widowed father in a Midlands
city in England. He is later joined by a Mr. Raj, a Ceylonese,
who may be the same man that was casually mentioned in
The Long Day Wanes: "He was a man of rich culture of
which he would give anybody the benefit in long, slow,
rolling, monotonous monologues." Together the "exiled"
Englishman and the cultured Ceylonese confront the modern
suburban landscape of contemporary England.

Burgess chose to use the first-person narrative, so
Denham tells his own tale. This is a master stroke, since
Denham and his own obsessions and torments are clearly
seen in the forefront of the novel. Unlike Ennis, Crabbe, and
Lydgate, he is not lost amid the actions and events of the
plot. His personal involvement in the world he perceives is
made readily apparent by his manner of telling the tale: "I'm
telling this story mainly for my own benefit." At once all
other characters and events become not subordinate to
Burgess's desires and attitudes alone, but to Denham's. Here
is a man who sets out "to clarify in my own mind the nature
of the mess that so many people seem to be in nowadays."

Denham is a businessman who cherishes stability above
freedom. He sees the world going to hell around him in "the
post-war English mess" and believes fervently that "those
who blaspheme against stability don't last very long." Consequently, he tends to treat life on the sly, superficially, and
somewhat cautiously. He enjoys his mistresses and prattles
on about the sacredness of marriage but is himself unmarried
and alone. He feels himself an exile from the English world,
but most of all he embodies a disspirited, wordly-wise

boredom and disillusionment. For him travel is merely "that illusion of liberation . . . the illusion of getting somewhere." He even describes it as a "brief illness." Home for him "is not a place but all places, all places except the one we happen to be in at the moment." He believes firmly that contact between people is an impossibility, "except briefly in bed, over a shared bottle." Loveless, tired, and expatriated, he returns to a suburban England, which half reflects his own cynical uninvolvement with life.

The carefully observed suburban world comes clearly into focus, a jaundiced, corrupted place. The closed, uninvolved world traps its inhabitants as surely as if they were prisoners in some padded cell. The suburban streets reveal "clean pavements like mortuary slabs," and the sun makes the landscape "seem flat, cardboard, not a necropolis, but something that had never lived." This is the world of Denham's sister, Beverly, the suburban housewife, where "the honest black telephone shone coyly from behind flowery curtains." It is the world of television, of aimless-eyed "zombies," lured "to submit to the blue hypnotic eye and the absence of the need for thought or sodality." Denham returns in the dead of winter, depressed by "the whole damp cabbagy essence of England" and sighs wearily to himself, "Ah hideous, corrupt, T.V.-haunted England."

In such an incommunicative and frozen world, people still have "a hunger for unifying myth." This need for communion seems to be satisfied by film stars, newspaper comics, weekend adulteries, but most of all by the English pub: "We pray in a church and booze in a pub: profoundly sacerdotal at heart, we need a host in both places to preside over us." The weekend drinking bouts in the pub are as close to communion as modern man can get, and the only remark someone makes about the church is that "the church spire interferes with their bloody television reception." The modern suburb is Burgess's version of a modern hell.

To this world returns J. W. Denham. He and his father, a retired printer—"they carry the miracle of the word to

generations yet unborn"—go drinking at the Black Swan pub
on Saturday night. The pub becomes the central arena for
petty suburban adulteries. Billy Winterbottom, a meek
printer, takes up with Imogen Everett, the daughter of a
failed poet, who's just fled her husband. Billy's wife, Alice,
parades with her weekend lover, tough Jack Brownlow, while
Mrs. Brownlow carries on with nondescript Charlie Whittier.
Imogen's father, Everett, the poet, asks Denham for a loan
to get his poetry published, but Denham refuses and is called
away on business to Ceylon.

On the flight back from Ceylon Denham runs into Mr.
Raj, or rather Mr. Raj insinuates himself into Denham's
presence. He looks like an "Apollo in frozen milk chocolate,"
has a B.A., is attempting "to write a thesis on Popular
Enceptions of Racial Differentiation," and is on his way to
the same town in England where Denham is headed. Raj is
a fascinating character, at once sycophantic to Denham and
highly intelligent. Denham describes him as both "gentle
and formidable." He talks of love and reciprocity and yet
pursues his own interests with a quiet, skillful vengence. He
is marked by gracious manners and a "deadly Eastern
realism." He despises the Negro as a member of a lowly
race, while he himself is black. Burgess admitted that Raj's
presence in the novel acted as an alien element tossed in
amid the adulterous suburban labyrinth, a catalyst in the
mixture, but he also realized that "the character dominated
the book. This I didn't intend."

At first back in England Denham views Raj merely as
"a breath of turmeric and coriander to season our cold meat"
in the suburbs. He believes, more or less with Raj, that
"twain can meet, despite inordinate tensions created wantonly
by demagogues in both East and West." When Raj begins
making complimentary remarks about the size of Denham's
manhood at the pub, however, (strictly a common courtesy
in Ceylon) Denham advises him that is it not the time and
the place to do so. Likewise, when Raj pursues Alice
Winterbottom to rent a room from her, Denham tells him that

this would be impossible. When Jack Brownlow turns on Raj as a "one-time imperial master" would turn on "insolence from a member of a subject race," Denham realizes that perhaps things are more complicated than they appeared. It is when Raj has been ambushed by a group of English teenage toughs, who are left far worse off than he, that Denham decides to take Raj home to spend the night. He also decides that his father should take Raj in as a lodger to keep him company. Raj cooks up a magnificent curry; old Mr. Denham loves it; Denham sees that everything is in order, and he leaves on a business trip to Singapore.

In Singapore Denham receives a telegram that announces flatly, "Dad dying." He hurriedly flies back to England. His father has died, literally, from Raj's rich curries. While he surveys his father's coffin in the parlor, Raj enters drunk and confused. He had written to Denham to ask his advice about how to befriend Alice, and Denham had sent back a humorous cryptogram in which the first letters of each world spell out the flippant message: "Can Oriental People Understand Love. Are They Innocent Or Not. Not Only Women." Raj, lost and confused, points a gun at an outraged Denham. Denham strikes out at Raj's race, his blackness, seeing in old Denham's death, Raj's revenge. Raj is stunned, while Denham rails on: "Despite all your bloody talk about us all being brothers . . . one half can't understand the other half." Raj staggers out. Shortly thereafter Alice walks into the room and says that Raj has shot Billy. Denham calls the police, but they think he's been watching too much television. He hurries to Winterbottom's house and finds Raj in the bedroom with the gun standing over Winterbottom's body. Raj asks Denham's advice. Denham advises him to walk out into the garden and shoot himself. Raj sees no need to wait for the garden: "He put the neat lady's pistol to his right temple and squeezed the trigger, with a delicate milk-chocolate finger."

At the end of the novel, Denham finally realizes that in supporting stability over freedom, he has chosen detachment from life instead of the possibility of love, "for surely that sneered-at suburban life was more stable than this shadow life of buying and selling in a country where no involvement was possible." What of love? "Even the word was better than this emptiness, this standing on the periphery and sneering." Perhaps Denham's "conversion" comes too quickly, too neatly, and undercuts all too easily his delightful, low-keyed satiric language, which has carried the book along. Yet he has committed the same sins he sees in others; his overcompensation for his lack of roots, his own tepid noninvolvement, has generated the death of three people: his father, Billy Winterbottom, and Mr. Raj. He is left with a scrap of Mr. Raj's writings, which closes the novel: "The capacity of people for hatred can never cease to astonish . . . Love seems inevitable, necessary, as normal and as easy a process as respiration, but unfortunately . . . "

Beneath the antisuburban veneer and the clash once again of East and West, Burgess has painted a fairly grim picture of man's existence in the modern world. Man is homeless, isolated, in no real communion with his fellow man. He has fallen from the intimate grace of old traditions, of Christian faith. In such a world "You have had no action, you have had merely J. W. Denham on leave, eating, drinking, unjustifiably conscious, meeting people, especially Mr. Raj, recounting, at the tail of the eye, almost out of earshot, the adultery of small uninteresting people." It is a world in which there can be no right answer; the question itself "is not easy to define." The only reality in the modern world seems to be "the high explosive that lies hidden underneath stability," the crude lusts and addled passions of "just silly vulgar people." This is a world in which, if there is a God, he seems to be only a God of wrath and punishment. Punishment is all; "that way everyone of us is a little bit of God." And love is nonexistent.

Reinforcing the sense of detachment throughout the novel, Denham describes the things he sees as if he's watching a film. Scenes appear as "trick photography rather than bad continuity"; action continues "like a dull and

endless film." People make film entrances, and one acts "as
though he were a television programme." On his plane ride
back to England to find his dead father, Denham meets
Monique Hugo, film star, a "whipped-like-cream, spun-like-
sugar, crackly crunch product of the shiny mythopoeic
machines of our age." Perhaps these references reveal once
again Denham's own detachment from life. He views the
world around him as unreal and disconnected. His snappy,
crafted prose is not enough finally to connect him either to
love or understanding, even though his awareness of them
begins to surface at the end of the novel. He has been too
long gone from England, too little influenced by the East. He
remains a lost soul, an exile, in a world that eludes him. The
clash of East and West is no longer a mere matter of different
manners and different foods. It has left J. W. Denham in an
abyss of disillusioned loss, and the mess he sees all around
him is his own.

The Right to an Answer is one of Burgess's best novels.
Burgess's usual ironic distance, which in his previous East-
West novels had resulted in fictions more ingeniously reported
than fully realized, is here replaced or superseded by the
fully realized personality of J. W. Denham. Denham's ironic
detachment is viewed not only as part of his personality, but
also as part of the very suburban and modern landscape he
inhabits. The story, therefore, deepens and broadens because
of his involvement in it. A tale told in the first person
necessarily involves the reader more quickly, at the beginning
at least, than one told in Burgess's more clinical, objective
manner. And Denham's ironies and emotions reflect those
around him. Trapped in his cynicism, Denham cannot finally
understand or pity the people around him; trapped in theirs,
they cannot understand or pity him. The impasse is complete.

The parallels the reader discovers between Denham's
personal confession—"I'm telling this story mainly for my
own benefit"—his personality, and the people's lives that
envelop him yield a resonance and depth in this novel that
are lacking in Burgess's previous efforts. The comic, detached

tone of the narrator in *Devil of a State* and *A Vision of Battlements*, for instance, here resides in a participant within the novel itself. The tone is Denham's throughout; it never falters or grows frenetic and arch. Rather, Denham's personality builds and expands as the tale itself does. The two are finally inseparable. Like Burgess's Enderby in later novels, Denham remains a fully developed, fully realized character in his own right, and Burgess's creation of him, through which to view the East-West clash once again, lends the novel the human dimension and focus it needs to remain memorable.

3

•••

A Manichean Duoverse

Anthony Burgess likes to talk and write about the "fundamental divisions"[1] in life. He believes firmly that it is
necessary "to define life as subsisting in a duoverse in which
we maintain our stability by learning to cope with these
opposites."[2] These great opposites, part of the Western
Christian's outlook on the world, include good and evil, spirit
and flesh, heaven and hell. From this perspective life becomes
a dynamic dialectic between oppositions. We have seen this
already in Burgess's novels concerned with the irrevocable
clash between Eastern and Western cultures. His own
experience revealed the effects of that clash. To this theme
is joined also the clash between the individual and the
collective, between Ennis and the army, Crabbe and a
polyglot Malaya, Lydgate and the state of Dunia. One of
Burgess's principle methods of organizing a novel is to pit
a main character against an absurd, corrupt, and often comic
world, within which he must live. The "fundamental divisions"
in life can be seen, therefore, both in Burgess's themes and
in his fictional methods.

The process, however, becomes more complicated than
one of mere opposition. Burgess's world in his novels is one
in which good and evil, spirit and flesh, interpenetrate one
another. They are mixed and fused, not to the point of
ultimate synthesis, but to the point of continuing, unresolved
conflict. There are moments when good seems to conquer
evil, but these are only moments in an endless flux of time

and space, in which resolution is as uncertain as life itself. The interpenetration of mind and matter, good and evil, creates a universe of universal conflict and uncertainty, where no synthesis or resolution seems possible.

As a lapsed Catholic Burgess described himself many times as a Manichean: "I'm only a Manichee in the widest sense of belief that duality is the ultimate reality."[3] Manichaeism preached the ultimate dualism: God and the Devil were coequals. The Gospel of the Prophet, Mani, declared: "Light and Dark, Good and Evil, are the two opposite and coeternal Sources of all that is. They were mingled together . . . "[4]

The Devil created man and the visible universe. All matter was, therefore, evil. Man was not fallen from some Edenic paradise; he was spawned in evil from the beginning. There seemed to be no possibility of redemption. Body and Soul could neither be reconciled nor resurrected.

And yet a few stray sparks from God's forces of light at the moment of creation did manage to enter into the material darkness of the devil's world. Each man contained some glimmer of a soul within him, however overwhelmingly imprisoned in his own flesh and original corruption.

A Manichean believer could either entirely renounce the world or devote himself to the corrupt pleasures of it. The majority of believers or the Elect, the "Righteous Pure Ones" of Manichaeism, renounced the material world and turned their backs upon it. The Soul must "purify and free itself from the defilements of material darkness and ignorance."[5] Purification demanded withdrawal from the material, visible world. Devout Manicheans took monastic vows, dressed in a single black robe, depended on offerings from their followers, and became eternal wanderers. They accepted a completely ascetic, passive, and antisocial way of life. They opposed marriage, sex, property, meat, eggs, wine, labor, agriculture, killing animals and uprooting plants. Such a "deep urge to flee the world"[6] and a horror of materialism created "a religion of pessimism . . . without hope."[7] Their

creed was ascetic, more to save the spark of light of the
Divine within man than to save man himself.

Other Manichean heresies chose to enjoy completely the
material darkness of man's existence and practiced arcane
and elaborate sexual debaucheries. These saw no hope of
man's salvation at all and, therefore, celebrated only the
momentary pleasures of the flesh. The fables and myths the
Manicheans used to explain the origins of the universe were
rife with such elements as cannibalism, incest, and abortion.
Lust was the evil demon that propagated a world.

In either case Manicheans insisted on an either/or
decision. They could not tolerate the more "compromised"
Christian position, wherein both flesh and spirit are seen as
mutual and corresponding avenues toward grace and redemption. For the Manicheans the world is the site of a
constant, unrelenting war between opposites; it is as if the
universe had been polluted with conflict from the very
beginning. The tortuous interpenetration of good and evil, of
uplifting spiritual light and repugnant material darkness, in
a world basically debauched and demonic, remains for the
most part unresolved and unresolvable.

The influence of Manichaeism on Christianity has been
great. Much of the dualistic vision, though much less extreme,
can be found in the theology of St. Paul. St. Augustine
himself was a Manichean between the years A.D. 373 and
382. The ascetic ideals of Manichaeism affected the monastic
traditions in the Christian community. The very dualistic
nature of the Western mind, as opposed to the Eastern, in
many ways supported Mani's heretical beliefs.

Thanks to his Catholic background, strong Manichean
elements appear in Burgess's novels. Several of his characters
are sensitive, ascetic souls, who wish at times to withdraw
from the sordid, corrupt world around them. In *Tremor of
Intent* and *1985*, the main characters do just that.

In reaction against his Manichean outlook, Burgess at
one time was drawn very much to Islam. He admired its
austerity as opposed to the "debased Baroque" of his own

Catholic faith: "It's a very simple religion . . . Indeed the whole of Europe could have been Islamicized. The whole of Spain certainly was, and if you're living in the East, if you're living under hot skies and desert sands and camels, you can see the attraction of this very austere religion." And yet religious historians have suggested that the Manichean belief in the magic properties of numbers, its astrological notions, and its ritual practices were passed on to Islam.[8]

The attraction to Burgess of certain aspects of Manichaeism can, therefore, be accounted for both by his personal experiences and by his lapsed Catholicism. In fact, in many ways, his vision of the world as one of constant reversals and repetitions within the on-going conflict between good and evil reveals an essentially conservative Catholic eschatology. The somewhat vicious circle seems to uphold rather than to change the *status quo*. Burgess admitted, "I always loved dialectical materialism. But it was a structuralist love from the start."[9] This "love," indeed, may be more aesthetic than moral, more a way of constructing the world in his novels than an article of essential belief.

In any case, his essentially comic view of existence, despite all its absurd and tragic notions and events, presents a world far less pessimistically "felt" and far more hopeful than the Manicheans allowed for.

If the first group of novels we have looked at essentially dealt with manners, in particular the manners of East and West, the second group of novels deals essentially with matters. Those matters reflect the Manichean dualism of the world at large. In both *Honey for the Bears* (1963) and *Tremor of Intent* (1966), Burgess wrote about commitment and choice in the Cold-War world of spies and agents. In *1985* (1978), *A Clockwork Orange* (1962), and *The Wanting Seed* (1962), Burgess confronted the problem of individual free will and choice in the monolithic and completely socialized states of the future. In these anti-Utopian or cacotopian novels, he created fables about what might happen if the State were allowed to triumph. In each case the State's ideas of good and evil or right and wrong contrast violently with the individual's. Paul Hussey, Denis Hillier, Tristram Foxe, Alex de Lago, and Bev Jones oppose their versions of individual morality to the State's.

In each of these Manichean novels Burgess still believed that the ultimate human right is the right of choice. St. Paul's primacy of conscience still loomed larger in his outlook than the more pessimistic certainties of Mani's prophecies. The true enemy was not the Manichean but the man or institution that forced an individual to choose against his will or the neutral observer who avoided making any choice whatsoever. Both suffered the wrath and vengeance of Burgess's Manichaen point of view.

Honey for the Bears (1963): "What I seek is the continuum, the merging."

The plot for *Honey for the Bears* was more or less suggested by Burgess's own trip to Leningrad with his first wife in 1961:

We did a trip to Leningrad by boat, and there she was taken ill. This was probably the beginning of the cirrhosis. God knows what it was. She collapsed. She knew no Russian at all, collapsed in the street, and I was not there. It was nightmarish. And was shoved into a hospital, a very good hospital. They really look after you. I was left more or less on my own and was speaking Russian, got the material for *Honey for Bears*, which is pretty well based on fact, except the homosexuality and so on . . .

His wife's sudden illness and nightmarish misadventures in Leningrad are clearly reflected in the incidents and tone of the novel.

The Manichean "alternation of aimless spasmodic action and sheer paralysis, the craving for exotic sauces thus becoming cognate with a sacred huddling into the dusty dark of the past," as Burgess in the novel described the manic-depressive cycle of the major character's, Paul Hussey's, dashing about Leningrad at all hours of the day, clearly are

reflected in the nightmarish rush and tumble of the plot of
the novel. Paul, a thirty-seven-year-old antique dealer in
East Sussex, and his wife, Belinda, an American girl from
Massachusetts, have come to Leningrad on a cruise ship to
help the widow of a friend. Her husband, Robert, whom Paul
knew during the war, has died of heart failure, leaving his
wife, Sandra, alone. Robert had been to Leningrad before to
sell dozens of drilon dresses on the black market at consid-
erable profit. These consumer goods, which the Russians
lack, become the honey for the Soviet bears. Paul has stashed
ten dozen of these dresses in his luggage and while in
Leningrad hopes to meet Robert's Russian contact there, a
P. V. Mizinchikov. While the cruise ship steers toward
Leningrad, Belinda comes down with a painful rash, which
is treated by the ship's doctor.

The novel picks up speed and careens from incident to
incident once the ship docks in Leningrad. Doctors aides
cart Belinda off to the hospital by ambulance. Zverkov and
Karamzin, two members of the Soviet Secret Police, confront
Paul in his hotel room and announce that Mizinchikov has
been arrested and has revealed Robert's scheme with the
dresses. Paul pleads innocent, rushes to the hospital, and
gets involved there in a long psychological interview with Dr.
Sonya Lazurkina. She wants to know all about his childhood,
reveals that Belinda, under drugs, has confessed that she
hates men, and suggests that Paul is himself a homosexual
whose only meaningful sexual relationship was with his old
war buddy, Robert. Belinda must remain in the hospital for
observation. Paul goes away stunned, checks out of his hotel,
and moves in with Alexei Prutkov, an interpreter for Intourist,
who works at the Hermitage and whom Paul ran into in a
crowded restaurant during his running to and fro.

At a party at Alexei's everyone gets royally drunk. Paul
drinks an entire bottle of vodka while hanging upside down
outside the window, held only by his left ankle, to prove his
courage. But then he shouts that everyone should get stripped.
In the morning, hungover and repentent, Paul is kicked out

of the apartment by Alexei for having revealed such sexually perverse instincts. Alexei is disgusted with Paul's apparent homosexuality.

Paul is sent by Alexei to meet a man at the House of Books, to whom he can sell his dresses. The man mentions Mizinchikov's name, which he could only have known if informed by the Secret Police. Paul realizes it's a setup, that Alexei is an informer, and spotting Zverkov and Karamzin across the street, waiting for him to take the money, begins giving the dresses away. He hands them to people who are passing by, proclaiming Anglo-Russian friendship forever. Zverkov and Karamzin carry him off to headquarters, interrogate and beat him, and finally realize that he is not part of a major conspiracy but only a small-time, amateur criminal. After a night in a cell, he is released, only to find a letter from Belinda, saying that she is going away with Sonya Lazurkina, the doctor, and will not be returning to England with him.

The novel concludes with the farcical and bizarre episode of Paul's smuggling out of Russia the apparent son of a famous but discredited Russian composer, Opiskin, disguised as Belinda. The deal is arranged by the mysterious Dr. Tiresias and his companion, Madox, an odd pair Paul met on the cruise ship coming to Leningrad. Tiresias, involved on a major scale with smuggling and crime, pays Paul five hundred pounds to deliver the disguised son of Opiskin safely to Finland on a boat leaving that night. The disguise is discovered on board the ship, Paul and Opiskin are locked in the honeymoon suite, and Leningrad authorities, in particular Zverkov and Karamzin, are summoned by radio. By the use of secret messages, Paul relates what is happening to a returning group of football enthusiasts. At the right moment these men block Zverkov, Karamzin, and the ship's officers, and Paul and Opiskin hurry down the ramp to free Finnish soil.

In the last scene Paul meets Zverkov and Karamzin at a beer garden and learns that Opiskin is really Stephen V.

Obnoskin, a very dangerous criminal and gangster. His act of heroism turns out to be one more deceptive and illusory action in the confused and uncertain actions of his entire life. Paul, Zverkov, and Karamzin drink a toast to freedom and add, "Whatever it is."

Paul's trip to Leningrad proves to be his initiation into a world filled with contradictions: "He had never been more aware of everything necessarily containing its opposite. What was he, then, and what was he in the world for?" Before disembarking from the ship when it arrives in Leningrad, he gets caught up in a nighttime revel, the "Atheists' Ball." Here students are disguised obscenely as nuns, priests, and bishops. The blasphemous dance throws Paul into confusion: "Dancing was going on there: priest with nun, saint with martyr, friar with monk." Old reliable traditions are being mocked and undercut, a pattern that the rest of the novel continues to reveal.

The world becomes a Manichean nightmare for Paul. Those things which appear on the surface to be opposites are really more similar than different. Those things which appear to be the same are in fact very different. Russia and America seem to be the great opposites in the political and cultural structure of the world, but as Alexei suggests, "What's the difference? It's all the State. There's only one state." Paul realizes this as well: "The West wanted sex and avatars; Russia the opium of progress. Ah, nonsense. The State was a twisted wire coronal a child would wear on its head. People were people . . . In different ways our societies move towards the same goal—the creation of a new kind of man who shall be sinless." Similarly, America and England, represented by Belinda and Paul, seem to be very dissimilar, and yet, Belinda tells Paul in her final letter to him: "You fell for the Big American Glamour like you all do and pretend not to . . . you just become the Big American museum . . . Dear Old Mother England, matrix of American Culture . . . Meanwhile moon with your wartime boy-friend and sing the old sad songs . . . keeping a Stiff Upper Lip what what chaps."

Alexei's rebellion against the Soviet establishment—complete with his paltry American slang, his "hip" existence, and his craving for jazz—turns out to be a mere charade. Not only is he in the occasional pay of the Secret Police, but "the trouble was that the language of rebellion was also, in the USSR, the language of the Establishment."

On the other hand, things which appear to be relatively stable and similar turn out to be very different from one another. The roles of men and women, particularly in the Husseys' marriage, turn out to be false; both are strongly, if intermittently, homosexual. The policemen, Zverkov, and Karamzin turn out to be the most reliable and honest of Paul's friends. The drab sameness of Leningrad and its inhabitants turns out to be subjected to the curious Slavic temperament, a manic-depressive cycle that rises and falls constantly between euphoria and paralysis.

Opposites and contradictions abound in this Manichean world. Zverkov is a philosophical, thoughtful man; his cohort, Karamzin, is a man of force and physical strength. Alexei offers Paul jazz and his apartment but turns him in to the police. Sonya Lazurkina offers Belinda real love and understanding and keeps her dependent on drugs and medicines. Dr. Tiresias proclaims that freedom of choice is what he believes in and yet masterminds a massive criminal network. Russia suggests a great family enterprise yet maintains a huge Secret Police. Paul and Belinda's marriage is parodied by Paul's and the disguised criminal's escape under the cover of newlyweds. Dr. Tiresias's mysterious bisexuality—the doctor can never be identified as male or female in the novel—epitomizes the sexual ambiguity at the heart of the book. The only synthesis possible in such a world is to recognize a universe that is at once thoroughly dualistic and so thoroughly interpenetrated by good and evil that all becomes ultimately ambiguous.

Paul's journey forward into Leningrad is also a journey backward to a recognition of his own past. If drab, run-down Leningrad has "at least the *look* of Orwell's fantasy world,"

it also, in many ways, reminds Paul of his childhood in the
slums of Bradcaster: "He smelt his school days in Bradcaster—a whiff of brewery, tannery, burning potatoes, dust,
a bourdon of tobacco which suggest Christmas." A horsehair
sofa in Dr. Lazurkina's office reminds him of his Aunt Lucy's.
A cabdriver is "the spitten image of an out-of-work called
Fred whom Paul sometimes met in a Sussex pub." In fact,
"he was shocked to his soul as the grimy past enfolded him
deeper and deeper."

Russia becomes the past incarnate. "The old solid
Russia preserved in Tsarist decor" is everywhere, no more
so than in the huge labyrinth of the Hermitage, with its "gilt
and matchite and agate, the walls of silver velvet, the
rosewood, ebony, palm and amaranth parquet, the frozen
Arctic seas of marble veined and arteried like some living
organism." Belinda, lying in her hospital bed, daydreams
about her past and thinks, "It was as though they were just
taking me into the family as some of these big slum families
were so big already they used to take in just any poor kid
from the street." The anonymous Leningrad landscape "was
all nameless the way everybody in a family was nameless;
names were for strangers." Belinda's talk of family and love
arises from her awareness of "the great family archetypes
which brooded over this strange yet familiar country." Belinda
realizes, "Love is about the only thing these people have."
"Perhaps," says Paul, "Russia is really everybody's past.
Not everybody's future but everybody's past."

This journey of self-recognition within which the present
slowly reveals the past (another Manichean dualism, which at
first seems a pair of opposites, then seems all too similar, and
at last remains an interpenetration of both opposite and similar
characteristics) reveals to Paul his love for Robert. This step-
by-step series of revelations is symbolized by the wooden
peasant-woman doll Paul buys for Belinda. Within each doll
there is another, smaller doll, "until the innermost peasant-
woman doll, which was the size of a walnut. This was probably
deeply significant of something in the Russian psyche."

Also like the Russian psyche—the doll within the doll—
is Paul's ritualistic unveiling of his own past, his own sexual
ambiguities, and uncertainties. At one point Burgess wrote
that his novels dealt with a single character's "stripping-off
of illusion."[10] This is precisely what has happened to Paul
Hussey, and even though at the conclusion of the novel he
proclaims, "I'm going back to an antique-shop . . . somebody's got to conserve the good of the past," the reader
realizes that whatever good existed in the past, it too is
tainted and complicated by the ambiguous and unresolved
tensions and uncertainties of the human condition.

At one point Dr. Tiresias proclaims:

I am tired of categories, of divisions, of opposites. Good, evil; male,
female; positive, negative. That they interpenetrate is no real
palliative, no ointment for the cut. What I seek is the *continuum*,
the merging. Europe is all Manichees; Russia has become the most
European of them all.

Such a proclamation is attractive; it promises unity and
continuity, but in the mouth of the evil Dr. Tiresias it is
revealed for what it is: another false illusion of unity and
oneness. Tiresias's desire for a continuum includes and
justifies his greed, his lust for power, and his criminal
enterprises. In a universe spawned out of conflicting and
shifting opposites, such a statement for unity can only be,
however attractive, a mask for future evil designs.

While in jail for one night, Paul tells a tale to the other
inmates of a world which is divided between two tsars. "Each
has great shows of magic and strength to frighten the other.
But each did not wish to fight the other." Between them lived
a solitary man in his own small house. He seems to have had
the best of both possible worlds, for he could shop in either
tsardom. His was "the way of life with everything open." His
was the genuine human way. Freedom of choice thus becomes
the genuine human attribute in this Manichean world. The
parallel with the relationship among America, Russia, and
England is made more obvious when Paul relates how the

man took a wife from one of the tsardoms, who then "said to her husband that he must join the right tsardom." She leaves, leaving him stranded without having taken a stand.

Like the men in his story, Paul chooses not to act, more than he chooses to act, leaving him at once the butt of comic circumstance and the victim of his own inertia. His failing to choose is, in effect, a kind of choice, although his lack of character in no way strengthens the reader's regard for him.

Paul's proclamation of conserving the past in his English antique shop, "before your Americanism and American's Russianism make plastic of the world," may illustrate the idea of choice as expressed in his fable in jail, but it is at once too pat and too unrealistic to fit the novel itself. The past as revealed is more than just a collectible series of *objets d'art;* it is a confused and troubled place, made palatable only by its having passed. Belinda's and Paul's search for love leaves them both at large in ambiguous circumstances. Perhaps Paul's final pronouncement, though it may sound somewhat noble and possible, is just another example of human gullibility and pride, akin to Tiresias's desire for a continuum, yet another attempt to deal with the essentially Manichean nature of man and the universe. Yet choices must be made, however ultimately ambiguous and uncertain.

Honey for the Bears reveals a thoroughly Manichean universe on many levels, the political, the sexual, and the personal, although as one critic suggests, "the Manichean issues . . . are often secondary to the comedic emphasis."[11] At times the novel seems too schematic, too carefully programmed to bear out the Manichean vision. Paul's zigzagging from place to place, from person to person, in a strange and alien land for awhile focusses the reader's attention more on him than on the palpable design. And yet Paul is such an incomplete character, almost a cartoon stick-figure pushed from point to point, that even he begins to evaporate within the twists and turns of the tale. What Paul lacks in personal interest, Burgess makes up for in this novel with his comic skill at creating a zany, episodic, almost absurdist roller-coaster of a plot.

The recognition of the essential duality of all experience and intention and the unswerving belief in the sanctity of individual free will emerge as the major theme of the novel. Choice in such a complicated world epitomizes what it means to be human, even though the freedom necessary for that choice remains as ambiguously uncertain as life itself. "Freedom," toasts Paul at the end of the novel. "Whatever it is."

Tremor of Intent (1966): "Ultimate reality is a dualism or a game for two players."

If *Honey for the Bears* revealed a Manichean world, and if Hussey's attempts to deal with that revelation appear to be more a matter of avoidance than commitment, Denis Hillier, the British spy in the world of intrigue and espionage in *Tremor of Intent*, meets the moral crisis head-on. While Hussey drifts, as characters in comedies often do, Hillier commits himself fully to the Manichean vision he sees. His is a committed moral quest, filled with self-questioning and self-doubt, in a world which all too easily appeals to the appetites of the flesh and the palette. Hillier's moral regeneration is one that Hussey only half completes. Hussey wonders about what he should do. Hillier acts.

Burgess fashioned Hillier's moral battle within the structure of the spy novel. Hillier regards himself as a "superior technician," "a void, a dark sack crammed with skills." He's a "fallen Adam in his forties," a man branded like Cain with a telltale "S" burned into his left flank from some long-ago espionage assignment. He swigs a whiskey called *Old Morality*, believes in Original Sin and free will—"I believe in man's capacity to choose"—and suffers from both gluttony and satyriasis. He has an old-fashioned Catholic's sense of the reality of evil and resists any system or

ideology of explanation, blame, or denial. His final assignment, before he retires, is to rescue a rocket fuel scientist,
defector, and old school friend, Edwin Roper, from a scientific
conference in Yarylyuk in the Crimea. To effect this, he
boards the cruise ship, *Polyolbion*, in Venice disguised as
a typewriter expert, Sebastian Jagger.

The plot unravels with all the sensuous delights and
surprising betrayals of the spy genre. On board the *Polyolbion*
Hillier meets Mr. Theodorescu, a fat, many-ringed homosexual and buyer and seller of information (as mysterious
and ominous a figure as Dr. Tiresias in *Honey for the Bears*)
and his luscious Indian companion-secretary, Miss Devi.
Theodorescu challenges Hillier to an eating contest, a lavish
gluttonous splurge. The loser, the man who eats less, must
pay the winner a thousand pounds. Theodorescu wins and
demands his payment in cash. Hillier, distraught, and after
throwing up over the guard rail, dances with Miss Devi, who
seduces him and leads him into a range of sexual experiences
he has never enjoyed before. Theodorescu, however, comes
upon them in Miss Devi's cabin, spies the "S" on Hillier's
flank, gives him a drug to make him relax, and demands that
Hillier tell him all the espionage information he knows.
Hillier reveals some information, is paid $12,000 for his
efforts, and is rescued by Richard Wriste, the steward. As
a parting shot Theodorescu tells Hillier that he has alerted
the Soviet authorities in Yarylyuk of Hillier's coming, that
he and Miss Devi will leave the ship tomorrow by helicopter,
and that if he wants to get in touch with them further he
should meet them in Istanbul.

Hillier the next day reveals his dilemma to Alan and
Clara Walters, whose father, a flour baron, has suffered a
stroke the previous evening and whose avaricious step-mother
is already off with some other man. Alan is a precocious
American boy, fresh from a triumph on a television quiz
show. His sister, sixteen-year-old Clara, passes the time
reading sex manuals but is herself still innocent. Hillier
needs a Russian police uniform to slip ashore at Yarylyuk

and get to Roper. First Alan tries to lure a policeman to his
cabin to sell him something. When this fails, Clara resorts
to seduction and gets a drunken policeman into her cabin.
Hillier knocks him out, drags him into Mrs. Walters' bed,
slips on the uniform, and leaves the ship.

At the Chornoye Morye (Black Sea) Hotel the scientific
conference is in full swing. Hillier locates Roper being sick
in the garden. Roper refuses to leave. Suddenly Wriste
appears, prepared to kill them both. The British want Hillier
dead, because he's no longer any use as a spy, and he knows
too much. The whole plot to restore Roper was a set-up to
destroy him and Hillier. A certain cabinet minister in England
wants Roper dead, because, as it turns out, Roper caught the
minister, Sir Arthur Cornpit-Ferrers, in bed with his (Roper's)
German wife, Brigitte. Brigitte had left Roper in London to
become a prostitute and was forced by East German spies,
who had taken her relatives prisoner, to get information out
of Cornpit-Ferrers. To salvage his reputation, Cornpit-Ferrers
gets Roper delivered into the hands of Russian agents and
forcibly exiled from England. Wriste, an agent for Panleth,
some secret organization for assassinations, wants to shoot
both Hillier and Roper and take back a finger of each to his
superiors to verify his success. Suddenly Alan Walters
appears with a gun and kills Wriste. He got the gun by
stealing it from Theodorescu, when that swollen pederast was
having his way with Alan. Hillier marks Wriste's body with
the "S," Roper is determined to remain in Yarylyuk, and
both Hillier and Alan flee back to the safety of the ship.

On board ship, after Hillier has finished reading part
of Roper's autobiography, which Roper handed to him and
which revealed the sordid affair between him, Brigitte, and
Cornpit-Ferrers, Clara comes into the cabin to announce that
her father is dead. Hillier comforts her and finally makes
love to her, not in the voraciously selfish manner he did with
Miss Devi, but in a very gentle and initiating way. Hillier's
final act is to get to Istanbul, reject Miss Devi's latest offers,
fill Theodorescu with veritable tons of information, and then

kill him. He injects him with a drug that makes him euphorically drunk, leads him down to the dark docks of Istanbul, and watches him fall into the sea and drown.

When we last see Hillier, he has become a priest living in Ireland. He welcomes Alan and Clara, who have stopped by before Alan is to take up of medieval studies and Clara is to marry a sculptor. Roper has been reunited with the sexually promiscuous Brigitte in East Germany. At the novel's conclusion, Hillier has left the espionage game for good and contemplates the greater battles between good and evil.

Burgess craftily prepares for Hillier's regeneration from burned-out technician and spy to priest, from materialistic to spiritual concerns. There are signposts throughout the text. His belief in Original Sin, his description as a "fallen Adam," his awareness of being on his last assignment as a spy, and his recognition that as a spy he is "always ready to use people as if they were things" instead of human beings, prepares the way for his conversion. His growing realization that he loves Clara, or at least an idealized image of her, in contrast with his overwhelming lust for Miss Devi suggests to him that Miss Devi must represent "those fires of purgatory through which he had been permitted to pass to reach the beatifical vision." This is made even more explicit when he makes a reference to Beatrice's having led Dante "up to the glory of the stars" and views Clara as that "clear bright one," in whose presence "he was becoming respiritualized, made aware of an immortal soul again after all these many years." His initiating Clara (whose name means "light") into sexual experience is both tender and loving and prompted by her, a far cry from the lusty revels with Miss Devi: "This was no girl for the big sweating engine of phallic sex . . . He gave without taking . . . This was an act of love." Hillier's declaration to Roper—"We've got to forget history. It's a burden we've got to shed. We can't get anything done if we carry all that dead weight on our backs"—his making a final confession to Theodorescu in their final meeting—Theodorescu says, "You're turning me into a priest"—, Wriste's

calling himself an angel of death, and then proclaiming that
"it was all ritual," clearly reveal the pattern of Christian
redemption and regeneration.

When Wriste declares that "perhaps all of us who are
engaged in this sort of work . . . seek something deeper than
what most people term life, meaning a pattern" and proclaims,
"Our aseptic rational world does not have to be a mirror of
ultimate reality," the spiritual progress of Hillier is made
even clearer. Hillier's decision to settle in Ireland—"It's the
only place for a Catholic Englishman forced into exile . . .
With the Irish . . . history is timeless"—further underlines
his decision to opt out of the "aseptic rational world" of
espionage and intrigue and apply himself to a deeper, more
mysterious "mirror of ultimate reality," the realm of the
spirit.

Hillier's regeneration is paralleled by the initiation of
the children, Alan and Clara, into the mysteries of death and
sex. As Hillier explains, "Both your baptisms have been
heroic." It is appropriate that he should be the one to oversee
and participate in their initiation. As Alan explains in comic
understatement, "Well, you've certainly shown both of us
how the other half lives." The precocious Alan has seduced
the evil Theodorescu to get his gun and then arrives in the
nick of time to kill Wriste. Clara surrenders her "terrible
innocence" to her sexual encounter with Hillier. Hillier is
aware that real innocence can be dangerous, that youth can
be cold and heartless, because of its being committed to no
cause or to no person. He realizes that "they were too vigorous
but also too honest, the enemies of intrigue." Their baptisms
under fire fully initiate them into the all-too-human complexities of the modern world. They are humanized, even
though the price they must pay is a stiff one.

Alan, whom Hillier describes perceptively as one who
"seduced yourself into becoming a member of the modern
world," is yet fully aware of the consequences. When Hillier
upbraids him about playing at an adult world—"Sex-books
and dinner-jackets and earrings and cognac after dinner. You

talk about *me* playing games"—Alan counters almost heart-
breakingly, "We are only children. It was up to you to
recognize that. Games are all right for children."

Burgess makes it very clear in the novel why Hillier is
the one who can be saved and why Edwin Roper cannot be.
The difference between the two of them goes back to their
schoolboy days in Bradcaster, where Roper and Hillier were
fellow-pupils at a Catholic school whose patron saint was St.
Augustine, and which was run by Father Byrne. Hillier more
or less bought most of the Catholic dogma, the belief in
Original Sin and freedom of choice, the necessity of recognizing the reality of evil, and the inclination to believe that
sex and lust—"this damnable sex, boys," as Father Byrne
describes it—are very much a part of man's fallen and
unredeemed state. Roper, ever the skeptical rationalist,
questions the faith at an early age. His logical and scientific
mind cannot accept the miracles and beliefs of the church.
He seeks a rational, logical, and unified universe in which
everything has its place and there are no contradictions, no
mixed motives.

Roper's pursuit of logical explanations, however, cannot
explain away the fact of evil. His coming upon the piles of
corpses in Nazi concentration camps overwhelms him in just
the same way that the entire Nazi experience has overwhelmed
Europe: "We didn't want to believe, since belief that a
civilized nation had been capable of all this must overturn
everything we'd ever taken for granted about civilization,
progress, the elevating power of artistic, scientific, philosophical achievement." Stunned Roper marries the German
prostitute, Brigitte, and goes along with her idea that all are
responsible for the war, that Bolshevism is the great logical
conspiracy behind the scenes. When she deserts him, having
slept even with Hillier on the sly, Roper is again at a loss
to explain the meaning of existence. Gradually he falls under
the influence of a group of scientists who believe in a world
state and international science, yet another pipe dream to
succumb to. Hillier describes Roper's great failing: "What

counts is the willingness and ability to take evil seriously and to explain it." This Roper cannot do. He is doomed to yet one logical scheme after another, believing man's rational nature will save the world. His blindness prevents the kind of spiritual growth that Hillier can and does experience.

What Hillier comes to realize is that the universe is ultimately Manichean. The spy game is only a pale replica of the real battle between absolute good and absolute evil:

"Beyond God," said Hillier, "lies the concept of God. In the concept of God lies the concept of anti-God. Ultimate reality is a dualism or a game for two players. We—people like me and my counterparts on the other side—we reflect that game. It's a pale reflection. There used to be a much brighter one, in the days when the two sides represented what are known as good and evil . . . But we don't believe in good and evil any more. That's why we play this silly and hopeless little game!"

"We're too insignificant to be attacked by either the forces of light or the forces of darkness. And yet, playing this game, we occasionally let evil in. Evil tumbles in, unaware. But there's no good to fight evil with. That's when one grows sick of the game and wants to resign from it. That's why this is my last assignment."

Sin and goodness seem to be no longer available to modern man in his corrupt world of espionage and intrigue. Hillier suggests that "We need new terms. God and Notgod. Salvation and damnation of equal dignity, the two sides of the coin of ultimate reality." In such a world the real villains are the neutrals, those who refuse to take sides and live merely to further their own ends. These include Theodorescu, Wriste, Cornpit-Ferrers. The spy game may be a pale reflection of the real battle, but it is, in *Tremor of Intent*, the only game in town. To avoid sides in that dangerous game or to play both sides off against one another for personal power and profit constitutes the real villainy. In a particularly Manichean statement, Hillier concludes, "Don't you think we'd all rather see devil-worship than bland neutrality?"

Tremor of Intent ranks as one of Burgess's best novels.

It is masterfully constructed. The espionage framework and plot of the novel reflect and embody Burgess's larger Manichean vision. The language of the novel is often lyrical and rich, especially when recreating the sensual lusts of the cruise—the food, sex with Miss Devi, the epicene elegance of Mr. Theodorescu.

The plot begins with a fifty-one-page letter written by Hillier to his superiors. The language reflects his imagination and thoughts, especially his tiring of the spy game and his eagerness to be done with it. It suggests St. Augustine's own confessions of the man grown tired of lust and sensuality and turning to more lasting, spiritual truths. Similarly the chapter of Roper's autobiography, which Hillier reads, reveals in its flat, point-by-point narrative and language the kind of unenlightened, logical mind Roper has. Hillier speaks of games, sin, evil, and innocence; Roper prattles on totally unaware of such larger concerns. The very language each man uses reveals his state of mind and outlook, very cleverly recreated by Burgess.

Burgess's world is here complete; there are no loose ends, no unnecessary details and dangling incidents. It is a corrupt, contemporary world that knows "the difference between the eucharist and what the breadman delivered" but also realizes that in the smell of roses "were pledges that life went on in universal patterns below the horrors of power and language." It is a world celebrating its own appetites but realizing that at the last this is not enough: "Seek to possess the body of the loved one and you might as well be in a brothel. The act could not be ennobled into a sacrament in the way that bread could be transubstantiated." In such a world Hillier's decision to reject contemporary values is both noble and heroic. His intent to do so, though timorous and uncertain at first, finally becomes his committed action. If, as one critic has suggested, the essential tension in Burgess's novels posits "the vital drive to commit oneself to a moral absolute opposed by the craven urge to lurk in solipsistic twilight, nourishing the ego on the phenomena of the surface world," [12] Hillier has resolved that tension heroically. His is an act of Burgess's own faith.

1985 (1978): "We have to be on our guard."

Of Burgess's three futuristic, anti-Utopian or cacotopian novels, *1985* is both the most recent and the least effective. The book is divided into three sections: a series of essays, such as "Clockwork Oranges," "State and Superstate," and "The Death of Love," about society in general and George Orwell's *1984* in particular; the short novel, *1985*, Burgess's own view of the world ahead; and an epilogue consisting of an interview with the author. The essays make explicit Burgess's themes: the battle between individual free will and the state, the Pelagian and Augustinian world views about man's place in the universe, the conflict between the individual self and the behavioristic psychologies of men like Pavlov and B. F. Skinner. In the essays Burgess also discusses Orwell's *1984*, seeing it more as a fable about the death of love in postwar Britain in 1948 than as a real prophecy of things to come. The epilogue, a series of shrill warnings and dire prophecies from Burgess—love, language, freedom will decay as the state increases; war is the inevitable tool of the state—concludes with Burgess's warning, "We have to be on our guard" and his hope that man will ultimately prevail: "Man has survived the first thirty-three years of the Era of the Bomb. He'll survive whatever new horrors are in store for him. He's remarkably ingenious."

The novel begins in the city of London, which is owned by the Arabs, in 1985. A famous pub is now called the Al-Bulnbush. England is run by the Trade Unions, a kind of ultimate closed-shop environment in which "holistic syndicalism" is the norm. The Unions battle the State in never-ending conflict, which thoroughly submerges the individual within the collective scheme of things.

Worker's English is the flat, simplistic language of the

era, combining lazy slang with bureaucratic jargon. Hamlet's famous speech becomes "To get on with bloody life or not to, that's what it's all about really." Kumina gangs ("Kumina" means "teens" in Swahili) roam the streets and form underground classrooms to teach themselves Latin and Greek. King Charles III, "a rather podgy bat-eared man in his late thirties," sits on the throne.

Into this state of affairs comes Bev Jones, a former history teacher, who believes passionately and firmly that "the only things of importance are subversive. Art is subversive. Philosophy, too. The State killed Socrates." He also believes in "the right of man to loneliness, eccentricity, rebellion, genius; the superiority of man over men." Bev's thirteen-year-old daughter, Bessie, sits stupefied before the television and babbles on precociously about sex. Bev's wife, Ellen, burns to death in a hospital fire because the firemen are on strike. Just before she dies, she tells Bev, "Don't let them get away with it." Bev resigns from his union, tears up his union identity card, drops out of society, and sends his daughter to a Girls' Home. Caught stealing gin, he is sent to the Crawford Manor Rehabilitation Center, where he is beaten in a cellar because of his unwillingness to cooperate.

When he is released from the Rehabilitation Center, he goes to join the British Free Army, a private army led by a mysterious Colonel Lawrence. Bev discovered the existence of this private army, organized to maintain essential services during all kinds of national strikes, in an underground newspaper, *The Free Briton*. Lawrence is planning to move his forces in and take over all public services on the day of a General Strike in Britain, when even the regular army will lay down its arms. When workers go on strike and refuse to complete the new mosque in downtown London, the regular army is sent into the fray. A massive General Strike occurs, but King Charles III restores order swiftly in a speech delivered to the country. Colonel Lawrence is unmasked as an Islamic conspirator. All along he'd planned to take over Britain for the Arabs and establish an Islamic state. He is convicted of manslaughter. Bev, meanwhile, is captured, tried, and sent off for a life sentence to Purfleet Castle. He commits suicide by thrusting himself up against the electrified fence outside the castle. Once again the state has triumphed over the individual man of conscience.

1985 reads more like an essay than a novel. Its design is clever, but the characters are mere cardboard cutouts; they engage in conversations, arguments, and debates as if they were mere puppets representing the cause of the State or the cause of the individual. This "juiceless," "text-book-y" quality never rises above the level of matter-of-fact discourse. In one of the opening essays Burgess declared that the language of *A Clockwork Orange* was "too linguistically exhibitionist." The problem with the style of *1985* is that it reflects what Burgess at one point wrote about the way Bev was conducting one of his dialogues; it is "in the schoolmaster's way that not even impending death can kill."

While *1985* is a curiously inert novel, its explicit treatment of Burgess's themes and concerns does make it a good general introduction to those themes and concerns. These are better realized in Burgess's other cacotopian novels, *The Wanting Seed* and *A Clockwork Orange*.

The Wanting Seed (1962): "A sort of perpetual waltz."

In some future time the world is divided into two empires: Enspun, the English-Speaking Union, and Respun, the Russian-Speaking Union. In England, London has grown so huge that its administrative center is located in Brighton at the edge of the sea. People live in small, functional apartments, tiny cubicles with all the furniture built into the walls. They wear wrist microradios, watch television on the ceiling, and drink a cheap vegetarian drink called alc. The government is in the hands of the liberal party, led by the Right Honorable Robert Starling. The great crisis is overpopulation.

The problem of overpopulation is so overwhelming that

the Starling government has devised some startling cures. The Ministry of Infertility has decreed that there should be only one child born to a family and even that is one too many. The ministry recompenses the family when a child dies, thereby supporting infanticide. Corpses are turned into phosphorus pentoxide for food. Sexuality is so frowned upon that homosexuality is celebrated and openly practiced. "It's Sapiens to be Homo" proclaim wall posters. Women must wear solemn black dresses with tight bodices and powder their faces a dead white. Burgess himself believes firmly that homosexuality is a perversion, that it is "a kind of radical chic" which encourages the "genuine madness" of a "homosexual mafia." Such a radical cure to the problem of overpopulation is, therefore, pictured as dangerous and degenerate.

In its single-mindedness of purpose and policy, such an all-powerful State denies the "essence of man, bifurcation." It denies the fact that "we are both God and the Devil, though not at the same time." The essence of life remains "the division, contradictions," and to deny this essential confrontation—"Instincts tell one thing and reason tells us another"—especially in the sexual act itself, and to rely solely on a rational but preverse policy to solve the problem of overpopulation is to risk dangerous and unforeseen consequences.

Tristram Foxe, the novel's protagonist, a thirty-five-year-old history teacher in London, named perhaps for the author of the *Book of Martyrs*, believes that consequences can be foreseen. He views history as essentially cyclical, a Manichean dialectic between Pelagian and Augustinian beliefs. Pelagius, the man of the sea, believed in man's ultimate perfectability; Original Sin did not exist. This belief fostered the liberal faith in politics. The State would administer wisely to all. Cooperation replaces coercion. St. Augustine, on the other hand, believed in man's inherent sinfulness; Original Sin not only existed, but it could be redeemed only with the intervention of divine grace. Man was desperately in need of God. The Augustinian faith fostered conservative politics. Man must be coerced to do good. The Augustinian army

replaces the Pelagian police. Capitalism, not socialism,
thrives under such a system. It's each man for himself.

Foxe explains that the cycle of history is continuous. In
the Pelagian phase or the Pelphase, man comes to realize
that cooperation is finally futile. With a problem as explosive
and pervasive as overpopulation, liberal tactics lead to
inevitable disappointment. This period of disillusionment
leads to the Interphase, in which citizens are forced to obey
the laws. A secret police is created; their excesses lead to
further disruption in the State; power struggles erupt and
society collapses into an era of chaos and disorder. Slowly
the army is increased to restore order; individual men begin
to set up their own independent schemes and businesses; the
State enters a period of laissez faire, believing that selfishness
is the way of all mankind. This is the Augustinian phase or
Gusphase. Once order is restored, the ideal of cooperation
begins to reassert itself once again, and the Gusphase,
therefore, materializes into the Pelphase. And thus, the
historical cycle: "Pelphase, Interphase, Gusphase, Pelphase,
Interphase, Gusphase, and so on, for ever and ever. A sort
of perpetual waltz."

The Wanting Seed, a novel in five parts, traces the
political cycle Tristram Foxe describes. In part one the
problem of overpopulation is not being solved, despite the
lavish homosexual campaign launched by the government.
Slowly the Pelphase draws to a close. Unemployed hooligans
are drafted into the police and are called "grey boys." Prime
Minister Starling on television calls for strong repressive
measures. Poppol or the Population Police is created to ferret
out and destroy people who insist on having more children.
The grey boys attack a group of strikers on the docks to beat
them into submission.

During the Interphase things go from bad to worse. The
grey boys and Poppol are everywhere. Pregnant mothers are
carted off. Food becomes severely rationed. On top of the
growing unrest and use of force, a mysterious blight begins
to affect the entire world: wheat won't grow in Ohio; famines

spread in China; the herring catches in England become less and less; hens won't lay, and farm animals are dying. State ministers go on television to pray to "the forces of death which at present are ravaging the esculent life of this planet." The belief in Original Sin begins to appear once again, a sign that the Gusphase is on its way. Before it comes, however, an orgiastic era of cannibalism and human sacrifice occurs. Fairs celebrate copulation; pagan festivals erect May poles. Priests, long out of favor during the Pelphase, are returned to the countryside to conduct Masses and lead the people back to a celebration of fertility and rebirth. The State admits defeat with its use of the police, "so now it's the priests they call on . . . We're right down to essential function now, the sacramental function."

Gradually order is restored. The blight ceases. The Gusphase opens a new Ministry of Fertility. Private enterprise flourishes. The problem of overpopulation, however, remains. The new solution is war. The State stages massive battles, artificial wars of men against women to wipe out the excess population. War replaces homosexuality as the new plan to cure the problem. These "Extermination Sessions" are staged somewhere on the Irish coast, complete with fireworks, amplified and recorded sounds of battle, and elaborate stagesets of destroyed buildings and villages, all neatly enclosed within a huge electrified fence. Poppol is replaced by the Global Population Limitation Authority; the police state becomes a "free state, order without organization, which means order without violence. A safe and spacious community." The Gusphase is complete.

Tristram Foxe undergoes his own cycle within the phases of society, which he himself has outlined in his history lectures. He is married to Beatrice-Joanna Foxe, a fecund earth mother who has an "aura of fertility" about her. She loves Tristram but also enjoys a sexual liaison with his brother, Derek. It's as if, in good Manichean fashion, she must have both men.

At the beginning of the novel, Beatrice-Joanna's and

Tristram's infant son, Roger, dies of meningeal infection.
Beatrice-Joanna suspects that the doctor, ideologically opposed to overpopulation, has let him die. On the day of her
son's death, she is comforted by Derek. He makes love to
her in her apartment, at the same time Tristram is being
denied promotion as head of the Social Studies department
where he teaches, because of his heterosexuality. Later in
the day, Tristram returns home to Beatrice-Joanna to make
love to her. She becomes pregnant, although it's difficult for
her to decide who is the father. Captain Loosley, a captain
in Poppol and involved in the power struggles of the
Interphase, tells Tristram that he has intercepted a letter
from Tristram's wife to his brother, Derek, filled with erotic
references. Loosely wants Tristram to kill his brother. Tristram
refuses but confronts his wife with his discovery in the street.
Suddenly he is carried away in a battle between grey boys
and strikers and lands in jail. Beatrice-Joanna hurries off to
her sister's home to hide during her pregnancy. Derek,
learning of his brother's incarceration, decides not to release
him and keeps him there.

While the blight covers the world and cannibalism
thrives in the streets of London, Tristram manages to escape
and starts off on a long journey to find his wife. Meanwhile
she has given birth to twin boys, Tristram and Derek
(Manichean justice!). Loosley, however, discovers them and
takes Beatrice-Joanna and the twins back to London to
discredit Derek once and for all.

Tristram's trip is a nightmarish journey through cannibalistic conclaves, all-too-public barbecues, pagan celebra-
tions of fertility, and sexual romps in fields under the moon.
He discovers at his sister's-in-law home that his family has
been taken away, and on his way back toward London is
inducted into the army. Almost before he realizes it, he's
trained and quickly shipped out to some mysterious coast.
No one will answer Tristram's questions about the nature of
the enemy or the reasons for the war. He's caught in one of
the Extermination Sessions.

During the battle at the trenches, everyone is killed, except Tristram, who lies beneath the corpses of his colleagues. He manages to crawl out and escape back to London. In London he gets a job teaching the history of warfare at a technical school and, having received a letter from Beatrice-Joanna while he was in the army, returns to her in Brighton. She has been living with Derek in a splendid apartment with her two sons but misses Tristram—"She needed two men in her life, her day to be salted by infidelity"—and feels neglected by Derek in his obsessive pursuit of his career. Derek thrives in the Ministry of Fertility, Loosley gets unceremoniously demoted, and at the end of the novel Beatrice-Joanna and Tristram, having survived his dark night of the soul, are reunited at the edge of "the life-giving sea."

Through out the novel Beatrice-Joanna walks down to the sea to restore her faith in the ultimate beauties and mysteries of the natural world. She is very much a creature of the sea herself, for "the sea spelled life, whispered or shouted fertility; that voice could never be completely stilled." She invokes the sea in her private reveries: "We're sick, O Sea. Restore us to health, restore us to life." In the Gusphase, war becomes "the great aphrodisiac, the great source of world adrenalin . . . a massive sexual act . . . the justifier of fertility." Yet it is the eternal sea which embodies all life, fertility, the cycles of nature and the hope of mankind: "There it stretched all before her, endowed with delirium, panther-skin, mantle pierced with thousands of sun's idols, Lydia absolute, drunk with its own blue flesh, biting its scintillating tail in a tumult like silence . . . Break waves. Break with joyful waters . . ."[13]

The cycle of the novel from blighted wasteland to fertile renewal suggests, as one critic wrote, "the vegetation myth of the cyclic rebirth of nature." This nature cycle parallels but undercuts the political and social cycle of the State. While the State thrashes and vacillates, the natural cycle of growth takes its own true course. Tristram and Beatrice-Joanna are reunited, while the State still faces the problem

of overpopulation. The individual may undergo a genuine
rebirth and emerge more than a mere survivor, but the State
can only ricochet back and forth between Pelagian and
Augustinian phases.

The relationship between art and sexuality in Burgess's
view reveals once again why the State must fail. As Tristram
explains, "Great art is a kind of glorification of increase
. . . tragedy and comedy had their origin in fertility ceremonies . . . the sacrificial goat . . . and the village Priapic
festivals." As if to support this thesis, during the pagan
ceremonies and the parades of copulating couples throughout
England in the Interphase, live drama begins to spring up
once again: "Well, thought Tristram, leaving the tent at
twilight, soon men would be dressing up as goats and
presenting the first neo-tragedy. Perhaps in a year or two
there would be mystery plays." The final word is Burgess's:
"One could not perhaps, after all, and it was a pity, make
art out of that gentle old liberalism. The new books in the
[Gusphase] were full of sex and death, perhaps the only
materials for a writer."

The one problem with *The Wanting Seed* is that it is
very much a novel with a thesis. At the very beginning
Tristram explains the Pelagian-Augustinian cycle of history,
and the novel neatly proves that his design is right. Consequently the characters tend to become mere cardboard figures,
each clearly representing some facet of the thesis. As one
critic aptly suggests, "They suffer but never transcend or
understand their suffering."[14] The game plan of the novel,
however artfully laid out and designed, still smacks of
contrived allegory, and the full-bodied, emotional impact of
the best of novels doesn't exist.

As if to "flesh-out" his concept, Burgess delights in a
genuine verbal lyricism. His description of the sea, of
cannibalistic revels, of the tenor and fear of battle, and of
an Easter sermon suggest the rich, emotional center the novel
lacks. Too often Burgess also uses words for the sheer sound
or bizarre quality of them. Words such as "bathcolpous,"

gnathitinancy," "allomorph," "exophagy," and "anabasis"
pepper his text. These unusual words only draw attention to
themselves, as if Burgess were showing off his verbal
dexterity. They detract from the design of the novel and seem
tossed in at random for no other effect than to reveal the
author's playfulness. They also make more obvious the
separation between the novel's thesis and the novel's language, as if the two were more at war with one another than
in conjunction with each other. The careful plan of historical
cycles and the almost random sprinkling throughout the novel
of lyric descriptions and *portmanteau* words never come
together in any complete narrative fusion.

At one point in the novel Burgess remarks that the
Manichean duality of all things "could be tragic if we allowed
it to be. But it's better to see it as comic." The thesis of the
novel, as well as the language, obviously distances both
reader and author from the authentic sufferings of the
characters involved. Comedy always demands distance, as
do satire and irony, for if the reader is allowed to identify
personally and emotionally with the characters, he loses the
ability to laugh at them. Burgess's novel is certainly a kind
of black or dark comedy, but it fails to create that final
emotional enjoyment which lies at the center of all great
literature. *The Wanting Seed* raises fascinating questions
about man's political nature, the cycles of history, the very
real problem of excess population, and the necessary com-
promises of bureaucratic survival, but in the end it does not
touch the heart.

A Clockwork Orange (1963): "Real Horrorshow."

From any point of view, *A Clockwork Orange* (1963),[15] what
Anthony Burgess once referred to as "very much a *jeu de
spleen*,"[16] has become the most hotly debated and famous of
all his novels. Burgess wrote the novel in 1961, after a trip

to Russia, but it did not achieve worldwide attention until Stanley Kubrick filmed it in 1971. (In fact, Burgess sold the film rights to Kubrick for about $500, after Kubrick read it with fascination in the summer of 1969.)[17] The story of the fifteen-year-old hoodlum, Alex, his "conversion" to goodness by a government-sponsored operation, and his reconversion to terrorism and violence, has been taken as a prophecy revealing the tendency of our modern age and as a warning against the futuristic world of the welfare state.

The novel, in the first of three parts, begins in a local milkbar. Alex and his three "droogs" (friends) are drugging themselves with specially laced milk in order to gear themselves up for another night of "crasting" (robbing) and "tolchocking" (fighting). They purchase masks to disguise themselves and then head out into the night. They rob a shop, pummel an old professor, and savagely strike and kick an old drunk. Next they come upon Billyboy and his gang of thugs, who are about to rape a ten-year-old girl, and attack them with razors and chains. Then Alex and his droogs steal a sportscar, go careening through the dark countryside, stop to kick a couple making love under a tree, and arrive at a house with a shiny white sign on the front gate: "HOME." Once inside they attack the writer who lives there, and Alex rapes the writer's wife. They speed back to town and return to the Korova Milkbar. At the milkbar Alex becomes upset at his friend's filthy appearance and strikes him for ridiculing a woman at the bar who is singing an excerpt from an opera. Alex returns to his parents' apartment in Municipal Flatblock 18A, its lobby ravaged by filth and graffiti, and before going to sleep listens and masturbates to Beethoven.

In the morning the truant officer, P. R. Deltoid, comes to speak to him, but Alex ignores Deltoid's ineffectual preaching. Later in the day he picks up two ten-year-old girls at a record store and brings them back to his bedroom to rape them while listening to Beethoven's Ninth Symphony. That night, Dim and Georgie, two of Alex's droogs, challenge Alex's leadership of their gang, but Alex retains his control by thoroughly thrashing them and slicing Dim's wrist with his razor.

The night's plans include a trip to a house called the Manse. There an elderly woman lives with her cats and many valuable art objects. She refuses to fall for Alex's faked cry for help, so Alex, by standing on Dim's shoulders, crawls into the house through a window above the front door. Once inside, he finds the old woman, who rushes toward him to defend herself with a bust of Beethoven. He knocks her unconscious with a silver statue and amid a swarm of yowling cats and spilled milk, hears a police siren, rushes out the door, is knocked out by Dim with Dim's chain in an act of angry revenge for his sliced wrist, and is carried away by the policemen. At the station the police hit him. P. R. Deltoid, delighted that Alex has been finally brought to justice, spits in his face, and finally Alex is carried off to a cell. Later he is awakened to learn that the old woman has died. "That was everything. I'd done the lot, now. And me still only fifteen."

Part Two of the novel describes Alex's life in prison. In jail, Alex passes on information of possible uprisings and plots to the prison chaplain, who grows fond of him and lets him listen to his favorite music on the chapel stereo. In his cell Alex accidently kills another prisoner, who has been making homosexual advances toward him. The warden and state officials decide to turn him over to Dr. Brodsky at the hospital for the Reclamation Treatment, which is called Ludovico's Technique.

Ludovico's Technique is an experimental state-author-ized program of brainwashing and physical reconditioning. It consists of injections of a drug that causes Alex to become violently ill whenever he begins to respond pleasurably to violent thoughts. As part of the treatment Alex watches certain violent films, complete with various musical back-grounds, after he has been injected. The intent is to prevent him from wanting to participate in any such actions ever again. Unfortunately, Beethoven's Fifth Symphony is the musical background for one of the films. Thus, whenever he hears it, after the completion of the treatment, the violent sickness will overwhelm him.

At the conclusion of the treatment, Alex is presented before a panel of doctors and state officials and ends up licking the boots of a tormentor sent to attack him to see if the procedure has worked. He also grovels before a beautiful woman, because his sexual instincts create only pain and sickness for him now. He is at last released from prison, having become in Dr. Brodsky's words, "your true Christian . . . ready to be crucified, rather than crucify."

In Part Three, the former victimizer becomes complete victim. Alex's parents have taken a boarder to live in Alex's old room, so he is homeless. In his wanderings he comes upon the old professor, whom we met during the first night of violent revels in the novel. The professor and some of his friends attack him. He is rescued by two policemen, who turn out to be Dim and Billyboy. They drive him out into the country to attack him, and leave him for dead. He manages to walk through the darkness of a farm village to a country house with shiny white letters on the gate: "HOME." The writer, who recognizes him from a photograph in the morning paper as the person who has undergone Ludovico's Technique, takes him in and decides to use him to help "dislodge this overbearing Government." The writer, F. Alexander, calls in his liberal friends, who espouse the cause of individual liberty, to discuss how to use Alex as a public witness against the government's repressive actions. Slowly, Alexander begins to realize that it was Alex who raped his wife and plans his revenge. With the help of his friends, he installs Alex in an apartment in town. Alex falls asleep and awakens to symphony music. Immediately the pain and sickness begin. Finding that he has been locked in, he leaps out of the window in a fit of suicidal panic.

He awakens in a hospital bed, realizing that the writer and his friends have tried to kill him. He also realizes that his love of sex and violence has been restored; the sickness no longer returns when such thoughts cross his mind. The

Minister of the Interior pays a visit and announces that the
writer has been imprisoned. To discredit the writer's political
party and to assure the government of Alex's public support,
he offers Alex a secure, well-paying job. Alex asks to hear
Beethoven's Ninth on the stereo, relishing his visions of
"carving the whole litso [face] of the creeching [screaming]
world with my cut-throat britva [razor]. . . . I was cured all
right."

The cyclical pattern of Burgess's book is apparent. In
Part One Alex is the violent victimizer. In Part Two he
undergoes his "cure." In Part Three he becomes the victim
of violence before his final "reversion." Alex begins as a
rebel against all law and order, upon which the state is based,
becomes a victim of the state's conditioning techniques, and
winds up fully sponsored and protected by the state with a
job. The parts are also unified thematically. Each begins
with the question, "What's it going to be then, eh?" a phrase
that is repeated twelve times throughout the book, empha-
sizing Burgess's thematic interest in individual choice and
free will and the uncertainty of what can happen next in this
strange and alien world. This is a crucial theme, and one to
which we will return later.

Other actions and themes recur in the individual chapters
in much the same way that the symphonies, which Alex
loves, repeat certain motifs. For instance, each first chapter
in each of the three parts begins with Alex's going somewhere:
out on the town, into prison, or out free once again. There
is a fight scene in each of the second chapters. Loneliness
is the motif in the third chapters, from the droog rebellion
against Alex to the beginning of the treatment in the hospital
to his having no place to go. Dreams and nightmares haunt
Alex in each of the fifth chapters.

What strikes one first about the book, however, is the
language. Burgess invented a slang he chose to call "Nadsat."
He reported in an interview:

I went to Leningrad and discovered that they had these *stiljagi*
there, they had teenage riots and gangs, cult of violence, so it

struck me that if I could combine East and West in a single persona, teenage person, it would be appropriate to use a composite dialect that is Russian and English . . . What I tried to do was to present a state which of course had to become a future state because of the dialect, which was neither West nor East. I think it comes up mostly West.[18]

In the novel itself the language is described as "off bits of rhyming slang . . . but most of the roots are Slav. Propaganda. Subliminal penetration." To the Western ear, the Slavic roots provide a strange and alien sound, and the Russian flavor of the vocabulary connects almost subliminally with the Westerner's fear of repressive governments and state authority. The authoritarian socialism of Burgess's futuristic society comes to us through this harsh, unnerving speech.

Because of its language, *A Clockwork Orange* begins as a puzzle to be solved, a message to be decoded. This strange language, therefore, distances the reader from the action in the book, because it automatically disconnects him from the world he is used to. He wonders why this strange language is being used. What kind of world exists in which people talk in this outrageous fashion? In short, when the reader grapples directly with Burgess's language, he must also try to figure out what kind of a world Burgess is writing about.

Nadsat itself is a language of objects: its vocabulary, like that of most slang, consists of words for concrete and physical things or actions, rather than abstract ideas or thoughts. Here is Alex raping the writer's wife and listening to his cries: "Plunging, I could slooshy [hear] cries of agony and this wri:er bleeding veck [man] that Georgie and Pete held on to nearly got loose howling bezoomy [mad] with the filthiest of slovos [words]." The use of Nadsat distances the reader from the actual rape itself, reducing the scene to some other-wordly action, some strange incident in some alien place. We would react violently and directly to the more commonplace phrase, "howling mad," and would relate immediately to the writer's pain and sense of outrage. When he is "howling bezoomy," however, that strange word calls attention to itself and in doing so diverts our attention from the full force of the horrible event. This jargon also suggests Alex's own inhumanity and distance from the feelings of his victims, for his relationship to his own act remains detached and coldly objective.

Our response to Alex is carefully controlled and manipulated by Burgess in more ways than just through the use of Nadsat. We are first of all shocked by Alex's actions. He is violent, detached, amoral, and criminal. He is a creature of the night: "The night belonged to me and my droogs and all the rest of the nadsats, and the starry bourgeois lurked indoors drinking in the gloopy world-casts, but the day was for the starry ones." He delights in his own self-serving capabilities and admires his own superiority, as he sees it in contrast with the ignorance of others: "I had a real horrorshow smeck [good laugh] at everybody's like innocence." He appears as a self-indulgent, unrestrained, and callous adolescent, celebrating in his own mind the interpenetration of sex and violence:

Oh, it was gorgeousness and gorgeosity made flesh . . . I was in such bliss . . . I was smecking [laughing] all over my rot [mouth] and grinding my boot in their litsos [faces] . . . I broke and spattered and cried aaaaaah with the bliss of it.

Any character who must carry an entire novel cannot be entirely unsympathetic. Burgess uses many devices and images to make Alex a far more sympathetic character than he perhaps deserves to be. For instance, the novel is written from his point of view: he narrates his own adventures, automatically justifying and explaining his actions as every first-person narrator does. When he weeps, the first-person narration manipulates and encourages our sympathy for him. He playfully refers to himself as "handsome young Narrator" or "your humble Narrator." He frequently addresses the reader to implicate him more fully in his tale, referring to him as "brother." Alex also possesses a perceptive intelligence, in comparison to such fellow droogs as Dim, a "clowny animal," and a sense of his own authority: "So they knew now who was master and leader, sheep, thought I." Events within the plot also enable the reader to sympathize with Alex, for instance when he is rejected by his parents upon release from jail.

Burgess has also made Alex more sympathetic by giving him an artistic consciousness. When Alex goes to fight with Billyboy and his gang at the beginning of this book, he chooses a razor for his weapon instead of tne usual knives, so that "I could flash and shine artistic." We are led to admire his style in preference to that of the dim-witted bully boys. Even during the fight he enjoys not so much the mayhem but the ordered balletic quality of it: "And, my brothers, it was real satisfaction to me to waltz—left two three, right two three."[19] This artistic appreciation in Alex culminates in his love for classical music, especially for Beethoven. Such music produces "a cage of silk round my bed," instant bliss, "like silvery wine flowing in a spaceship, gravity all nonsense now."

There are, then, at least two Alexes confronting the reader. Is he merely a clockwork automaton, a creature of his mechanized society, whose violence is merely an extension of his own boredom and sense of worthlessness? Or is he, in fact, better than his clockwork society, an artistic and intelligent person? His appreciation of music emphasizes this dichotomy:

Great Music . . . and Great Poetry would like quieten Modern Youth down and make Modern Youth more Civilized. Civilized my syphilised yarbles [genitals]. Music always sort of sharpened me up O my brothers, and made me feel like old Bog [God] himself.

For Alex the appreciation of music and the more restrained manners of civilization are antithetical. Alex himself believes that violence is the essence of the individual self:

More, badness is of the self, the one, the you or me on our oddy knockies [lonesome], and that self is made by old Bog or God and is his great pride and radosty [joy]. But the not-self cannot have the bad, meaning they of the government and the judges and the schools cannot allow the bad because they allow the self. And is not our modern history, my brothers, the story of brave malenky [little] selves fighting these big machines? I am serious with you, brothers, over this. But what I do I do because I like to do.

Burgess has suggested that the basic issue of *A Clockwork Orange* deals with the idea of free will or choice. He declared: "Choice, choice is all that matters, and to impose the good is evil, to *act* evil is better than to have good imposed."[20] And again: "I was merely trying to point out the very real danger, an imminent danger, that is, that the State is taking on more and more control."[21] And finally: "I lean toward anarchy; I hate the State."[22] This absolutist doctrine, which urges "the defense of self, no matter how twisted it may be, and the condemnation of the state, no matter how benevolent it pretends to be,"[23] seems at first glance to be supported by the text and certainly appeals to our Western ethos and cultural heritage. The Western "cult" of the individual does side with impulse, however violent, as opposed to conditioning, however benign.

Three of Burgess's characters clearly express their opinions about the matter of choice. The prison chaplain and the writer, F. Alexander, express their faith in free will and individual choice. The doctor for the treatment, Dr. Brodsky, expresses his faith in the state's right to compel man, if necessary, toward the good.

The chaplain insists:

The question is whether such a technique can really make a man good. Goodness comes from within . . . goodness is something chosen. When a man cannot choose he ceases to be a man.

He wonders: "Is a man who chooses the bad perhaps in some way better than a man who has the good imposed upon him?" F. Alexander agrees, believing also that what makes man human is his ability to choose. He links this belief to the tradition of liberty and insists it must be maintained and safeguarded at all costs.

Dr. Brodsky, on the other hand, rejects such arguments. In defending his use of Ludovico's Technique, he declares, "What is happening to you now is what should happen to any normal healthy human organism contemplating the actions of the forces of evil, the workings of the principle of destruction. You are *being made* sane, you are *being made* healthy." (italics added) He believes that an individual should be impelled toward the universal or socially acceptable good, as defined by the state.

In the dramatic context of the novel, however, the idea of choice is not presented so schematically. For one thing, Alex chooses the treatment himself, in an effort to get out of prison. Dr. Brodsky tells Alex, "You made your choice and all this is a consequence of your choice. Whatever ensues is what you yourself have chosen." At the same time, the advocates of individual choice are thoroughly discredited. The chaplain, an alcoholic, works hand in hand with the warden and the prison authorities, repeating to them all that Alex as his informer reports to him. Similarly F. Alexander, the writer, in his campaign to overthrow the government, is willing to exploit Alex, even to the point of murdering him. These two witnesses for free choice and human liberty are as inhuman and as much clockwork oranges as anyone else.

Brodsky describes one of Burgess's main ideas in *A Clockwork Orange* when he suggests, "The world is one, life is one. The sweetest and most heavenly of activities partake in some measure of violence—the act of love, for instance, music, for instance. You must take your chance, boy. The choice has been all yours." Violence remains at the heart of things, or at least is so inextricably intertwined with everything else that F. Alexander's notion of man as "a creature of growth and capable of sweetness" seems at best naive and at worst dangerously wrong-headed. The world of the novel is so totally mechanized, controlled, and dehumanized that the only reality seems to be that of coercion and power. Nadsat and the state, Alex and F. Alexander, the chaplain and Ludovico's Technique, all appear as the different manifestations of certain primal drives, such as the thirst for violence and the will to power.

Burgess reinforces this bleak outlook on man's instincts by using nightmarish images. Alex is continually haunted by nightmares and visions of rebellion, violence, and terror. When he and his droogs go speeding across the countryside during their first night of violence, Alex is eerily aware of "winter trees and dark . . . a country dark, and at one place I ran over something big with a snarling toothy rot [mouth] in the headlamps." After the writer is subdued and his wife raped, Alex and his droogs flee, "running over odd squealing things on the way."

In *A Clockwork Orange* Burgess displays once again his Manichean world views. The self is as much a reflection of and extension of the state or society as the state or society is of the self. The only reality remains a constant struggle of forces, most clearly seen here in the form of the individual self against the collective power of the state.

What Burgess points to here is a reality of chaos and control, the two contenders for man's soul, constantly and irrevocably at war with one another. What he seems to have written is a startling critique and expose of the Western liberal faith in the inherent goodness or good intentions of the individual. Burgess clearly undercuts the belief in individual free will. Perhaps the true vision of the book is as much a "subliminal penetration" of our faith in this belief as Nadsat is of our language.

When Stanley Kubrick filmed *A Clockwork Orange*, his major task was to find cinematic equivalents for Burgess's prose. To achieve the same kind of stylized and futuristic atmosphere Kubrick brilliantly used such cinematic materials as color, light and dark, music, setting, and pacing. Bright reds alternate with dark shadows; hospital-bright rooms alternate with black scenes on city streets; Purcell's "Music for the Funeral of Queen Mary" provides a gloomy, ponderous background throughout the film, and Alex's singing of "Singing in the Rain," while he kicks the fallen writer, is both funny and chilling. The Korova Milkbar, the writer's house in the country, and the "cat woman's" mansion filled with sexual *objets d'art* reveal a harshly lit, modernistic architecture of plastic and fiberglass; and in scenes of violence and sexual athletics Kubrick speeds up or slows down his film to resemble a madcap frenzy or an almost graceful ballet respectively. All these cinematic touches make Kubrick's world as eerie and as fantastic as Burgess's. It is, as one critic has called it, a film of "pop-rococo art,"[24] a hedonistic violent landscape of the worst aspects of popular contemporary culture.

Kubrick's vision of Alex, however, is far more sympathetic than Burgess's. For one thing Malcolm McDowell has a handsome, sly, boyishly mobile and roguish face which the spectator cannot easily resist. McDowell uses a quirky smile, a mixture of malicious sneer and adolescent bravado, evil and shy at once, that immediately sets him apart from the other less attractive faces in the film.

The violence that Alex inflicts on others is far more stylized in the film than the violence inflicted upon Alex. When Alex's gang attacks Billyboy's, Kubrick films the scene as a rollicking ballet. When Alex rapes the two young girls, Kubrick speeds up the scene and plays "The William Tell Overture" in the background. When Alex kills the woman with the cats, he acts out of self-defense, since she has come at him with a bust of Beethoven, and he kills her with a huge white statue of a phallus: so much for her "pornographic" art! In all instances the violence Alex inflicts appears like a dance, a wildly good time, or a strike against the decadence of the cultural scene. When Alex undergoes Ludovico's Technique or when Dim and Georgie drag him out in the fields to beat him up, the violence is graphic, close-up and bloody. We see Alex's suffering immediately without any stylized distortions of it.

There are several other modifications in Kubrick's film which load the dice in Alex's favor. P. R. Deltoid and the prison guard display homosexual affectations. Deltoid feverishly grabs Alex's genitals while he and Alex, clad only in his underpants, are seated and talking on Alex's bed. When later at the police station he spits in Alex's face, it almost seems a gesture of sexual frustration and revenge. The prison guard, Hitlerian in his goose step and a fiendish martinet in his attention to rules and regulations, purses his lips and marches Alex around, as if he is totally some new toy to command. The rectal examination, while totally unerotic, nevertheless suggests sexual possibilities, which are further suggested in the homosexual prisoners' leers and winks at Alex during chapel. The writer, F. Alexander, is clearly mad, and his psychotic facial gestures suggest that Alex, instead of being an object of mere revenge, is in the hands of a madman.

The final scene in the film reveals Kubrick's siding with Alex even more. In the book Alex envisions "carving the whole litso of the creeching world with my cut-throat britva." In the film we see Alex frolicking sexually with a naked blonde woman in black stockings, while a crowd of proper Victorian men in top hats and women with parasols stand around and decorously applauds. Alex's intended violence is eradicated altogether, and the apparent joy of sex, when contrasted to the "up-tight," fully clothed Victorian onlookers, appeals to our modern "liberated" sympathies.

The devilish or Manichean balance of Burgess's novel is lost in Kubrick's film. Kubrick seems to be capitalizing on the modern psyche's rage against all authority and all values, that same romanticized view of rebellion which at first appeared to be the vision of the novel. Kubrick admitted as much:

Alex's adventures are a kind of psychological myth. Our subconscious finds release in Alex, just as it finds release in dreams. It resents Alex being stifled and repressed by authority, however much our conscious mind recognizes the necessity of doing this.[25]

In many ways both Burgess and Kubrick seem fascinated with the style of their hero's world and being, if not by his actions. This separation between style and action, between form and content, indicates a decadent or mannerist sensibility, which admires the trappings of style but views life only as a hopelessly cyclical drama of violence, coercion, power, and despair.

It's as if each artist, in creating a warning of some future state or in revealing the depths of man's depravity, has surrendered to these very forces and those very demons he seems intent upon identifying and destroying. In the apparent defense of free will, each has declared it an illusion. Kubrick's film remains visually stunning but emotionally chilling, a glacial Xanadu of man at his one-dimensional worst. As Alex is forced to watch violent films during Ludovico's Technique, Kubrick seems to be suggesting that we depraved souls have become as depraved and as soulless in our choice to watch him. It's as if all these carefully contrived images have nothing beyond them but a nihilistic cynical *ennui* and spiritual impotence, as if a garish neon sign were illuminated to proclaim the spiritual vacancy of neon.

Burgess's novel, on the other hand, while portraying a brutal and brutalizing world of force, at least demolishes the simplistic opposition between self and society. The Manichean interplay between good and evil conjures up a world of characters and society far more complex and intimately related than Kubrick's film. It is this almost demonic complexity that Burgess leaves us with, chilling our apprehension of the intricate world around us, not merely our emotional reactions to it, with the diabolically assertive final line, "I was cured all right."

When the W. W. Norton Publishing Company published the American edition of *A Clockwork Orange*, the seventh chapter of the third part was omitted. Burgess himself agreed to the omission: "Whether I'd say 'Yes' now, I don't know; but I've been persuaded by so many critics that the book is better in its American form that I say, 'All right, they know best.'"[26]

The seventh chapter of the English edition reveals Alex

at eighteen becoming bored with his violent, youthful activities, looking forward to the experiences of marriage and
children, and viewing his former life as an episode outgrown:
"Youth is only being in a way like it might be an animal
. . . Being young is like being like one of these malenky
machines." Burgess has said that when he grows up, Alex
"would realize that aggression was just a mode of youthful
activity."[27] Juvenile violence is something to go through but
to grow out of. This chapter makes *A Clockwork Orange* into
a tale of adolescence, experienced and surpassed, in contrast
with the bleaker American version, which suggests that Alex
will remain violent forever. Burgess added: "He's turned out
in the American edition to be a mere clockwork figure, I
suppose, who's just impelled towards evil by some determin-
istic force, which is not what I intended at all."[28]

In the final chapter of the English edition, Alex concludes
that his son will probably act just as he did. He will be
unable "to stop his own son, brothers. And so it would itty
on to like the end of the world, round and round and round,
like some bolshy gigantic chelloveck, like old Bog Himself."
The Manichean cycle will continue; violence will continue
to play an important part within it. Alex's failure to recognize
the evil inherent in such a cycle leads the reader to believe
that he has not really learned much from his experiences. In
retelling his tale he has merely viewed it as part of an
inevitable cycle, for which he is not responsible.

The popularity of the novel obviously is related to the
popularity—and controversial nature—of Kubrick's film. Yet
looking back on the novel, Burgess found it "too didactic,
tricky, and gimmicky." That it may be, but the creation of
Nadsat and the character of Alex is a novelistic triumph.
"It's had a mythical impact of some kind," Burgess mused.
Perhaps the Manichean roots of that myth reflect all too
clearly the roots of our own contemporary malaise.

4

●●●

The Mythic Method

In general terms, Anthony Burgess considered himself a modernist. He identified his own work with the themes and techniques of literary modernism. For Burgess modernism "relates to a particular period in history, the First World War. We can't forget it, even if some of us didn't experience it. It's one of the most traumatic experiences the world has ever had."[1] Burgess explained that Modernism "expressed itself as a rejection of the doctrine of Liberal Man—progressing, mastering his environment, finding salvation in science and the rational organization of society . . . The human instincts were now to be more important than the reason: Natural or Animal or Unconscious Man replaced the planning intellect . . . Everything had to be re-made—the language of literature, the sonorities of music. . . . "[2]

It may be difficult for us, living as we do in an age of constant warfare and anxiety, to realize the shock the First World War produced throughout Europe. As Burgess suggested, "the First World War was a more terrible war, because it was a meaningless war." All the Victorian and nineteenth-century beliefs in civilization and cultural progress collapsed in the face of unrelenting trench warfare. Millions of lives were lost in a war of attrition, at times existing within only six miles of one long series of trenches and artillery. Such a bloody and endless contest seemed to reveal the complete breakdown of every nineteenth-century belief in patriotism, civilization, and cultural achievement.

The Great War produced a new mood, a new outlook,

in literature. Writers confronted the depths of a new sense
of anxiety, isolation, and collapse. In the poetry of Pound
and Eliot, in the novels of Hemingway and Fitzgerald,
appeared themes like the death of love, the futility of
existence, and the failure of human progress. A new world
of decay and nightmare appeared in the long bloody trenches
of a ravaged European landscape. Distrust, chaos, and
disbelief became the order of the new day.

The Great War seemed to create a decisive break
between the world of the civilized past and the world of the
chaotic present. The past was shattered; order and coherence
seemed irrevocably lost. The present appeared as Eliot's
Wasteland; chaos and insignificance threatened man's image
of himself and of his society. Nothing remained but fragments
of a shattered civilization in the trenches of Europe.

Time itself seemed split in half. The past had always
been regarded from a chronological and progressive outlook;
things added up and went forward. Events happened in a
logical, rational sequence. Now, suddenly, the present
seemed to deny all that. Now the world seemed fragmented
and disrupted. Time seemed to be only a cyclical, repetitive
trap, no longer progressive but regressive. Suddenly time
and the world stood suspended. The Great War shattered
man's civilized facade and revealed a primitive, violent
reality that seemed to deny the possibility of all progress and
all of time's forward motion.

In order to explore and present this new and pessimistic
vision of life, the writers after the Great War had to discover
new literary techniques. Several of these new techniques and
often the pessimistic vision which produced them preceded
the war itself, but only after it did they become more widely
popularized and publicly recognized. The writers themselves
could no longer rely on the nineteenth-century language of
sentiment or nineteenth-century literary forms, such as the
progressive, chronological novels of a Dickens or a Tolstoy.
New forms and new methods had to be found to express the
new, darker visions of the twentieth century.

One of these methods was called, particularly in poetry, Imagism. Imagist poets attempted to get away entirely from old sentiments and conventional literary language. They insisted on creating short, explicit, almost photographic poems. They wished to focus sharply upon one instant or moment in time and describe it as precisely and as economically as possible. Pound's description of faces in a Paris subway station may be the supreme example of the Imagist technique: "The apparition of these faces in the crowd/Petals on a wet, black bough." The poem focusses upon two separate images—the faces and the petals—which are dramatically juxtaposed like two parts of a mathematical equation: faces are to petals as crowd is to bough. These photographic images make up the poem and replace the more traditional and romantic poet's description about how these images subjectively affected him. Pound wished to capture this dramatic effect, or as Hemingway later described it, "the real thing, the sequence of motion and fact which made the emotion."

A second literary technique or method T. S. Eliot defined as "the mythical method." The idea of using a myth as a point of comparison or contrast to try to explore the chaos of the present is precisely the literary method discovered by James Joyce and Eliot.

In *Ulysses* James Joyce evoked parallels between the heroic odyssey of Homer's *Ulysses* and an ordinary day in Dublin, Ireland, in 1904. He consciously juxtaposed the older Greek myth with his own tale of modern Dublin, evoking both ironic contrasts and mutual comparisons. Eliot at once recognized the technique for what it was:

In using the myth, in manipulating a continuous parallel between [the present] and [the past], Mr. Joyce is pursuing a method which others must pursue after him . . . It is simply a way of controlling, or odering, of giving a shape and significance to the intense panorama of futility and anarchy which is contemporary history . . . Instead of narrative method we may now use the mythical method. It is, I seriously believe, a step towards making the modern world possible for art, towards . . . order and form.

Thus both Joyce and Eliot used older myths and literary forms
to make comparisons between the lost past and the futile
present, and they insisted that such a method brought to an
exploration of the present a sense of order and form that it
otherwise entirely lacked. It's as if myth provided the skeleton
upon which the flesh of the present chaotic age could be
grafted.

Anthony Burgess, because of his belief that the Great
War was so terrible, because it seemed so meaningless,
suggested that "you have to find the meaning of the war in
a myth or something, the old men against the young. Anything
will do." He has been an avid student of Joyce all his life.
His own critical works on Joyce, *Joysprick* (1973) and *ReJoyce*
(1965), make that clear. Thus his own use of the mythic
method in many of his novels—his debt to the literary
modernism of Joyce—derives in part from study and celebration of Joyce's achievements. It derives also from his own,
as well as Joyce's, Catholicism, since Burgess believed that
"Joyce's attempts to build for himself an order . . . is a
substitute for the order he abandoned when he abandoned
the church."[3] He believed that if one studied the past closely
enough, "the discovery of patterns emerge, perpetually
emerging patterns, repeated patterns."[4] In these patterns, in
these older literary forms or myths some sense of historical
continuity might be found with which to confront the modern
meaningless world: "The fundamental purpose of any work
of art is to impose order on the chaos of life as it comes to
us,"[5] Burgess declared, and in this he paralleled the views
of Joyce and Eliot.

"Joyce's aim was to exploit myth, symbol and language
and to eschew the contrivances of plot."[6] Joyce "created
systems of correspondences,"[7] almost in place of plot,
constantly seeking correspondences between his present story
and the past. Such a method appealed to Burgess: "Action
has to come from an exterior myth, like that of the *Odyssey*
. . . which suggests, even if it does not fulfill, an image of
purposive movement."[8]

In his novels Burgess delighted in playing off a present situation against or within a wider and larger context. He once wrote that the novel form gets its narrative strength from older, epic forms in ancient poetry and folktales, and that the focus of the modern novel reveals a continuing "tension between heroic form and unheroic content."[9] This tension occurs in the contrived parallels the author creates between some universal pattern of human experience or some archetypal framework, namely a myth, and the story, which occurs in the present age.

Examples of the mythic method in Burgess's novels can be seen in some of those we have already explored. In *A Vision of Battlements* Burgess constantly manipulates parallels between the story of Richard Ennis in the army and Vergil's *Aeneid*. In *The Wanting Seed* Burgess uses certain vegetation myths and the idea of history as a mythic cycle. In *A Clockwork Orange* Burgess works with the myth of Utopia. In *Tremor of Intent* he manipulates the literary form of the spy story, itself a kind of generic myth. In each case Burgess uses his mythic method ironically, pointing out the discrepancies between the futility and chaos of the modern age and the more satisfying sense of purpose and order in the older myths.

This method produces a plot which at best appears constantly fragmented and ragged, yet allows for moments of genuine insight and revelation, and which at worst borders on the incoherent and the confusing. Burgess's plots have a tendency to twitch and gyrate, opening up into an almost random series of absurd episodes tumbling one upon the other. At the center of the often black comedy lurks one harried soul, struggling for some way out, some accommodation with meaning and his own bewildered identity. Around him swirls a shattered world, caught between lost truths and present absurdities.

For Burgess the use of a myth to order and organize his novels has helped to reconcile his Manichean views. He believed with Levi-Strauss, the French anthropologist, that

all myths share a primary structure. That structure is based
on the reconciliation of opposites. All myths, therefore,
attempt to heal the division between flesh and spirit, good
and evil, men and women by resolving these divisions in
some kind of narrative framework. Thus each opposite pair
is seen as primarily a unity. Flesh becomes part of spirit, as
sunlight is but the other side of shadow. As Burgess explained,
"Structuralism is the scientific confirmation of a certain
theological conviction—that life is binary, that this is a
duoverse . . . The notion of essential opposition—not God/
Devil but just x/y—is the fundamental one."[10]

If modern history since the Great War has recorded only
decay and collapse, then perhaps discovering mythic or
universal patterns within it can lead to hope in the future.
For Burgess to find mythic parallels in his novels is to find
the promise of yet a new cycle or rebirth and transformation
in modern history. To write about a present time, with its
themes of uncertainty, futility, and spiritual isolation in a
mythic framework, with its suggestions of repetitious patterns,
newer cycles, and continuous rebirth, is to attempt to
reconcile the narrow-minded despair of modernism with the
more open-minded, universal pattern of myth. History dies
and changes; myth lives on and recycles itself.

In relating this to his own literary technique, Burgess
declared

Never present a tune or theme, however lowly or fragmentary, unless
you intend to repeat it at a later stage—or, preferably, transform
it, develop it, combine it with other thematic material . . . [Any
detail is] a little figure, that, worked into one corner of the carpet,
must eventually appear in another corner for the sake of formal
balance . . . Time changes things; hence the balance achieved by
identical repetition of the same motif is out of place; there has to
be a transformation, however slight.[11]

Transformation remains the key. Eliot and Joyce attempted
to transform a muddled, chaotic present into human significance by using myth as a framework, in Eliot's case pagan
cycles of the season and Christian tales of resurrection; in

Joyce's, Homer's *Odyssey* and the Catholic Mass. Burgess's Catholicism, however lapsed, propels him in the same manner. The shape of its liturgical and religious forms, such as the Eucharist, and the essence of its Christian myth, such as resurrection and rebirth, he used as an ironic counterpart to the lack of both shape and essence—and, therefore, ultimate significance and hope—in the modern world. He, too, hoped to transform modern chaos, the legacy of the Great War, into universal significance, the ultimate achievement of any great myth.

The Doctor Is Sick (1960): "A Man on the Run."

The Doctor Is Sick, one of the five novels Burgess wrote during his "terminal" year, is, as he has suggested, "based on my experiences in hospital, not all that much fantastic, really. On the whole there's a lot of truth in that one." The experiences in the novel occur to one Dr. Edwin Spindrift, a Ph.D. lecturer on linguistics in a college in Burma with the International Council for University Development, who has passed out while lecturing on folk etymology in one of his classes and has been sent back to England to be examined by neurologists for a possible brain tumor. The truth of the novel deals with his self-discoveries as a person and his recognition of what it means to be fully human during a comic nightmare of a quest for his missing wife in a seedy and derelict London. Throughout the novel Burgess parallels Spindrift's personal experiences with the more universal or mythic quest for self-identity and understanding.

After a series of tests, including a grim spinal tap, an electroencephalogram to monitor his brain, and an arteriogram to examine his blood vessels, Spindrift feels "unmanned" in the "subterranean world of female technicians." In the middle of the night, he decides to escape and sneaks out through the cellar door. Thus begins a wild flight across London in search of his wife, who has written to him that she has run off with a bearded artist.

The rest of the plot spins and drifts in an absurd series of coincidences, confrontations, and circumstances. Spindrift rushes about on his quest from pubs to strange apartments, from cinemas to subways, hounded by strange characters and stranger incidents. He meets two Jewish twins, Leo and Harry Stone, in a sleazy underground nightclub; Bob Courage, a watch smuggler, who kidnaps him and locks him in his apartment to indulge in some homosexual carryings-on with whips; Renate, a big gin-guzzling German whore; and his former employer, a Mr. Chasper, whom he meets in a public toilet. He escapes from Courage's clutches, stumbles into the Bald Adonis of Greater London competition at a local theater and wins, escapes again, and arrives at a bar in a huge Edwardian hotel. In the luxurious marble men's room, he comes upon Aristotle Thanatos, an old friend, who is crowned with vine leaves as a part of a Bacchian celebration in the hotel. He offers Spindrift his hotel room to sleep in and a job in public relations in the morning. Forever grateful Spindrift, exhausted, makes his weary way to Thanatos's room and discovers there Sheila, his wife, making love to an unknown man. He faints dead away.

When Spindrift awakens he finds himself in a new, all-white hospital ward. It's the postoperative ward. His escapades have been part of some nightmarish dream. Sheila arrives and wants a divorce. Spindrift, confused, lets her go. Once again he awakens at night, sneaks out of the hospital, and goes in search of Mr. Thanatos, hurrying off into the "freedom of London night."

What are we to make of all this? At certain moments Burgess seems to be satirizing the modern world—its music, its low life, its plastic culture, its frivolous art. At one point Spindrift stumbles upon "a long narrow gallery full of pleasure machines," with such games as "H-Bomb" and "a most compulsive game in which the player battled against lung cancer (diagram of chest and bronchial tubes with flashing lights for zones of infection)." In the hospital ward every man is reduced to a thing, an object to be treated and operated upon, "impotent on a cellar table." But such a theme is hardly the only "truth" of this crazy-quilt work.

The wider experience of *The Doctor Is Sick* includes Spindrift's personality and outlook on life and his mythic descent into a psychological underworld of the mind to discover the limits of that personality and outlook. Toward the end of the novel a clergyman refers to Spindrift's name as "a sort of riddle." Chasper, his former employer, describes it as "the most poetical name in the whole department." A woman at a hotel thinks it's "a good name for a washing machine." An advertisement on a sign, which Spindrift sees form the height of Bob Courage's apartment, reads "SPIN-DRIFT MEANS CLEAN" and "THINGS COME CLEAN WITH SPINDRIFT." And when Sprindrift tears up one of Courage's pornographic magazines, he watches "with satis-faction the spindrift of odd isolated words as they snowed to the worn carpet."

In his hallucinatory ramblings Spindrift is indeed coming clean. He is learning all sorts of ugly things about himself: "It seemed that coming into contact with life made me into a liar, a thief, a whoremaster, a cheat, a man on the run!" He at once spins and drifts, sometimes actively pursuing his quarry, at other times allowing himself to be carried away by events seemingly beyond his control. This active-passive conflict in him suggests a kind of running-in-place and getting nowhere, a suspended animation, which leaves him breathless but remarkably static: he just seems unwilling or unable to direct his own actions.

Spindrift is, after all, a linguist, caught up in his own intellectual "spindrift of odd isolated words." His doctor accuses him of being obsessed with words. He'd rather preach than understand, and at moments of crisis, he characteris-tically passes out. He is mesmerized by "divine philology" and "could grow more excited over the connotatory differences between the two words [nude and naked] than he could over the nude, or naked, flesh itself." Such intellectual dedication makes his wife's pursuit of men more understandable. And the ensuing sexual impotence, which seems to be a part of Spindrift's "disease," reflects his spiritual impotence as well.

His adventures in his hallucinatory nightmare make clear that in loving words as separate objects he has neglected life itself. In loving the etymology of the word, "love," for instance, he has neglected the complicated actuality of human love itself. Amid the swirl of absurd episodes in the novel, Spindrift's sin comes into focus:

Let him loose in the real world, where words are glued to things, and see what he did: stole, swore, lied . . . And then all that business about resenting being treated as a thing. That was very much the pot calling the kettle black-arse, wasn't it? He'd treated words as things, things to be analyzed and classified, and not as part of the warm current of life.

At the conclusion of the novel Sheila berates him: "You don't care enough about hanging on to me. You only really care about bilabial fricatives and semi-vowels and all that rubbish." He realizes too late that "a bundle of bilabial fricatives is just a *thing*, isn't it? You can't love a thing."

Spindrift's journey toward self-revelation shapes the eccentric curves and seemingly random episodes of the novel. This journey is given mythic significance by Burgess as a journey into the underworld, somewhat similar to Bloom's adventures in Nighttown in Joyce's *Ulysses*. The myth of the descent into the underworld is an ancient one, similar in its form to the Christian pattern of the dark night of the soul. If the wanderer survives the trip, he is restored to his own world with new and deeper insights into his own soul and identity.

The mythic pattern begins early in the novel. The "subterranean world of female technicians," where Spindrift is "unmanned," introduces that realm of the underworld. He escapes from the hospital by descending into cellars; a telephone booth in which he rests momentarily becomes a "glass coffin"; he travels throughout London on the Underground; at the theatre "deep in the earth was a great cold tomb of people"; and he acknowledges at one point that "cellars were playing a big part in his life." Before he descends into this psychic underground, into the comic nightmare of his own diseased mind, his head is shaved, his clothes are taken, and his watch is stolen. Stripped down to the barest essentials—his pajamas and his doctor's diploma, the latter characteristic of his early conception of himself— he enters the timeless world of myth. Burgess refers to him as a "lost traveller," just as Spindrift, seeing the other patients in their turbans in his hospital ward, refers to them as "Mecca pilgrims."

In a fine essay on literature and myth, Northrop Frye suggests that "while the interpreter or commentator on a myth finds the profundity of the myth in its meaning as *allegory*, the poet, in recreating the myth, finds its profundity in its *archetypal framework*."[12] This is precisely what Burgess as novelist was up to in *The Doctor Is Sick*. Sprindrift's night journey doubles as a mythic quest for self-revelation. References to Odysseus, Prometheus, and Adam—at one point Spindrift, "remembering his James Joyce," dials EDEnville 0000, "and asked for Adam"—only strengthen and intensify the ritualistic aspects of man's eternal quest for self-knowledge.

In such a hallucinatory or mythic realm, "the insignificant becomes, when doubled, the significant."[13] Burgess doubles and redoubles his tale with a vengeance. The Stone twins represent one violent, less articulate personality and one more thoughtful personality, blessed with a "patrician overlay." Both are aspects of Spindrift's Jekyll and Hyde personality. Bob Courage steals watches; there is no clock in his apartment; Spindrift thinks someone has stolen his watch. And Thanatos's wine party mixes the celebration of Bacchus with overtones of death, since his own name means "death." Doubling and redoubling persist throughout the novel, achieving a mythic significance in their own right, for

throwaway, seemingly random details take on more significance when they're repeated and transformed.

Spindrift's wanderings within the darker, violent labyrinth of his own mind lead to his realization that he must
accept the darker, more violent essence within him. To
remain a linguistic purist, a Dr. Jekyll of philology, and to
deny the existence of "the warm current of life," complete
with all the complex and violent desires of a Mr. Hyde, is
to settle for bilabial fricatives in place of genuine, human
love. Sheila recognizes that "you're a kind of machine, and
the world needs machines," but Spindrift acknowledges the
passionate darkness within him and in everyone.

Or does he? Spindrift believes that he can change.
Sheila feels that he cannot and leaves him. Running "off to
find Mr. Thanatos" at the conclusion of the novel suggests
that he is still pursuing death instead of life. Or perhaps life
for him now without Sheila is something to be newly
experienced: "There was no hurry, of course. Plenty of time
for plenty of piquant adventures."

Unfortunately, the novel is too crammed with "piquant
adventures" to fit the mythic framework. It seems too often
to wander off aimlessly, undirected and at loose ends. The
scramble of absurd encounters too often appears gratuitous,
a grab bag of incidents too loosely tied. The absurdity often
outweighs the mythic dimension, and Spindrift and his
journey sink beneath the on-going rush of weird characters,
crazy encounters, and undigested bits and pieces of episodes
and incidents. Still, as an early novel it does point the way
to Burgess's developing use of myth and clearly places him
in the mainstream, however flooded here, of literary modernism.

Beard's Roman Women (1976): "What a curse sex was."

Burgess's nineteenth novel is a kind of ghost story and tale
of resurrection. Ronald Beard, a fifty-year-old scriptwriter,

who has been married for twenty-six years to Leonora, has suddenly become a widower. His wife dies of cirrhosis of the liver on the first day of spring in a London hospital, having collapsed for the first time of the disease on a rainy day in Rome. He has her body cremated and is flown to Los Angeles to discuss the possibility of a musical film based on the lives of the Shelleys and Byron. At a Bel Air mansion, Beard meets Paola Lucrezia Belli, a dark Italian photographer, who comes to his hotel room the next morning to make love. She's off to Rome to pursue her photography, and even though Beard is wary of a return to Rome—the city reminds him of his wife's death—he follows her there.

In Rome Beard delights in the rebirth of his sexual desire with Paola, but she suddenly is called away to take photographs of the latest Arab-Israeli war. Beard receives a call from Gregory Gregson, an old friend in the import-export business from Brunei, who invites him for a drink. Gregson maintains that he saw Leonora coming out of Barclay's Bank in London just a little while ago. When Beard returns to his apartment, he receives the first call from "the authentic voice of Leonora," half-singing a Christmas carol Beard had made up, singing of Brunei and its "brown men busy with axes and knives" to the tune of "Silent Night." He thinks the voice must be a recording, since he and Leonora did record his Brunei carols.

The next morning Beard receives a second call from Leonora, singing "Come All Ye Faithful" with Beard's satiric Brunei lyrics: "Pay homage at the Yacht Club,/That snottier-than-snot club . . . " Shaken, he and Gregson head off to the airport bar to see Gregson on his way. At the bar Beard spots an earlier lover of his, Miriam, but she now is older, ravaged with cancer, and cynical. Back at the apartment alone, a third call comes from Leonora. In this one she says that she's not dead, that there's been some mistake, that she is now living with her cousin, Ceridwen, in Manchester, and that she intends to come to Rome. Beard, shaken even more, suspects some kind of conspiracy.

Then Leonora telephones again, saying that she has collapsed in the airport bar and Ceridwen had to take her back home. She also prattles on about her sexual needs. Beard hangs up. Three days later Paola returns and decides to take in a group of refugee children from the Arab-Israeli War. Beard, loving orderliness and quiet, wants no part of such a plan. The phone rings. Paola answers it. It is again Leonora, and Paola explodes: "You said your wife was dead."

Time passes. At the conclusion of the novel, when we next see Beard, he has married Ceridwen, a woman who seems to combine Paola's dark sensuousness with Leonora's orderliness and common sense. "Leonora" turns out to be Leonora's sister, Mrs. Gwyneth Isherwood Hanson, who out of spite has been telephoning Beard and who borrowed the Brunei tapes several years ago and failed to return them. She still calls Beard, babbling incessantly about her sexual needs.

Beard learns he has a terminal illness, a bad heart. He is summoned to Rome to write a television script on Spinoza, meets Gregson there again, and runs up and down the steep stairs of Paola's apartment to try to bring about his own death quickly. He fails, and the novel concludes when he returns to the hotel bar with Gregson to get drunk: "Getting into the cab with Greg he was, he supposed, as happy as he had ever been in his life."

Again Burgess takes potshots at the slick modern world of "demotic media," Hollywood scriptwriters, chic parties and vacuous "California goddesses who gloried in belonging to the two-dimensional culture that smelt of nothing." But his real subject is the complex desires and repulsions that occur betwen men and women. Sex becomes a curse, the fratricidal war between the Arabs and Israelis merely another form of incompatibility and conflict: "You know they're the same race really." He denigrates the "clockwork toy called Pre-destinate man, wound up by God and arbitrarily set by Him on a path leading to salvation or perdition," a mere object mechanically reacting to sexual stimulation and desire. And Beard himself is accused of not really liking women.

Women, according to the clear-eyed Miriam, "move about too much, they have needs and ideas of their own," which upsets the self-centered man's desire to use them for his own pleasure.

Beard seems lost in a world of women. He harbors immense guilt about his wife's death, guilt for dragging her out to Brunei, for all the major and minor infidelities in which he indulged himself, for merely outliving her. These feelings certainly parallel Burgess's own. Beard is haunted by her memory, already half believing that as a ghost she will return to haunt any attempt he might make to begin a new life: "The widower's sex could not really be guiltless, the wife having in a sense been put away so that flat belly and firm breasts could now be enjoyed in fact not merely fantasy. The guilt a murderer's guilt."

Beard's return to Rome is at once a return to the scene of the crime as well as to the possibility of a new life with the sensual Paola. Rome, "a city of robbers," full of "vapid bloody insolent Roman bloody handsomeness and useless idiotic youth," represents at once both death and desire, a rainy ghostly place, which Paola captures in her photographs of the city reflected in puddles, and also the eternal city of Christianity and, therefore, resurrection and rebirth. The odd-angled, eerily photographed pictures by David Robinson, which are included in the novel, capture the two-faced city of Rome, both gloomy and vibrant.

Beard undergoes a kind of mythic journey into the underworld, much the same as Spindrift's in *The Doctor Is Sick*, although Beard's is more closely allied with the battle between the sexes. Burgess makes reference to the search for the Holy Grail and the Fisher King's resumption of his power and sexual potency. In the apartment at one point Beard is stripped naked as is the apartment itself; he feels naked and imprisoned and at some sort of "a cross-roads, if you waited, you never knew." Here he writes his script about Mary Shelley, is deserted by Paola, is telephoned by the dead Leonora, and is raped by a gang of four girls, who think he's destroyed their boyfriend's motorbike. The apartment overlooks the crypt of Saint Cecilia, where the "matron saint of music" is supposedly buried.

Beard's women represent every facet of female sexuality. Leonora, a northern blonde, prided herself on her Welsh tidiness. Paola, whose last name means "of the family of beautiful ones," suggests a dark Mediterranean sensuality and is consistently messy in her personal habits. St. Cecilia suggests the purity of music and spiritual longing; Beard listens to Dryden's St. Cecilia's Ode set to music from within Paola's apartment, as he tries unsuccessfully to kill himself running up and down the stairs. Mary Shelley, the creator of Frankenstein, in Beard's mind stands for the "dream-stuff" of art and the creative imagination. References in Beard's mind to Salome and Judith recall the female sex's vengeance on John the Baptist and Holofernes and foreshadow the aggressive "gang of four." Gregson's latest lover is named Isa—"it means Jesus of course"—who is the daughter of a former lover, Aminah. And Aminah spelled backwards without the "h"—anima—is the Jungian name for the female side or projection of man's complete psychological self.

The men in the novel, though less sympathetic than Beard, nevertheless mirror his own male righteousness. Schaumwein, the Hollywood producer, is described as a "Genghis Khan." Pathan, Paola's former husband, abuses her and seeks pederastic pleasures elsewhere. Gregson embodies the old colonial paternalism of the British abroad. Speaking of the natives in Brunei, he sputters, "Whip them. Tread on them. Sort of language they understand . . . put the little swine back under colonial rule."

In many ways Beard's sexual desires for Paola parallel his past affair with Miriam. His present rejuvenation may be merely an illusionary throwback to remembered passion. Is his resurrection merely a resurrection of the romanticized past, or is it a genuine resurrection from the dead? The disillusioned Miriam, now an Israeli radio newscaster, who has lost her left breast to cancer and who is killed two hours before the cease-fire is declared in the Arab-Israeli War, states the problem to Beard in the airport bar: "You love what I was—present tense married to past tense, an impossible marriage." To evoke the past is to fall victim to illusion; there can be no going back. As for Mary Shelley, Miriam concludes, "It took a woman to make a Frankenstein monster. Evil, cancer, corruption, pollution, the lot. She was the only one of the lot of them who knew about life."

Beard emerges from his dark night of the soul, or in this case perhaps of sexual appetite, and marries Ceridwen. He admits in a letter to Paola, after they have broken up, that "You restored me to life in a bad time." At the same time he realizes that he could never have lived with her: "I remain at the end a monoglot Englishman . . . I thought I was ready to be stripped naked and imbued with a new chivalry . . . but I was too old and too weak and too frightened." To him Ceridwen—a "*new direc*tion" perhaps? (Ceridwen backwards is "new direc")—"possesses your charity and your passion and something of your beauty, as well as belonging to the one world I knew." Deliverance? Self-knowledge? Yes, in a subdued conservative manner. Beard recognizes his limitations, at the same time he has exorcised the guilt over his first wife's death. He realizes, in talking to Dr. Bloomfield on the day he is told he hasn't long to live, that he's failed "in chastity, knowingly, deliberately" to Leonora, Paola, and perhaps to Ceridwen. Bloomfield suggests he must learn to truly love himself in the remaining months ahead, that love is "symbiosis . . . the sense of a single living entity. The desire to be part of it, the desire for a part of you to be a part of it." Perhaps in his third attempt to commit suicide at the end of the novel, in that one frail glimpse of a feeling of happiness, Beard has finally realized the essence of love.

Throughout the novel Burgess once again confronts the many forms of art and life. His Brunei Christmas carols, his interplay between the text of the novel and David Robinson's photographs, Pathan's (the novelist's) attack on Beard's (the scriptwriter's) art—"All you have to do is to write down Scene

Ninety-two or whatever the hell it is, medium close shot or
some such bloody mumbo-jumbo"—and his comments on
Beard's final script's transformation into Paul Newman's
film—"The Lovers of the Lake" become "Milord Lucifer"—
reveals Burgess's continued interest in the forms of art. Art
as form provides consolation and order, since it helps both
to explain life and to evade it. In either instance, life remains
an ultimate mystery.

Even the consolation and order of marriage, superior as
"complex semiotics to mere sex," creates its own "mythology,
a joint memorybank, a language . . . the end of a marriage,
whether through the death of life or of love, was also the end
of a civilization." Marriage, itself a sacred form of art,
transforms mere personal experience into its own universal
mythology.

Beard's Roman Woman remains a minor novel in the
Burgess canon, if only because of its concentrated thematic
unity. It is too easily unraveled and diagrammatically arranged. It seems ultimately thin and all too carefully prearranged, as if Burgess were using modernist techniques and
methods with one hand tied behind his back. Yet it serves
as an example, however simplistic, of that method, which
reached its fullest scope in Burgess's hands in the artful
failure of *MF* and the resounding triumph of *Napoleon
Symphony*.

MF (1971): "Riddles are there for a good purpose."

The task that Burgess set for himself in writing *MF* clearly
reveals the modernist's desire to use myth as the framework
for a novel:

Is it possible to take an Algonquin myth like the one Levi-Strauss
presents in his novel talk at the Sorbonne, and make a modern
naturalistic novel out of it? The aim is to try and make it look like
a straight-forward, traditional, realistic novel. If it could only

function through the mythical structure of it, then the whole thing's a failure.

If we look at the novel as "straight-forward, traditional and realistic," then we have to conclude that it is a decided failure, however artfully and cleverly contrived. If we look at *MF* in terms of the Algonquin myth, which Burgess used as his framework, then we can clearly see how literary modernism is supposed to function.

Without a clear knowledge of the mythic background, *MF* seems like yet another gratuitous romp through absurd encounters with oddball creatures in some popculture landscape, leading only to dissolution and chaos. At one point in the novel, Burgess writes, "A sure sign of amateur art is too much detail to compensate for too little life," and in the plot of *MF*, this certainly seems to be the case.

Miles Faber, the MF of the title, is a twenty-year-old college student who has just been dismissed from college for publicly fornicating with someone named Carlotta as a form of unspecified protest near the college library. He acknowledges that his is a "formless mind . . . a medieval quarter crammed with junk shops," that he wishes to "get beyond structure and cohesion" in all things, and that "I recognized in myself a certain histrionic gift, another term for exhibitionism." He seems to be Burgess's evocation of a typical addlepated student of the late Sixties. His present desire is to get to the Caribbean island of Castita, there to find the poetry and paintings of the Castitian poet and painter, Sib Legeru. He looks upon Legeru as a prophet promising significance and hope.

After some difficulties, Faber decides to fly to Miami and work his way on a boat from there to Castita. On the bus to LaGuardia he notices a suspicious man in a black suit, who also appears on the flight to Miami. The man accosts Faber in Miami and delivers him into the hands of a Mr. Pardaleos.

Pardaleos reveals a remarkable tale. It seems that Faber's father, who died in a plane crash, had committed

118 Anthony Burgess

incest, not just once with his sister, but twice. Faber's aunt-
mother, filled with remorse, then drowned herself. Faber has
a sister, and his father had worked hard to make sure they
would always be separated from each other, so that incest
would not recur. The sister is somewhere in the Caribbean;
so is Castita. Faber manages to elude Pardaleos's men and
arrives in Castita, having survived an apocalyptic storm at
sea.

Faber arrives on Castita during a celebration day, the
feast of Senta Euphorbia, complete with parades and carnivals,
priests, a circus troup, and a soccer team. In a bar a man
known as Mr. Memory, who plays mind-reading games at the
carnival, complains about the oppressive dictatorship on the
island and is arrested by the police. Faber, penniless, sets
himself up as Mr. Memory Junior to make some money and
enjoys the riddles and questions which are tossed at him.

Faber is asked out to dinner by the deformed man he
meets at the fair, a Dr. Gonzi. Gonzi, an idealist, is appalled
that he's been offered money to appear as a freak in the
circus that is presently in Castita. He gets drunk and suicidal,
asks Faber a riddle, and declares if Faber can answer it,
he'll shoot himself; if he cannot, he'll shoot Faber. Faber
knows the answer but refuses to divulge it. Gonzi fires at
him, but Faber dashes off into the alley, only to be arrested
by the police. A Mr. Dunkel from the circus delivers him to
a certain trailer in the circus area. Faber is stunned. In the
trailer he comes face to face with his physical double, Llew
(short for Llewelyn), a vulgar and obscene troublemaker,
whose mother is Aderyn, the Bird Queen, in the circus.

Events tumble forward. Faber checks out of his hotel,
ready to leave Castita, on the day of a sudden miracle at
Dwumu, the local mosque-cathedral. Blood has been seen
to flow from the penis of the statue of the infant Jesus there.
The President and the faithful turn out to view the miracle,
which later proves to be a hoax. As Faber is talking in a
local bar, in walks Miss Emmett, the old woman who had
raised him as a boy.

Fate intervenes. Across the street in Miss Emmett's house lives Faber's sister, Catherine, a plump, unattractive, seventeen-year-old girl. She and Miss Emmett came to Castita to see a doctor for Catherine's psychological problems; her father made a pass at her, and Miss Emmett stabbed him with the scissors she always carries with her.

Still searching for the works of Sib Legeru, Faber discovers the key to his house and he learns that it is the very house in which Miss Emmett and Catherine are staying. Faber locates Legeru's manuscripts and paintings in the garden shed in back of the house. The hodgepodge of surrealistic poems and pictures delights Faber. To his misguided mind they all "showed similar acts of daring that soothed my soul by their disdain of what the world calls meaning."

Fate still calls the shots. Faber hears a woman's scream. He rushes back into the house to find Llew trying to rape Catherine. She'd called him in out of her bedroom window, thinking it was her brother. Miss Emmett rushes at him with her scissors, he topples out of the third-story window and cracks his skull on the birdbath below. Faber hides Llew's body in the shed and drives back in Llew's car to the circus, hoping to pretend he's Llew and not alert the already anxious police to the accident. He kisses Aderyn good night, drives her to a doctor's appointment in the morning—she's aware that her Llew seems less obnoxious, more articulate—and rushes to see how Catherine is doing. Aderyn surprises him there. He immediately states that he and Catherine mean to wed, and Aderyn, still suspecting something, declares that they shall marry that night at the circus.

Incest hovers in the wings. The absurd, surreal wedding occurs in one of the center rings, attended by the circus folk and various animals. Faber and his sister are led to a trailer to consummate the marriage, but Miss Emmett arrives just in time to pound on the door and save the day. She takes Catherine back to town. Aderyn, furious, confronts Faber, accusing him of Llew's murder, having insisted on the wedding as his punishment. Faber realizes that he and Llew are twins, when Aderyn admits that she is not Llew's real mother.

Back at Miss Emmett's house Faber has a long talk with a Z. Fonanta, who has hovered around the circumference of events in the book mysteriously. He has cured Catherine and is now a poet. At the beginning of the novel back in New York, Faber had overheard him speaking French into a recorder at a restaurant. He now reveals himself as Faber's grandfather, explains that Llew was indeed Faber's twin, and that Fonanta had committed incest with his own mother.

The novel ends in 1999 in a castle in Italy by Lake Bracciano, where fifty-year-old Miles Faber now lives with his Chinese wife, Ethel. Miles and Ethel have adopted several children "of varying colors and nationalities," and we learn for the first time that Miles, Aderyn, and Fonanta are black. Out of "creative miscegenation" and incest seems to have emerged a new order of love and responsibility, far from the mindless ravings and paintings of Sib Legeru. In fact Fonanta has revealed that the old Anglo-Saxon word, "siblegeru," means incest, and that in fact the dead prophet was merely a creation of the Fabers, delighting in "a suprious creation, followed by the salutary horror of seeing how mad and bad and *filthy* the pseudo works were."

In his essay, "If Oedipus had read his Levi-Strauss," Burgess discusses the myth he used in *MF*. In a folk tale of the Iroquois and Algonquin Indian tribes, a girl accuses her brother of trying to sleep with her. He insists it is a double and kills him. The double's mother, however, is a powerful sorceress, "the mistress of magic owls who ask difficult riddles under pain of death,"[14] and comes to avenge her son. The brother weds his sister to avoid her revenge, and the two of them run away. The mother, meanwhile, cannot even conceive of such a thing as breaking the taboo against incest. Burgess recognizes the similarity between this tale and the Oedipus story: "In both legends there are riddle-asking, half-human creatures: owls, the sphinx."[15] And in both to solve the riddle is to bring about certain death:

The man who solves the insoluble puzzle has, symbolically, disrupted nature. Since incest is the ultimate perversion of nature, nature is shocked to death . . . if you avoid the riddles you avoid the penalty for incest . . . To the 'primitive' mind, the puzzle and the sexual taboo have an essential factor in common—the knot that holds the natural order together.[16]

Burgess saturates his novel with images from the two myths of Oedipus and the Algonquin Indians. Owls appear throughout: Catherine has a little china owl; Aderyn's name in Welsh means "owl." Faber dreams of a squaw making the sounds of an owl, a foreshadowing of his confrontation with Aderyn. References to Oedipus's clubfoot abound. Lion imagery suggesting the Sphinx is everywhere: it is suggested that Llew's name is the reverse of Nowell, since he was born on Christmas Eve, and Nowell or Noel backwards is leon or "lion"; Dr. Gonzi is described as lion-faced; Llew has been smuggling drugs in the bottom of lions' cages. Burgess multiplies and reduplicates these images endlessly throughout *MF*.

Miles Faber prides himself on his ability to solve riddles, and as Burgess describes him, is "the boy who was bound to commit incest because he could answer all the riddles correctly."[17] Besides the riddles that he himself devises, Faber is asked to solve five riddles in the course of the plot. He answers only one, the first one, presented to a college class in literature by a Professor Keteki. A reference to a play in an old diary of 1596, which reads, "Gold gold and even titularly so," Faber decides refers to Marlowe's *Jew of Malta*. His somewhat tortuous reasoning wins him twenty dollars. The other riddles offered to him for solution by a family lawyer named Loewe, Dr. Fonanta, Dr. Gonzi, and Aderyn he refuses to answer. With Loewe he feels involved in a deceitful set-up; with Fonanta he feels the answer is too obscene; with Gonzi he knows if he answers, he'll be responsible for Gonzi's suicide; and with Aderyn, the answer involves unriddling the mysteries of the universe, and either choice—

god or the devil—would be ultimately wrong. She has asked
him, "Who was the final final, say,/That was put back but had
his day?" A dog has his day; reversed would make it "god."
But "if you've had your day, you've lived" and the reverse of
"lived" is "devil." Faber is spared the act of incest, however,
when Fonanta informs him that his answer to Keteki's riddle
is wrong. This failure to solve the first riddle—the answer is
never revealed—eventually saves Faber from his incestuous
fate, since in the old myth, to solve the riddle is to break the
taboo and bring down on oneself severe consequences.

The significance of *MF* remains the same as the earlier
incest myths. Incest is "the negation of social communion,"
according to Pardaleos. As Fonanta adds, incest signifies
"the breakdown of order, the collapse of communication, the
irresponsible cultivation of chaos." Burgess identifies incest
with the narcissistic attributes of contemporary culture—the
casual sex, the frivolous self-centered culture, the muddled
pop-art of Sib Legeru. And Faber himself is a product of this
culture. At one point, when Pardaleos informs Faber about
his incestuous heritage, Faber quips nonchalantly, "Primal
sense isn't revolted, except perhaps aesthetically. It's ideas,
words, irrational taboos, pseudo-ethical additives . . ." He
seems to choke on his own jargon, as yet uninitiated into the
heart of disorder and collapse that incest symbolizes.

Faber, whose name means skilled workman and who is
clearly resolved, at first, to solve every riddle that comes his
way, begins to realize that life itself may be an ultimate,
unresolvable riddle. Perhaps, he surmises,

Riddles are there for a good purpose—not to be answered. They are
like those do-not-touch wall panels set in the great buildings of the
modern world, which you can take as a rationalized translation of
the natural order.

Life is not a mere riddle to offer up one omnipotent solution;
it constantly frustrates us with its mixture of both good and
evil. This Faber at last realizes: "Order has both to be and
not to be challenged, this being the anomalous condition of

the sustention of the cosmos. Rebel becomes hero; witch becomes saint . . . You've got to have it both ways, man."

Burgess's plot in *MF* is itself a riddle, filled with coincidences, mysterious characters, and double dealings. Everything is doubled and redoubled. The most obvious example is, of course, Miles and Llew, the identical twins. Doubleness lies at the very heart of things. To deny this reality in search of one great explanation is to seek only the ultimate chaos and narcissistic self-immolation of incest. Faber realizes that both God and the Devil are at work here, that reality is an insoluble riddle not to be tampered with, and that the penalty of tampering with it could be death. He thinks to himself at one moment, "The fear of solitude is at bottom the fear of the double, the figure which appears one day and always heralds death." Yet that double must be recognized, or else one is left only in his own self-centered, incestuous soul.

Why doesn't *MF* work as well as it should, given the incredible artful dodging and careful planning on Burgess's part? Faber tells his own story, so that the reader can more easily sympathize with his search for clues and desire for meaning. He realizes that he's "imposing the postures and language" on events that have already happened to him a long time ago, but this lends his tale the aura of a mystery to be solved. He even includes the reader in his own musings: "What, incidentally are you like?" But the device seems forced and haphazard.

MF reads more like a crossword puzzle than a novel. The mythic allusions are too self-conscious, too obvious on the page. They are not subsumed within a real human character. They stand out as signposts along a fanciful yellow-brick road to some absurdist fairy-tale world. The bones of the myth protrude through what should be the flesh of believable characters and recognizable emotions. As one critic has suggested, one "appeal of puzzle-solving" is the

pleasure one can get simply from having solved the puzzle. This is a pleasure that on rare occasions is equal to deep esthetic satisfaction, because in the works of a writer like James Joyce, solving a literary puzzle is equal to penetrating some universal mystery. But it isn't always, so it's risky to assume that the unscrambling of any anagram or the tracing to its source of each literary reference are tantamount to experiencing art for its own sake.[18]

Based on their interest in literature as game and puzzle, several critics have discovered what they call a "post-modernist" trend in contemporary literature. They believe that contemporary writers, unlike Eliot and Joyce, delight in artifice for artifice's sake, in treating literature as an elaborate game. Perhaps *MF* would fall into this pop-art, comic-strip camp, as several critics have tried to suggest. Perhaps *MF* does reveal a "new sensibility," which may be called "post-modernist" and which delights in "blatant artifice, two-dimensional characterization, black comedy, manufactured camp . . . [and] linguistic distortion."[19]

Burgess, however, considered post-modernism, a "ridiculous phrase." He clearly intended to use myth as an archetypal framework in many of his novels but at the same time insisted on holding fast to the character at the center of the story: "You've got to have some sort of meat there, and solid meat is character." He believed as well that much contemporary fiction suggests a universe which is arbitrary and discontinuous, and he firmly denies that vision of the deep-seated disorder of things. If *MF* fulfills a "post-modernist" recipe, it is to Burgess's chagrin and not to his credit.

In discussing *Napoleon Symphony* one critic suggested that there is an "odd *outsideness*" to Burgess's writing and that most of his characters, beyond "a single vivid character," are "sawdust."[20] This criticism seems justified in describing *MF*. Faber, however, is not a very vivid character, lost as he becomes amid the complications and gyrating twists of the plot. There is no "felt life" in the novel, as if the modernist use of myth has overpowered all other facets of the novel. *MF* remains an intriguing and artful failure. It is more fun to decipher than to read.

Napoleon Symphony (1974): "The essence
of the heroic . . . in music."

In "An Epistle to the Reader" at the conclusion of *Napoleon Symphony* Burgess explains in heroic couplets what he has attempted to do in the novel:

> . . . somehow to give
> Symphonic shape to verbal narrative . . .
> . . . to frame
> A novel on Napoleon Bonaparte
> That followed Ludvig Van . . . Third, in E-Flat,
> The Eroica. This novel, then is that:
> Napoleon's career, unteased, rewoven
> Into a pattern borrowed from Beethoven.

Burgess had always maintained that all his fiction could be viewed as the "novels of a failed musician," that they are extremely "auditory" and meant "to be read aloud."[21] He insisted that "we're only at the beginning of learning what music and literature can do together. We're still in the modernist period." To create a novel in symphonic form involves introducing certain images, actions, and symbols that, like themes or motifs in symphonies, must be repeated at a later stage. Thus the form of the novel achieves the "formal balance" of a symphony; that balance is "achieved by identical repetition of the same motif,"[22] at several points not merely repeating a phrase or an image but transforming it, developing and extending its significance in the narrative.

At the same time Burgess also develops the myth of the hero. He wishes to represent in the novel "the essential hero":

> My task as novelist? Restore that rogue ram,
> That bad colossus, to the symphonic program,
> Dealing in hard particulars but still
> Invoking what is always general
> In music, the Napoleonic presence . . .

Burgess believed that Beethoven in his "fiery" Finale in his

symphony celebrates Prometheus, the mythic, heroic figure,
who stole fire from the Gods and brought it down to men.
Thus Beethoven celebrated both the historic Napoleon and
the mythic Prometheus, the one a mere mortal and a failure,
the other that eternal symbol of heroism throughout and
beyond history. In fact Beethoven tore up his dedication of
his symphony to Napoleon, viewing him as just one more
earthly tyrant. In his own mind the "Little Corporal" just
could not measure up to the heroic sweep of his symphony.

Burgess carefully patterned his novel on Beethoven's
symphony:

What I have in front of me when I'm working is the score of the
Eroica. I will make the various sections of the novel correspond to
the various sections of the symphony, so that if I take, say eight
bars of Beethoven, it's roughly equivalent to three pages of my own
work.[23]

The overall pattern of the symphony can be seen in the novel.
The symphony is divided into four parts, the *Allegro*, the
Marcia Funebre, the *Scherzo*, and the *Finale*. The *Allegro*
moves vigorously and triumphantly. Part one of *Napoleon
Symphony* traces the rise of Napoleon from military general
to Emperor. The "irritable, quick, swiftly transitional"[24]
passages of the chapter parallel those in the *Allegro*. The
Marcia Funebre or Funeral March moves "slowly, very
leisurely, with a binding beat suggesting a funeral march."[25]
In Part Two of the novel Burgess traces Napoleon's retreat
from Russia across the snowy and frozen landscape. The
Scherzo passes quickly in a spirited, joyous manner. To
Burgess the horns suggest the dancing flames, which Prometheus brought to men. Thus in Part Three of the novel
Napoleon watches a play at the Paris Opera, a production of
the Prometheus myth. The *Finale* in its light touches suggests
almost a formal dance in its fugal repetitions, and it concludes
on a triumphant major tonic chord. In Part Four of the novel
Napoleon, now exiled to St. Helena, sits and reminisces in

the garden of an island estate. After Napoleon's death, Burgess writes a triumphant two-page hymn of praise to the mighty Napoleon reviewing his troops in the spring. The novel ends on that note: "And I say aga INRI ng bells bells bells bells and rejoice. Rejoice."

Burgess filled his novel with references to musical instruments—violins, trumpets, drums, flutes. The formal connection between Beethoven's symphony and his own is also very carefully made. For instance in Part Two, the opening lyric, which refers to Napoleon's corpse—"There he lies/Ensanguinated tyrant/O bloody bloody tyrant/See/How the sin within/Doth incarnadine/His skin/From the shin to the chin"—duplicates exactly the rhythm of the opening motif in the *Marcia Funebre*, as introduced by the violins. The dead Napoleon may awaken, Burgess suggests, to "the trumpeting of violets," the word "violet" suggesting perhaps the violins.

Beethoven's funeral motif moves in a slow, stately, majestic manner. Burgess parallels this with his use of images of heaviness and ponderousness. Napoleon lies on a mahogany board, drawn slowly on a farm tumbril by four asses: "These souls merely plodded, patient in immemorial asininity, gray and shagged and unwhipped." Napoleon's hearing a high fife could suggest the point where the oboe begins to carry the motif. This occurs almost exactly three pages after the opening lines—the repetition of the complete funeral motif—underscoring Burgess's plan to equate eight bars of Beethoven with three pages of his own text. The motif itself lasts eight and one half bars and, therefore, about three more pages. Finally, when the sombre violins begin again, Napoleon awakes in Moscow "to resignation," a mood very similar to the music's.

Throughout the novel the plot is often difficult to follow. It comes in fragments, glimpses, and a detailed rush of battles, armaments, political intrigues, names, military maneuvers and strategies. Clearly what Burgess attempted is the sweep of Napoleon's career, rather than a carefully

plotted, straightly narrated representation. The reader becomes caught up in the flow of events and characters as the
novel rushes forward.

The novel opens with Josephine waiting with friends for
Napoleon to arrive and marry her. This quiet prelude precedes
the novel itself and concludes with Napoleon's arrival and
his command, "Begin!" We are off and running. In Part One
Napoleon, still full of desire for his new bride, defeats the
Italians, improves his military strategy with his famous pincer
movement (he splits the opposing forces and then attacks
their flanks), sails to Egypt to encounter black flies, defeated
Turks, and a British blockade, and returns from Egypt to
liquidate the Revolutionary Directory and become one of a
new triumvirate to rule France. At the same time Josephine
has been having an affair with Lieutenant Hippolyte Charles.
Napoleon, cuckolded, is furious but decides against divorce
as his career ascends. He crosses the Alps to defeat the
Austrians at Marengo, dallies with an opera singer, and is
made First Consul for life because of his daring military
victories. On the way to the opera a bomb hidden in a cart
in fromt of him explodes. He decides to form a secret police,
has Louis Antoine, a prince of the House of Bourbon, arrested
and executed, and crowns himself Emperor at Notre Dame.
All of this rushes along in bits and snatches, constant leaps
and juxtapositions, scenes following other scenes at a rapid
unrelenting rate.

In Part Two Napoleon dreams that he is dead but
awakens to encounter a German student, Stapps, at Schon-
brunn in Vienna, who has tried to kill him. Stapps babbles
on and on about German nationalism as opposed to the
antinationalistic, revolutionary principles of the French, and
refuses to retract his statements. Napoleon has him shot.

On a floating pavilion in the middle of a river at Tilsit,
Napoleon meets Czar Alexander of Russia to decide the fate
of Europe. Napoleon's Continental System is basically an
economic and trading program to isolate England and keep
her out of European trade. The effeminate Alexander betrays

Napoleon's scheme, and Napoleon decides to invade Russia. His choice proves disastrous.

The rest of Part Two deals with the terrible retreat from Moscow. Snow, icy rivers, collapsed bridges at Berezina, and the savage, relentless Cossacks destroy the French army. Bodies litter the landscape. Napoleon, as he did from Egpyt, returns to France disguised as a humble French citizen, M. Leon Lavol. He talks with the common folk at local cafés and realizes how desperate they and the French economy have become. In the interim he's divorced Josephine, his true love, who has not been able to produce an heir for the Emperor, and married Marie-Louise of Austria. She produces a son for him, but the cause is nearly lost. The section ends with Napoleon dreaming once again of funerals.

Fireworks and a grand ball at the Tuileries to celebrate the anniversary of the Emperor's coronation open Part Three of the novel. Napoleon attends a performance of the Prometheus myth, in which Prometheus steals fire from the gods, teaches men the art of war, and is finally bound to a cliffside where eagles torment him by pecking at his liver. Napoleon is outraged and demands that the actors set Prometheus free. The scene shifts to a satiric play in London, which mocks the Napoleon-Prometheus similarities. Again the scene shifts to the Concert of Vienna; Napoleon has been sent off to Elba, and Castlereagh and Metternich are dividing up the European spoils in the new post–Napoleonic age. Napoleon upstages them by returning from Elba. The restored King Louis XVIII flees from the Tuileries to Belgium. Napoleon is then once and for all trounced at Waterloo, and the French Empire collapses.

In Part Four Napoleon, exiled to St. Helena, a barren volcanic island, dies slowly of a bad liver. The parallels with the Promethean myth are obvious. He cultivates his own garden, talks about his days in Corsica and his European plans to a young English girl of fifteen, Betsy Bascombe, and rails at his hateful jailer, Sir Hudson Lowe. Lowe insists on giving him milk, not at all a proper remedy for a diseased

liver. At Napoleon's autopsy the enlarged liver stuns the
Corsican doctor, Dr. Antommarchi, but the English doctors
wish to report that he died of stomach cancer, like his father
before him. One of them, Dr. Shortt, agrees with Antommarchi, but the statement is signed to hide any British
involvement in Napoleon's death. Sir Hudson prepares a
blank tombstone. Much later Sergeant Trouncer, who has
been at St. Helena, reports Napoleon's last words to Betsy
Bascombe at home in her London garden: "France. Army.
Head of the Army. Josephine." And in the final coda Burgess
ends on a note of general jubilation for the dead hero.

Burgess's Napoleon is a feisty, impatient, decisive
military man who sees himself as a Republican liberator:
"I'm the spirit of the French Revolution, the American
Revolution, any damned revolution you please . . . blessed
with the enlightenment of the republican principle, from the
machinations . . . of ancient, corrupt and jealously feudal
monarchies." He has a fierce and fiery temper, a product of
his Corsican blood and Corsican sense of honor and blood-
feuds. At times he appears demonic, pushing his armies on
to greater and more impossible tasks, a titanic stage manager
directing his forces through the nooks and crannies of his
beloved maps: "He was prowling round the map that glowed
inside his skull, every river and even the most inconsiderable
township glinting obediently." He does everything too fast,
from eating—hence the unrelenting heartburn—to making
love. His lusty nature wages war as violently as he makes
love: "The conduct of war was, to him, a highly extravagant
mode of self-stimulation. It is conceivable, that Austerlitz
contrived for him a modest ejaculation, but the massive
slaughter . . . of the Russian campaign must, one hopes,
have procured a truly satisfying orgasm." Others view him
as a "new kind of mechanical animal . . . He's there to turn
the age into himself," but he triumphs as a character over
such feeble categories.

Napoleon Symphony is crowded with images and symbolic particulars.[26] These add an amazingly fertile fictional

density to the novel, and it surpasses in its fictional fullness the "thinner" modernist novels, *MF*, *Beard's Roman Women*, and *The Doctor Is Sick*. Perhaps the most important pattern of images in the novel is the one in which Napoleon is consistently represented by the elements, earth and fire, and consequently fears the element of water. His resemblance to the Promethean figure is underscored by such images. Neptune in the play about Prometheus speaks the lines, "The mighty billowing ocean stays exempt/From any would-be conqueror's attempt." An old woman warns Napoleon that "the earth would be my friend and the water my enemy." Russia appears to him as "a watery diffused kind of country." He dreams he is dead and dumped into the sea.

In Napoleon's mind "water was treacherous," and he identified it with "that woman-element." Josephine dreams of water and loves it:

To get to Paris meant that horrid jolting over land, somehow very *male* in its roughness. The sea, the warm spicy sea, she never feared the sea, the sea was her element, the sea was a woman, *la mère la mer*, and lapped round a man and enclosed him and made him yield, yes, yield all.

Napoleon rails against "the damned Seas, the accursed woman-element, the immutable boundaries of his Empire." The water imagery, of course, culminates in his decisive defeat at Waterloo: "It was the waters of an inconsiderable river that indirectly spoke the word Defeat, when a scared pressed fledgling of a sapper blew the bridge with premature haste." And Napoleon is sent in exile to St. Helena, imprisoned by the sea once and for all.

As the water imagery overcomes Napoleon's fate, the earth imagery shrinks to the size of the little garden he cultivates on St. Helena. He tells Betsy Bascombe that "a garden is what a man must win from the wilderness, it is the order he seeks . . . Once I sought to turn all Europe into a garden." In a savage rainstorm Napoleon's garden is destroyed. The wild storm suggests "that chaos seemed to have come again" and sounds like "the gods bellowing their ultimate rage at Prometheus." The water defeats the earth; the primal waters of chaos have come again to uncreate the man-made scheme of things: "There seemed to some to be a lesson here, and it was that a man may not make even a garden with impunity."

As European history shifts and changes, so do the styles of art. The minuet is replaced by the waltz. Napoleon's faith in "the classical spirit [which] rests on exactitude, on exact and accurate rendering of the world closely observed," crumbles in the in-coming waves of the romantic era, the "tempestuous formlessness" of a new age. Early in the novel Burgess writes a poem in classical, heroic couplets lauding Napoleon: "Mark how the Alexander of our age/Bids soldier's skill fulfill a lover's rage." When Napoleon is exiled on St. Helena, another poem recreates him in a romantic and sentimental manner and form: "Wherein I lie at summer ease, I see/that man again. . ." Wordsworth has replaced Pope. And toward the end of the novel Burgess writes a scene replete with all the endless, heavy clauses of the most stifling Victorian prose. The very language of *Napoleon Symphony* traces the changes in European history.

The rise of the German *Volk* and its sense of a nationalist, racist hegemony slowly overpowers Napoleon's battle with the old feudal monarchies in the novel. The failed assassin, Stapps, speaks of "the only pure race in Europe" and of a "mystical loyalty . . . to country as the country's gods that dwell in the forests and rivers, in sunrise and sunset." Romanticism and nationalism combine with the German sense of destiny, and Napoleon's more classical battle between republicanism and feudalism seems lost and abandoned in the "ever-moving stream" of history. The suggestions of German dominance foreshadow a darker future.

Toward the end of the novel in a kind of dream sequence just before he dies, Napoleon is confronted by a lady bearing a basket of roses. She may or may not be a kind of muse or the woman-element come to speak with him before his death. In any case she and Napoleon discuss the several aspects of heroism. Napoleon believes that "the nature of the hero has to be made manifest." He is a human being of "exceptional qualities," a decisive leader and a man of action. Without him there can be no separate myth of heroism. On the other hand she believes firmly that "the hero doesn't have to have existed. To nourish the imagination with the heroic image—this can be as well done through some superior (and hence perhaps heroic) imagination." She is arguing, in effect, for the mythic heroic ideal over the historic, and therefore mortal, reality. To Napoleon she suggests, "You could have been made, and made rather well, by some master . . . in words, you know. Then there would not have to have been all that cauchemar [nightmare] of flesh and blood . . . the essence of the heroic . . . in music."

Burgess has achieved that synthesis of mythic form and content he has sought in many of his novels in *Napoleon Symphony*. In doing so, he also managed to convey a full sense of Napoleon's flawed humanity, above and beyond the artful contrivances of the mythic framework. The sheer exuberance and richness of the language—one wants to stop and quote whole luscious sections of it—lift the narrative above a mere filling out of some modernist formula and into the higher realm of a fully articulated, emotionally created novel. In "dealing in hard particulars" Burgess reveals how sadly unrealized is the heroic image in human life, but that image itself remains untarnished in the stylized sweep of his narrative, the richness of his images and prose, and the size and reach of his Promethapoleon." History is transformed into myth; the mortal and flawed historical Napoleon becomes Burgess's—and Beethoven's—Prometheus, an embodiment of the human spirit. On the retreat from Russia a dying lieutenant surveys the bodies around him and "saw his left leg, from the knee down, actually break off, no pain, like a rotten tree-limb." And yet, weeping in the frozen Russian wastes he stumbles upon a simple truth: "The one part of the human system that could not break off and lie there in the snow was the Human Spirit." In its joyous exuberance *Napoleon Symphony* recreates and celebrates just that.

5

••

The Rituals of Language

In a recent review on a book about Joyce, Burgess insisted, "The mythic element in that book . . . is not important . . . [Joyce] was only concerned with finding pretexts (or the kind of excuse a man offers for the party behavior of a drunken wife) for the stylistic ports of call of his wandering muse."[1] In other words what Joyce really wanted to do was to "play around with language . . . the myth is a mere justification for what people nowadays probably call self-indulgent expression."[2]

At first Burgess's emphasis on language may seem to contradict his emphasis on the use of myth or form in his own fiction, until one realizes that the two are not mutually exclusive. In fact, Burgess maintained that Joyce merely used the myth of Homer's Odyssey "for a structural purpose." He used it to organize, shape, and give coherence to his otherwise more important interest in language and words: "Joyce's eyes were altogether on June 16, 1904 in a city concerned very little with truth—whether of myth, history or human character—but much concerned with words . . . we have some very solid verbal artifaction. And that's no myth."[3]

For Burgess, to manipulate language is to discover truth, as he himself suggested in his critical discussion of Shake-speare's life. An author's achievement should be based upon "the fundamental skill of putting words together in new and surprising patterns, which miraculously reflect some previously unguessed truth about life."[4] "Only through the exploration of language can the personality be coaxed into yielding a few more of its secrets,"[5] Burgess insisted. He admired both Joyce and Gerard Manley Hopkins for their manipulations of language, for their experimental daring with style and diction. "Both were so acutely aware of the numinous in the commonplace that they found it necessary to manipulate the commonplaces of language into a new medium that should shock the reader into a new awareness."[6] This awareness of what language can be made to do became for Burgess the most important aspect of modernist literature: "Prose and subject-matter have become one and inseparable; it is the first big technical break-through of twentieth-century prose-writing."[7]

Burgess believed that "every phase of the soul [has] its own special language."[8] Consequently, language should reveal or depict the movement and actions of a man's mind. If a character suffers in a novel, the language should suffer as well. It should not remain separate from the character's mind or feelings. The author's job "is making the language seem like a movement of the mind . . . it's very close to being an interior monologue, although you come in as an intermediary and shape it." Therefore, Burgess is opposed to "writing clearly contained, well-thought-out, periodic sentences," since if a writer writes in this manner—in declarative, strictly descriptive sentences—"You're not being true to the flow . . . In fiction there should be an element of doubt in the sentence. It shouldn't be sure of itself." For Burgess language creates a state of mind, the state of mind of the characters in his fiction. They are as they speak.

Burgess's sense of language is almost "more rhythmic than verbal . . . The rhythm determines the choice of words . . . It's like writing a new tune." Consequently he admired the style, not only of Joyce and Hopkins and Ezra Pound, but also of D. H. Lawrence: "You can feel the thing being made. He repeats himself; he repeats himself again, he's got to get the thing right; you're in the process of watching it happen." This sense of the continuing process of language being made—reshaped, repeated, stretched—we have already observed in such novels as *Napoleon Symphony, A Clockwork Orange,* and in sections of *The Right to an Answer* and *Tremor of Intent.* Burgess created new words, distorted his syntax, and in many cases reverted to poetic devices to convey his Manichean vision. In such novels as *A Clockwork Orange* and *Napoleon Symphony* language itself almost becomes the true subject of the story. The use of Nadsat in the former reveals exactly the state of society; the use of all kinds of rhythmic and musical devices in the latter reveals the rise and fall of Napoleon, as well as the changing shape of style and outlook in Napoleonic Europe.

Burgess finally looked upon his use of language in much the same way as he regarded his own use of myth. Both shape experience. Both give form to experience. In the final analysis, both create some sense of meaning and coherence out of the meaninglessness and chaos of life itself:

Language bears no relation to ultimate reality. It's a ritual-making device. It's a ritual-making process. You can make rituals out of language. And it is in the ritual that opposites are reconciled.

Language, therefore, can be used "to find the means of stilling the conflict" between Manichean opposites "through ritual forms." In his use of language Burgess tried to present both sides of his Manichean coin, at the same time recognizing that the coin is always a single object. That single object is the soul of one fictional character's particular perspective or consciousness. And that single consciousness is both revealed and created by the language Burgess used to tell that character's story.

Burgess believed, too, that in England language has always been associated with divisions between social classes. The upper classes have always spoken in the kind of clear, declarative, periodic sentences, which Burgess despised. British critics have always chided Burgess for writing English clumsily. He maintained that writers such as C. P. Snow and

Anthony Powell wrote with "an acceptable accent, whereas when I write, they're not quite sure where the hell they are." Consequently he praised such experimentalists in language as Whitman, Pound, Joyce, and Lawrence, all of whom, incidently, hailed from more or less lowly social backgrounds. And he regarded the social significance of the language in Shaw's "Pygmalion" as far-reaching and "incredible." When Burgess wrote of Nabokov that "lacking a country, he clings to a language,"[9] he may have been speaking in many ways about himself. The lanugage he created may be consciously wrought to break through the social illusions and verbal clichés of the English class system, which even when he lived in England, made him conscious only of his sense of exile.

It's not surprising that many of Burgess's main characters either are, or in many ways appear to be, artists themselves. Richard Ennis in *A Vision of Battlements*, Alex DeLago in *A Clockwork Orange*, Denis Hillier in *Tremor of Intent*, Miles Faber in *MF*, Ronald Beard in *Beard's Roman Women*, even the mighty Napoleon in *Napoleon Symphony*: all these characters pride themselves on their artistic achievements or outlook. And Victor Crabbe in *The Long Day Wanes*, Tristram Foxe in *The Wanting Seed*, Bev Jones in *1985*, and Edwin Spindrift in *The Doctor Is Sick* are all teachers, interested in either history or linguistics, both artistic fictions in their own ways. In this final group of works, the main characters are either poets in their own fashion, like Shakespeare, Keats, and Enderby, or they are shaped by the language they use so that they cannot see any further, as though they were antipoets. This is particularly true of Janet Shirley in *One Hand Clapping*. In *The Eve of St. Venus* Burgess is spoofing a kind of artificial or inflated poetic style he could only make fun of in a kind of fairy tale for adults. In each case, language itself becomes the major focus of these novels, two of which— *Nothing Like the Sun*, and in particular the two novels that make up *Enderby* (*Inside Mr. Enderby* and *Enderby Outside*)— are clearly Burgess's masterpieces.

One Hand Clapping (1961): "A nice decent life."

In Bradcaster, a large provincial industrial city in the
Midlands, Janet Barnes marries Howard Shirley. They appear
to be an ordinary, colorless couple. He sells cars at the Oak
Crescent Used Car Mart, she fills shelves at the Hastings
Road Supermarket, and they live in a modest council house,
eat ordinary food, like to dance occasionally, and watch
television. One of Janet's favorite television shows is "Over
and Over," a quiz program, where contestants each week try
to survive the competition and make it to the thousand-pound
question. The show comes complete with audience partici-
pation, a fawning M.C. named Laddie O'Neill, and an
isolation booth, in which the contestant must answer the
questions put to him. Janet knows that Howard has a
photographic brain and thinks that he'd make a superb
contestant on the show.

   Something, however, is wrong with Howard. He sleep-
walks and cries in his sleep. He sees modern existence as
a cheat and rages at the local newspaper. He announces that
he'd "like to live like a millionaire for, say, one month
. . . Then to snuff it . . . Because, when all's said and done,
there's not all that much to live for, is there?" Apparently
not, since his employer continually cheats his customers,
and Janet's sister, Myrtle, the lazy one with the sherry-
colored hair and Golden Frost lipstick, leaves her husband
and attempts suicide in the Shirleys' spare room one night.
Howard thinks Myrtle looks nice and peaceful and refuses
to disturb her. It's Janet who goes to call the police and,
thus, saves her sister's life.

   Howard writes to the quiz show and is accepted as a
contestant. His category is books, and he begins to memorize
every title and author in the local library. On television he
knows all the answers, wins one thousand pounds, goes on
to win eighty thousand pounds on the horses, and decides
to take Janet on a big holiday. On the eve of their journey,
an unkempt poet, Redvers Glass, arrives at their rented

house in Bradcaster. He's come to thank Howard for his largesse. Howard has donated one thousand pounds to a local newspaper to give to some deserving writer: "It's sort of a way of paying back all those dead old poets and writers and such like, that neither of us have even read. It's the least I can do."

Glass spends the night drunk at the Shirleys' house, and in the morning, pulls Janet into bed with him. She slips away but, aroused, meets him later at a local hotel. Howard decides that Glass can live in their house, while they're away on holiday. Throughout the endless trip with Howard to New York, Chicago, Miami, the Bahamas, Janet thinks often of Glass, gets sick on rich food, and feels very much uprooted and at loose ends. Howard spends his money lavishly, if only to prove in the long run "that there wasn't all that much you could to with money and that business about living pleasant was really a load of nonsense. Because the world's a terrible place . . ."

When they return to Bradcaster, the Shirleys find that Glass has allowed several of his friends to move in with him. Howard kicks them out, and Glass cautions Janet not to trust him. The next day is Janet's twenty-fourth birthday, and Howard insists he's planned something special. First of all he decided to send the remaining fifty-five thousand pounds to the local paper to distribute among various charities. Then he reads the poem he had commissioned Glass to write:

> We've all betrayed our past, we've killed the
> 		dream
> Our fathers held . . . clicking our off-beat
> 		fingers
> To juke-box clichés, waiting
> For death to overtake us . . .

In Howard's plan, death is not far off. He insists that he and Janet go to visit her parents and then Myrtle. When they return, Howard unveils his surprise: a murder-suicide pact for the two of them:

. . . we're getting out of the world as a sort of protest. Our deaths will sort of show how two decent ordinary people who'd been given every chance that money can give but no other chance, no other chance at all, how two such people felt about the horrible stinking world . . . We've got to be sort of witnesses, sort of martyrs.

Janet's response to Howard's madness is to brain him in the kitchen with a coal hammer. She goes to get Glass, whom she involves in the murder by allowing him to get his fingerprints all over the hammer. She's wiped her prints entirely off of it. Fearing what might happen if his fingerprints are discovered by the police, Glass decides to help Janet stuff Howard's body in a trunk. Janet retrieves the money, before the newspaper receives it, and she and Glass flee to Paris with the trunk. Glass buys a large Chinese camphor wood chest, and they put Howard into it. They then move to a bungalow in the French countryside. At the end of the novel, Glass may or may not be taking up with a neighbor, Madame Crebillon. In any case, if he starts complaining about the modern world as Howard did, Janet still has her hammer. They settle down to a decent, quiet, country life.

The world the Shirleys inhabit fits Howard's description of it. It is a dull, mechanical place, filled with the full routines of shopping, making money, and watching television. The name of the quiz program, "Over and Over," epitomizes the repetitive nature of the Bradcaster experience. The *Daily Window* looks out on nothing but dull celebrities and daily disasters. A play the Shirleys see in London, called "One Hand Clapping," is only a reproduction of this mindless existence. And even though "imagining the sound of one hand clapping for Zen Buddhists may may be . . . a way of getting in touch with Reality . . . proceeding by way of the absurd . . . supposed to be a way of getting to God," since no one can imagine it, it becomes as much an image of mechanical meaninglessness as the other habits in the Shirleys' existence.

Even Howard's photographic brain is "a sort of mockery, like having a machine fixed inside your skull." He has no

real interests in anything; he merely records the facts around
him. The reporter calls it "a sort of trick, a kind of deformity,"
since Howard has no real interest in or understanding of
books at all. It's Janet who dimly recognizes the truth: "His
photographic brain knew all about how many storeys there
were in these buildings, but he'd never actually seen them
before, and there's all the difference in the world between
knowing and seeing."

Television informs, or rather deforms, the Shirleys'
world. Janet and Howard know nothing. In school the courses
that counted included Make-Up, Deportment, Dress Sense,
Ballroom Dancing, and Homecraft. Mr. Thornton, the history
teacher, strummed his guitar. Mr. Slessor, the English
teacher, "said like he didn't dig the King's jive. Crazy, man,
real cool." Consequently "we'd not done any Shakespeare
. . . because the teachers said we wouldn't like it and we'd
get bored."

Television triumphs. To Janet when the set comes on,
it's "like a miracle." She stays home to watch Howard on the
quiz show, because "it would make it seem somehow more
real that way." When she dashes out to call the police
because of Myrtle's attempted suicide, everyone remains
glued to his own television: "Emergency Ward Ten would be
far more real to them than any real emergency like this one."
In fact, in various conversations and situations, Janet thinks
of herself as being part of a television show, part of a
courtroom scene, a medical melodrama, a crime adventure,
or even a murder mystery.

Janet is herself a walking cliché of the typical suburban
housewife. She cooks, she watches television, she fills the
shelves at the market. When Howard announces that he's
won about eighty thousand pounds, she can think of nothing
to say, except, "Come and get your tea." Her dreams emerge
as sentimental clichés, products of television commercials.
She thinks of motherhood "especially during the commercials,
showing mother and daughter both protected by the same
soap." When she spots herself in a shop window during her

vacation in the Bahamas, the "glamorous sunburnt blonde in white linen with dark glasses on" must be "like somebody out of a film." Happiness is "back in our little house in Bradcaster, sitting by the fire watching the T.V." And supreme happiness is doing the same thing on a winter afternoon,

dreaming a bit, romancing about who you might have married instead of the one you did. Seeing yourself in dark glasses and a playsuit in Bermuda or somewhere and a handsome rogue with white teeth and a bronzed Tarzan torso leaning over you with a cigarette-lighter . . .

True ecstasy: the sumptuous languor of a cigarette commercial on television!

When Redvers Glass appears on the scene, however, Janet seems to change. She giggles in his presence. She regards him as a bit of excitement, as something new. She views Howard as stern and gentle, and her "Red" as humorous and not gentle. She begins to think that "there's little enough in this life, really, and you only find it worth living for the odd moments," in this case, those few moments of sexual passion with Glass. He is so unlike Howard. Even his name, Redvers or Revers'd Glass, suggests this. Yet Janet quashes these new feelings. Security with Howard is much safer.

Even so, her vision of the world around her at first seems to expand. In America she notices how unlike the films of America the real America is: "The real thing had its own smell . . . less of a smell of people being dead . . . In any English town you can't help feeling that millions of people are dead and gone there, all through the ages, and their sort of ghosts are floating about . . ." Back home she complains to Howard: "You don't treat me like a wife . . . You just keep things to yourself all the time." And after she murders Howard, the manner in which she takes command of the situation surprises her: "Red was all right in bed, and that was about all . . . I'd really taken over now. I was really in charge and I was quite enjoying it."

Janet's vision, however, hasn't really changed at all,

and this is apparent in her language. Burgess, who has referred to the novel slyly as "a very British novel," wrote *One Hand Clapping* as a first-person narrative; Janet narrates her own story. From the very beginning the language reveals what kind of a character Janet really is. Here is the opening sentence: "I was Janet Shirley, *nee* Barnes, and my husband was Howard Shirley, and in this story he was nearly twenty-seven and I was just gone twenty-three." The persistent repetition of "and" flattens Janet's style of narration immediately. Everything comes out the same and is given equal weight. The language is as flat, as vacuous and as visionless as her own Bradcaster existence. When she questions the nature of her attraction to Redvers Glass, she writes, "It was an obsession, that was what it was, an obsession, and when I'd remembered that word I felt a lot better." She uses the word, "obsession," to pigeonhole and, therefore, kill the complexity of feelings surging within her. She stamps the word "obsession" on her desires to separate herself from them, to withdraw from them, thus using language to quash all experiences which might intrude on her colorless, habitual routines.

At the beginning of the novel Janet accepts the idea that "they always say that if you're a girl, and pretty like I was, you didn't need to know all that much. I could look smashing." After the long holiday with Howard, she realizes, "I was very ignorant, but because I was attractive that had never seemed to matter." Yet at the end of the novel, she is still encased in her flat, suburban language; there has been no real growth of vision or perspective. She has merely taken control of her life, instead of leaving it up to Howard. The language reveals that exactly the same life is being led. She relies on an old cliché: "What does it matter how long it lasts so long as there's still plenty of beer and fags?" "All I want is to live a nice decent life, getting as much pleasure out of it as I can. That's what we're here for, when all's said and done."

Decency is Janet's banner. It denies all else. It relies upon bourgeois habits and routines that should not be broken. At times Burgess manages to convey to the reader the incongruity between Janet's sense of decency and order and the strange events that have occurred around her. Nowhere is this more comic than in her response to having just killed her husband: "The best first thing to do, when you've got a dead body and it's your husband's on the kitchen floor and you don't know what to do about it, is to make yourself a good strong cup of tea."

Janet remains imprisoned in her shrunken state of suburban decency and the language which both supports and creates that state. In her travels the ultimate perception of things she manages to discover is "that wherever you went . . . people . . . seem to be pretty much the same . . . there's no place that's foreign any more. Mars is foreign, and Saturn . . . but no place on earth is really foreign . . . all people are the same. I tell you that now, so you've no need to waste your money on travelling." Janet's flat vision of the world, as Burgess makes clear in her language, is very much a product of her television-dulled, conventional lack of imagination.

Janet's story remains extremely unconventional and bizarre, yet her way of telling it is conventional and dispassionate. The comedy results because of the discrepancy between her style and the events that surround and include her. Such comedy makes for a lively spoof of conventional decency. She, however, murders with impunity and feels no sorrow for poor silly Howard, who in her mind "was just a handsome machine wanting to die." With no imagination whatsoever, she can understand only a shift in power, a change of control. She can comprehend neither compassion nor love. Such is the real price, Burgess suggests, of so mechanical and heartless a vision of the world and the language that embodies it.

The Eve of St. Venus (1964): "Your bride is a pagan goddess."

This slender, witty spoof of English country gentlemen and

their arch drawingroom speechifying was first written as an
opera in 1950. Burgess has always disliked the pretentious
poetic language of plays such as Christopher Fry's "The
Lady's Not For Burning"—"I always thought it was cheap
stuff"—and decided to write a parody of it. The novel is built
upon long, dramatic soliloquies and speeches in the arch
tradition of Noel Coward wit and country-gentlemen pom-
posities.

The plot transpires on the eve of Diana Drayton's
wedding to Ambrose Rutterkin, a decent if somewhat dull
structural engineer and rational fellow, at the Drayton's huge
country home. Sir Benjamin Drayton, fond of his food and
drink, preaches eloquently about the past, established order,
and genteel discretion in all things. He blusters about and
tyrannizes Spatchcock, the sharpeyed maid. Lady Winifred
Drayton remains sensible with a touch of irony throughout.
Julia Webb, a cynical, bitchy lesbian photographer and
bridesmaid, arrives to convince Diana not to marry Ambrose
and slip into a deadly suburban existence. Diana should
resist such conventional behavior and come away to see the
world with her. Jack Crowther-Mason, a politician and
Ambrose's best man, comes to keep his friend company on
the eve of the nuptial celebration. Benjamin's twin brother,
the alcoholic Bernard, arrives but retreats to his room to
drink alone and never appears. Throughout all this, Diana's
old nanny, five times wed, scurries about full of cynical and
sardonic comments. The standard crew of an English farce
in a countryhouse are here gathered at the Draytons.'

Outside in the garden stand statues of mythic gods,
given to Benjamin by the alcoholic Bernard. In a spirit of
jest, Crowther-Mason and Ambrose slip Diana's wedding ring
on the finger of Venus. The finger surprisingly curves back,
and they cannot get the ring off. Such is the beginning of the
revenge the old mythic gods—in this case, the goddess of
love—seem to have planned for these modern Christian
celebrants.

Ambrose goes to sleep in his room at a local pub. He

is awakened in the middle of the night by the smell of the sea and by the presence of a woman in his room, intoning quietly and mysteriously, "You're married to me." She disappears. He leaps out of bed and rushes back to the Draytons' house. There the sea smell is very strong. The vicar, the sensibly pleasant Reverend Chauncell, is called to rid poor Ambrose of his demonic possession. Venus has obviously possessed his soul. "The devil undoubtedly exists," Chauncell declares. "He normally shows himself as a sort of quick-change artist . . . or else something damnably desirable."

Chauncell decides to conduct an exorcism to drive out the devil. He leaves all the lights in the house on to keep the evil spirits away. While he goes to get the necessary equipment for the ceremony, Ambrose and Diana quarrel over Julia, Diana insists that marriage should not deprive her of a career, and Ambrose calls her "an undressed salad." Meanwhile, birds attack the car that the vicar and Crowther-Mason are riding in. They drive into a ditch and upon walking to the house find the place in darkness. Ambrose, meanwhile, has fallen asleep and dreams of chasing nymphs and tootling flutes. The vicar, armed with sprigs of garlic, a palm crucifix, a bottle of Jordan Water, and a black book, recites the words of the exorcism, but the Latin prayer he reads to attack Venus mysteriously comes out in praise of her. Clearly everyone is bewitched.

In frustration the vicar rips off his clerical collar after Crowther-Mason has concluded that there is nothing demonic about Venus's visit. Suddenly lightning strikes the statues. Venus is shattered. The sea smell vanishes. The vicar puts his collar back on but is still shaken by his own doubts and by the experience. The Christian exorcism has obviously worked but just barely. The ring cannot be found amid the rubble of strewn stone limbs, but Ambrose is free.

Diana, after a talk with her mother and caught in Julia's web of promises and enticements, decides to leave the house with Julia. On the road, however, an arrow mysteriously lodges in one of Julia's tires—Cupid's?—she cannot fix it,

and becomes the epitome of helplessness. Diana, missing
Ambrose's masculine strength, hurries back to his side.
Ambrose welcomes her, Crowther-Mason feels "a strange
desire for luxurious abandon," and everyone, discoursing on
the power of love, joins in singing a song about marriage:
"Tomorrow will be love for the loveless, and for the lover
love."

The bewitching eve draws to a close. Julia returns,
woeful and repentant, and still wants to be the head
bridesmaid, although she realizes, as in all good fairy tales,
"I'll always be there, like the irritant in the oyster, like a
witch at a christening." Spatchcock discovers a pigeon at her
window with the wedding ring tied round its neck, looped
through a handful of golden hair. She returns it to Ambrose.
At the conclusion of the novel old Sir Benjamin examines
"the mess of gods in the garden" at dawn, curses the loss of
the past and its gods, belabors the dreary mass entertainment
of contemporary society—"The gods in the garden, for all
the night's miraculous epiphany, were dead"—and prepares
for the wedding.

The old gods of myth have their momentary sport with
the "civilized" creatures of the English countryside. Crowther-
Mason, the slick but sympathetic politician, comes to realize
that "The past . . . is never discarded. The past is made
richer by the unfolding present. The gods are still alive,
aspects of the breathtaking, growing, moving, widening
unifying pattern." He also upbraids the fearful vicar: "We're
told to accept Vergil as an honorary Christian . . . myths are
not fairy stories. Our smug little hymns are too ready to suffer
a key-change." The vicar comes to realize the mythic power
of love, no matter its source, and even the decently dull
Ambrose comes to realize the sovereignty of Venus:

It's as though, while savouring the exhilarating three-dimensional
world, one were suddenly enchanted into a film. Now I'm just a
canvas. Or cardboard. Flat, monochrome. I was lifted above the
mechanical roundabout of time . . . sucked out of the steam of
history, raised by her to the timeless level of a myth.

Burgess's own modernist love for myth is here once again expressed.

The Eve of St. Venus is built upon a series of dialogues, interviews, and soliloquies, the "stuff" of drawing-room farce and manorhouse mannerisms. It reads more like a play than a novel, an obvious reflection of its being first the libretto of an opera. The fairy-tale quality of the story is further highlighted by Edward Pagram's pen-and-ink, Dickensian illustrations, exaggerating the characters' already exaggerated features.

As Burgess wrote in his foreword to the American edition, he wanted his characters "to speak a somewhat artificial 'literary' prose"[10] to mock the poetic dramas of Fry. This prose would be suitable for the kind of farcical comedy he was after, "manifested in a silly, ingrown, mainly non-existent rural aristocracy."[11] He romps through his language, drawing up long, poetic lists, delighting in Sir Benjamin's epithets—"Decerebrated clodpoles . . . you garboil, you ugly lusk"—relishing his descriptions of Venus and her mythic attributes:

Your bride is a pagan goddess. In the little bedroom over the public bar, over the darts and dominoes and detergent, over the luke-warm bitter and the packet of crisps, Venus was waiting for the dark. Foam-born Aphrodite . . . the laughing-eyed, delight of gods and men, waiting for Ambrose . . .

The midsummer night's enchantment is fully realized in Burgess's language and celebrates once again the power and delight of his wit and verbal exuberance.

Abba Abba (1977): "Dum pendebat filius."

In this minor but evocative short novel, which is really an imaginative introduction to the seventy-one sonnets by Giuseppe Belli (which Burgess has translated from Italian into English), John Keats, the English Romantic poet, meets Belli in Rome in 1820. Keats suffers from consumption and has come to Rome to avoid the harsh English climate. One evening Giovanni Gulielmi, a Roman man of letters, comes to Keats's apartment near the Spanish steps and tells him of a sonnet he's read that is written in the Roman dialect and that is in effect a catalogue of names for the male sexual organ. Keats becomes intrigued by the language of the piece, Gulielmi brings him a copy of the sonnet, and Keats translates it into English.

Keats knows that he is dying. The blasphemous sonnet is his way of passing the time. He is also intrigued by the Italian language. Gulielmi arranges for Keats to meet Belli in the Sistine Chapel beneath Michelangelo's ceiling. The meeting is pleasant but uneventful, though Belli is shocked when Keats, just out of curiosity, quotes from the blasphemous sonnet. Keats returns to his apartment, where he's waited on by his good friend, the pious Christian, Joseph Severn. He coughs up much blood and begs for laudanum to end his miserable life, but Severn out of Christian principles refuses.

Meanwhile Belli has been offered the position of head of the central bureau of censorship in Rome by Cardinal Fabiani. He's not exactly certain what he should do but thinks that perhaps if he accepts the office, he might be better able to write his own poetry.

Raving, Keats dies at last. All the furniture in his apartment must be burned, and the landlady must be repaid. The body is moved out at night, since Keats is not a Catholic and will be buried in the Protestant Cemetery. Burgess's own historical epilogue completes the lives of the other characters and traces the family tree of Giovanni Gulielmi to the present Joseph John Wilson, the fictitious translator of Belli's sonnets, who bears a remarkable resemblance to John Anthony Burgess Wilson.

We are told that Belli wrote 2,279 sonnets, and that in his attempt to present "realistically the demotic life of a great capital city," his work "may be regarded as kind of proto-Ulysses." Burgess's own translations of seventy-one of the

Biblical sonnets are blasphemous, ribald, and often extremely
funny.

The Manichean vision of life and art permeates *Abba
Abba* and accounts for its true nature. First among these
oppositions are Keats and Belli, the former "a poet of nature,
romance, fairyland, heartache, the classical world as seen
in a rainy English garden," the latter, a poet of "dirty cynical
suffering rejoicing Rome." Keats appears drawn to the music
of the Roman dialect—at one point he envisions writing a
poem about the changeless, eternal city—if only because he
admires the things that language can be made to do. Keats
is sent John Florio's *Queen Anna's New World of Words*, a
dictionary and pronunciation guide from Shakespeare's time
written by an Italian, which reveals that Shakespeare's
pronunciation of certain words was remarkably close to
present-day Italian. Belli is drawn to Keats, because he
recognizes that poet's interest in the sonnet form, having read
a minor Keatsian sonnet on a cat.

Manichean dualisms persist. "Hell is a city much like
Rome," and yet it is the seat of the church. Severn insists
to Keats that suicide is a sin, although Keats snaps back,
"Your damnable Lord did it. He knew he was to die and he
did not avoid it . . . He let himself be crucified, I call that
self-slaughter." Keats upholds the romantic faith that "the
earth and the heart and the imagination are all," that artists
"make truth, they *make* beauty . . . and in creating create
also themselves," while the Christian Severn responds: "You
have substituted something called Nature for God, and with
Nature there is nothing but Truth and Beauty and Goodness
till you fall sick, and then Nature becomes lying and ugly
and malevolent. You make Nature both God and devil . . .
according to your moods." Keats views Michelangelo's paintings as "all horror, all hell," a Christ more Promethean than
Christian. He thinks that "the painter has filled it with his
own guilt . . . He was too fond of broad shouldered boys."
And yet he rails against Severn's "bloodless Jesus" who lacks
"the Michelangelo muscles" to fight the devil.

Decay and impending death underlie Keats's final days. He believes fully in the sensuous realities of life, thinking of himself in terms of the "singing clarity" and joyfulness of the water in the fountain below his window, and yet within those sensuous realities lie the seeds of ever-present decay. He would uphold his delight in "the red din of an aching tooth as it engageth good hot meat [or] the dove-soft touch of a young lover's ripening breast," but beyond that he sees only nothingness and emptiness. Even the age has soured, the romanticism of revolution souring into an era of expanding nationalism and repression in the wake of Napoleon's defeat. Decay and disease permeate all things. Art, love, and religion seem to be perpetually at war with one another.

Belli himself embodies the dilemma as surely as Keats's faith in nature and horror of death do. Gulielmi describes Belli as torn between a love of Roman lowlife, of its life-celebrating obscenities, and a respect for the Roman papal rule and religion: "He is like two men always fighting each other . . . torn between his soul and his lower instincts . . . between the language of Petrarch or Dante and the rough speech he hears all about him in Rome." In the sonnet Gulielmi gave to Keats, Belli has used the word, "dumpen-nente," to describe the male sexual organ. The origin is from the Latin, "Dum pendebat filius," which describes Christ's hanging on the cross in a Latin poem. The "while he hangs" has become the one word for penis. The spiritual and the secular have met and transformed one another, yet still they remain essentially opposed.

Burgess insisted that art, myth, and language should reconcile these Manichean oppositions. As Belli insists, "A balance should be possible. Between the claims of the physically transient and the spiritually permanent. But finally it is the spirit that counts." First of all one must accept the dual nature of the self and of all things. Love is both "bestial" and "ecstatic." Subversion can become "the prop of social order." Belli must recognize and acknowledge that he is "a split man." And Keats rises to the occasion of this important revelation:

The way out is the way out of the conception of ourselves as unified beings. We are, in fact, unities in name and appearance and voice and a set of habits only . . . The dumpendebat self of our friend and the stabat mater self are but two among the many selves available.

True fusion occurs in art. Both Belli and Keats, however different as poets, admire and use the sonnet form in their work: "It seemed that two men, of language mutually unintelligible, might in a sense achieve communication through recognition of what a sonnet was." Belli believes in that "one ultimate perfect sonnet," the Petrarchan sonnet, from which the title of the book comes, with its ABBA ABBA rhyme scheme in the octet and its CDC DCD in the sestet. This form resembles for him "the terrible purity of God," since "in the recognition of the common form" of the Petrarchan sonnet both poets meet. In the Bible, the term "Abba Abba" is also Christ's name for his heavenly father. Each poet can write about whatever he wishes—fairylands or sultry, corrupt Rome—but they share the same form and, consequently, the same ceremonial aspects of writing poetry. The sonnet form has reconciled both Belli and Keats to each other's art and vision, even though their languages keep them apart.

Abba Abba is a kind of summation of Burgess's artistic beliefs. It is too much a series of conversations and dialogues to be much of a novel. But its explicit Manichean vision helps illuminate the murkier plots and themes of other Burgess novels, and it can serve as a distilled introduction to the best of these. The real appeal of the book is the Belli sonnets in translation. These surpass mere talk of art and language and achieve an artful ribaldry all their own.

Nothing Like the Sun (1964): "A potency of sharp knives and brutal hammers."

The subtitle of this fictional recreation of the life of William Shakespeare, "A Story of Shakespeare's Love-life," describes

both the emphasis and the scope of one of Burgess's best
novels. He has traced Shakespeare's growth from the son of
a glovemaker in Stratford to a heterosexual and homosexual
lover and a great poet of the stage. The novel ends in 1599,
at which point Shakespeare is on the verge of writing his
greatest tragedies, having come to his unique vision of the
world. The novel traces his development through the several
permutations of love to his fuller understanding of the human
condition.

At the beginning of the novel, Shakespeare ponders his
family's fortune. His mother, an Arden, always bemoans the
fact that she has married beneath her; she is acutely aware
that her family are of the gentry class. John Shakespeare,
Will's father, had once been Bailiff of Stratford, but now as
a poor glover is no more than a lowly alderman. Most of his
mother's property has been sold. Aware of his family's meager
condition, young Will feels that it is his duty to restore the
family name by achieving both wealth and respectability.

Will goes to see Old Madge Bowyer, a fortune-teller
who prophesies: "Catch as catch can/A black woman or a
golden man." This prophecy the novel bears out, when Will
becomes involved with Fatimah, a black prostitute, and
Henry Wriothesly, the beautiful, golden-bearded Earl of
Southampton. Will's later relationship with Fatimah adds to
his experience of lust and sensuality, while Southampton
comes to represent that image of wealth, position, and power
that the middle-class Shakespeare covets.

Before its fulfillment, however, a night of sexual revel
during a local Maypole festival forces Will to marry a red-
haired woman who is pregnant by him. The woman turns out
to be Anne Hathaway. In May, 1583, their first daughter,
Susanna, is born. Anne emerges as a lustful wench who will
not let Will alone. Will hopes to get away from home and
Anne to earn some money, but cannot think of what to do.

Eventually, after tutoring the five sons of a local Justice
of the Peace and being dismissed for sleeping with one of
them, Will witnesses a performance by the traveling troupe

of actors, the Queen's Men. He is drawn to the excitement of the stage. Shortly after Anne gives birth to twins, Hamnet and Judith, Will flees to London.

In London Will becomes an actor with the Queen's Men. On June 11, 1592 a riot in Southwark occurs. The Knight Marshal's Men have arrested a feltmaker's servant for making faces at them. An angry mob storms the jail, the Lord Mayor's Men arrive on the scene on horseback, and as a result of all the turmoil, the playhouses are legally closed. The plague is also growing in London, threatening the playhouses.

At the same time the reigning playwrights, Robert Greene and Christopher Marlowe, are in trouble. Greene dies of drunkenness and disease; Marlowe is subsequently stabbed to death under mysterious circumstances. Greene has left a posthumous pamphlet with references to Shakespeare in it, thereby indicating that Will is becoming noticed as both actor and writer in this London scene. Greene refers to him as an "upstart crow" with a "tiger's heart wrapped in a player's hide . . . he is as well able to bombast out a blank verse as the best of you . . . in his own conceit the only Shake-scene in a country." Shakespeare has arrived.

At a performance of his own "Harry the Sixth," Shakespeare is summoned to meet someone in the Lord's Box at the Theatre. Robert Devereux, the Earl of Essex, comments favorably on the ghoulish production of "Titus Andronicus" and introduces Will to the eighteen-year-old Henry Wriothesly, Earl of Southampton. Shakespeare is much taken by the sly, handsome young man and asks to dedicate a poem to him. Wriothesly accepts. Shakespeare goes off to write "Venus and Adonis" and has it printed by the enterprising young printer, Richard Field, of Stratford. Since the playhouses are again closed because of the plague, Shakespeare moves in with Southampton and writes his famous sonnets. Burgess suggests that they become lovers, although the exact beginning of this new relationship is only hinted at in the novel.

Southampton also takes Shakespeare to Tyburn one day

to see the hanging and quartering of the "evil" Dr. Roderigo
Lopez and two of his friends. In a bizarre and trumped-up
conspiracy, Lopez, Queen Elizabeth's physician and a Por-
tuguese Jew, is supposedly a spy for Spain, although this
may have been a plot hatched against him by Essex. Essex,
a soldier-statesman, increasingly threatens Elizabeth's reign
and seems to be on the verge of a revolt. In any case,
Shakespeare is appalled by the hanging, the drawing, and
quartering of the bodies, and the crowd's eager and blood-
thirsty enjoyment. A new group of players is established, the
Lord Chamberlain's Men, and while Southampton is increasingly drawn into Essex's plots and intrigues at court, Shakespeare decides to leave Southampton and takes a small house
in Bishopsgate in London.

Shakespeare discovers Mistress Lucy, a mysterious
black woman, who lives in his neighborhood. Southampton
gives him a thousand pounds to buy into a new theatre; he
writes "A Midsummer Night's Dream" and is working on
"Richard II," but all the while he dreams of Lucy. At last,
he courageously invites her to an opening of one of his
plays, and there seizes and seduces her. Sex reigns supreme
in all its various forms. While they are cavorting in Shakespeare's bed chamber, Southampton arrives. Lucy, whose
real name, she says, is Fatimah, is stunned by this splendid
nobleman. Southampton, bored with his pederastic intrigues
at court, takes to her immediately, summons her to several
of his parties, and makes her his mistress.

Meanwhile Hamnet dies back in Stratford. He is only
eleven. Shakespeare is stunned and returns for the funeral.
On a second return to Stratford he comes upon his brother,
Richard, in bed with his wife, Anne. This incestuous adultery
confirms in his own mind the sullied and vagrant patterns of
the flesh, and he returns to London, saddened but wiser.

In London Southampton wants him to write a play in
support of Essex's rebellion. Shakespeare refuses, and Southampton joins Essex in his schemes. Essex is later beheaded
and Southampton sent to the tower. Shakespeare and his

cronies dismantle the old theatre and cart the lumber to the south side of the Thames to erect the Globe.

Lucy returns and restores his sexual needs, even though he remains both cynical and weary. She's had a son, who might be either Shakespeare's or Southampton's, but keeps him away from both men, and later sends him back to her own land in the East. After one glorious sexual revel, Will discovers a red spot on his body. He suddenly realizes he's caught syphilis from Lucy, and she admits she probably caught it from Southampton: "We might all then, the three of us, be drawn into the one corruption." Shakespeare's vision of complete corruption and disease is intimately mixed with his sexual enjoyment and his belief in the order and beauty of art. At the close of the novel, the great poet dies with this vision explored and mastered in his great tragedies.

Burgess's sources for his novel include Stephan Dedalus's ideas about Shakespeare expressed in Joyce's *Ulysses*—that Shakespeare was cuckolded by his wife and his brother, Richard, and that the man can be know through the plays and the sonnets—and English folklore. In Oxfordshire Burgess "heard about this story, this popular story that Anne had been unfaithful with Will's brother":

In England history is very slow. Time stands still in England. 1660 is not so long ago . . . There's a lot of curious rhymes and stories that go around about Shakespeare, which I listen to with great attention, because they're in the folk; they must have been handed down.

Burgess's own additions to the story include his making the Dark Lady of the sonnets a non-Caucasian and Shakespeare a victim of syphilis.

Burgess also believed that "you can't be a genius and sexually impotent."[12] Since he also felt that "art is sublimated libido,"[13] it is only natural that sex plays such an extraordinary role in Shakespeare's growth as a poet. The very name, Shakespeare, suggested to Burgess the "image of some remote war-like progenitor, one full of both aggression and libido."[14]

The bisexual entanglements of Burgess's Shakespeare lead
him to his vision of the complex interpenetration of lust,
disease, mortality, and death. As one critic suggested, "the
crime of love is a necessary prelude to vision,"[15] and as
another adds, "sexual heat becomes the muse, the inspiration
to create."[16] Shakespeare's sexual awakening and talents
certainly indicate the depth and breadth of his own character
and his own propensity for artistic creation. For Burgess, sex
and art seemed flipsides of the same coin, as do disease and
talent.

Shakespeare's vision of the world in *Nothing Like the
Sun* parallels, once again, Burgess's Manichean vision. In
fact Shakespeare regards himself in the novel as two distinct
personalities, "sober WS aghast at drunken Will . . . Had
he not himself watched WS and WS watched Will? Where
was truth, where did a man's true nature lie?" WS seems to
represent Shakespeare's thoughtful, spiritual self, while Will
represents a deeper, more emotional essence. He feels
himself caught between flesh and spirit, between heterosexual
and homosexual love, and yet realizes he must pursue both
at once: "Our sin and our sickness is not to choose one and
turn our backs on the other but to hanker after both."

The Manichean vision haunts Shakespeare, just as it
did Belli, Hillier, and Burgess's other memorable characters.
Out of lust springs a new soul realizes Will, the father, "a
sleeping being called out of the darkness to suffer, perhaps
be damned, because of a shaft of enacted lust." He stands
in awe at the mystery of fatherhood: "A thrust of opal drops
in animal ecstasy unleashed a universe—stars, sun, gods,
hell and all. It was unjust." The horrible, stomach-turning
execution at Tyburn in front of the jeering throng can also be
viewed as an art, "far more exact than WS's own: the hangman
approached with his knife, fire in the sunlight, before the
neck could crack, ripped downwards from heart to groin in
one slash." The greatest riddle of all is love, "the beast's
heaven which is the angel's hell . . . love is a unity only in
the word . . . for love is both an image of eternal order and

at the same time the rebel and destructive spirochaete." The spark of divinity is often ignited "by a sort of quintessential beastliness." Somewhere, somehow "an infinite well of putridity" lies within man's soul and flesh: "We are, he seemed to say, poisoned at source."

And yet from this poisoned source that is man, springs the creative impulse of all art. There are "images of order and beauty to be coaxed out of wrack, filth, sin, chaos . . . To emboss a stamp of order on time's flux is an impossibility I must try to make possible through my art." The order of art can also help to purge all the contradictions in man's soul. As WS suggests, "There's a devil in all of us . . . We are full of self-contradictions. It is best to purge this devil on the stage." This is the voice of the creator of Hamlet, Macbeth, Othello, and Lear speaking.

Slowly throughout the novel Shakespeare awakens to the realities of language. If Burgess in *One Hand Clapping* reveals how the unimaginative use of language can imprison one's sensibilities and deaden one's perspective, in *The Eve of St. Venus* he makes fun of the overinflated, pseudo-poetry to which language can lend itself. And in *Abba Abba* he tries to suggest that literary forms are themselves eternal and can overcome even the differences between languages. In *Nothing Like the Sun* Burgess celebrates the possibility of language to create a world of complex and infinite mysteries in a manner similar to his celebration of language in *Napoleon Symphony*. He wrote the novel in a lusty Elizabethan style filled with poetic images and delights. Shakespeare's own male lust is described with anatomical vigor: "Out of the fork of this gentleman from a tangled auburn bush, thrust and crowed a most importunate Adam." And Burgess's description of country folk captures all the lusty phrasemaking we associate with the Elizabethans:

Drink, then. Down it among the titbrained molligolliards of country copulatives, of a beastly sort, all, their browned pickers a-clutch of their spilliwilly potkins, filthy from handling of spade and harrow, cheesy from udder new-milked, slash mouths agape at some merry tale from that rogue with rat-skins about his middle, coneyskin cap on's sconce.

Shakespeare, himself, becomes infected with this infectious speech.

Shakespeare begins to realize that words can and do create their own realm. He's entranced by Ovid and pleased with Plautus. He becomes intoxicated with the possibilities of language, of coining new phrases and creating new images. The style of his "Venus and Adonis" suggests "pure candy with honey sauce," just as his "The Rape of Lucrece" "raped the senses of its exquisite readers, overcame them in heady dispensations of rose-leaves and honeysuckle." As his vision of the human condition changes and darkens, so must his language. Sick of sweet rhymes, he describes his love-making with Lucy/Fatimah in sterner, hardier lyrics, speaking of "a burning hell of pleasure," "of pounded red flesh" and digging downward into some fiery center of earth. By the end of the novel his complex vision of disease and beauty, lust and immortality, directs him toward a "new language for its expression—jerking harsh words, a delirium of coinages and grotesque fusions . . ."

For the first time it was made clear to me that language was no vehicle of soothing prettiness to warm cold castles that waited for spring, no ornament for ladies or great lords, chiming, beguiling, but a potency of sharp knives and brutal hammers.

He has found his true language, the fierce images and speeches of *Lear* and *Macbeth*. Man may be "poisoned at source," but from that source springs his creative imagination. From poison comes great art, a Manichean mystery. As Burgess concludes in the novel, "Literature is an epiphenomenon of the action of the flesh."

The language of *Nothing Like the Sun* develops and changes just as Burgess's hero does. Shakespeare conquers and transcends his scalding vision of men's corruption and desires through his use of language, and the book traces that linguistic development from "sugar rhyme" to "brutul hammers."

The development of language in the novel is also supported and deepened by Madge Bowyer's original prophecy: "Catch as catch can / A black woman or a golden man." Images of black and gold permeate the narrative, both opposing and complementing one another. Blackness suggests not only the image of "a Goddess—dark, hidden, deadly, horribly desirable," the very image which begins the novel, but also the mysteries of the flesh, and Shakespeare's own rite of passage from boyhood to manhood, "through a dark tunnel of shame to that dark underworld where snakes coiled, heroes lay, a single goddess presided." Gold suggests Southampton's wealth, which Shakespeare covets, but also his own homosexual desires. The black goddess, at last viewed as a goddess of corruption and diesease as well as one of sensual delight and sexual abandonment, becomes for Shakespeare the muse for his art: "She had opened up these terrible Indies but remained as my navigatrix."

The frame within which the novel is created is a lecture given by Burgess as a farewell to some of his students in the East. As he spins his yarn, he imbibes more and more wine. Occasionally, he breaks into his own narrative to comment on the deliciousness of the wine or to leap hastily from one point in the narrative to another. At the conclusion of the novel he sums up his viewpoint on the dual nature of love and art. He insists that even though the listener, or reader in our case, may want to know "how ventriloquial all this is, . . . this is no impersonation, ladies and gentleman."

Burgess has obviously created a Shakespeare in his own image using what biographical facts exist—or don't—to fashion his own creation. The real Shakespeare was, in fact, however great a poet, nothing like the sun, but he was a great creater in his own right, in the language of his craft. Burgess's real last name is Wilson, which suggests that he may, as a writer himself, view himself playfully as Will's son in this honored craft.

At one point in the narrative Shakespeare thinks, "There was a reality somewhere to be encompassed and, with God's grimmest irony, it might only be grasped through playing at play, thus catching reality off its guard." Certainly the blatant artifice of a novel within a lecture indicates Burgess's playfulness and reveals how much a product of his own language and craft his Shakespeare ultimately is. And isn't this precisely the point? Burgess's language has conjured up a very definite image of Shakespeare; he is a creature of Burgess's spirit and craft, the essence sprung forth from the creative existence of Burgess's crafty Elizabethan tongue. The artifice of the novel emphasizes the role of language in inventing its own reality, however like or unlike the known or unknown.

In the novel, kites circle in the skies of London to feed on the plague-ridden corpses of the dead or the heads of traitors stuck on the spikes of fences. These are "the ultimate cleansers of the commonwealth, they attested the end of all noble flesh." While Burgess would never deny this reality, he yet believed, as expressed in his historical and critical account of Shakespeare's life, in the power of language and art to transcend, however momentarily, the kites' omniverous beak:

Take speech as a flickering auditory candle, and the mere act of maintaining its light becomes enough. Tales, gossip, riddles, word-play pass the time in the dark, and out of these—not out of the need to recount facts or state a case—springs literature.[17]

Enderby (1968) and The Clockwork Testament
or Enderby's End (1975):
He is not out of it at all."

What better hero for Burgess's masterpiece than a minor poet, the alchemist of language, the innocent idealist lost in the "gaudy meanness"[18] of pop culture and the modern world? Clearly Enderby is Burgess's most fully developed character in his fiction. He remains throughout his adventures "a kind of Blake sylph, a desperately innocent observer," whose compassion remains intact. He behaves, for the most part, politely, unless pushed or rattled by outside interference. He weeps for the defilement of the modern world around him and relies on poetry, his art, the writing of old-fashioned sonnets to see him through. He realizes that he is just a minor poet and yet believes in the high calling, the almost monastic discipline, of art:

Only the poetical enquiry can discover what language really is . . . The urgent task is the task of conservation. To hold the complex totality of linguistic meaning within a shape you can isolate from the dirty world.

And yet Enderby is all too human. He suffers constantly from heartburn: "In his view, if you did not get dyspepsia while or after eating, you had been cheated of essential nourishment." He remains virtually impotent and settles for solitary masturbation in place of life-generating sexuality. A the Muse tells him at one point, "You can't be blamed, if you've opted to live without love. Something went wrong early." He brings with him an inordinate amount of guilt, what he calls "creation's true dynamo," but which lies heavy upon his soul in its unrelenting presence.

Enderby can write poetry only when he retreats to the lavatory. That small, utilitarian, squalid chamber becomes his place of art, his escapist's refuge into solitary confinement. The smallest room in the house becomes his sanctuary. Minor art emerges from the results of dyspepsia and biological elimination. The poet is confined to his own wastes: the refuge of true art in a world gone mad with pop culture and high fashion. And here Enderby grapples with his great thoughts amid the daily clutter of his days, the artist's attempt to reach for the transcendence of great art out of "the sad, pretty, awful, tragic everyday."

Enderby, however, is no mere victim of circumstance. As his fellow lyric poet, Rawcliffe, suggests, "You wriggle out of the real striking of the blow by the operation of a time-wrap or space-woof or something. You fall on your feet."

There is something irrepressibly inventive about Enderby's "muddling through." His is a comic art, a Chaplinesque dodging of ultimate judgments. He remains an independent cuss, harmless, solitary, but prizing his own vision above all else, as he dashes from place to place, writes sonnets, dons disguises, flees the police, and takes up refuge in Morocco. He has a zany, quick-witted appeal, and we as readers root for his escape from and triumph over the furies that persecute him.

Enderby has always been a favorite of Burgess:

I've always liked . . . the character. People tend to say, this is you. You are the character. This is not really true. But for some reason, I took to the character. It came out of a curious hallucination. I was in Borneo. I'd probably had something to eat and drink, and I opened the bathroom door and found a man sitting on the toilet writing poetry. Of course there was nobody there. Just a pure hallucination. And out of that came the whole image. It's very curious how a purely imaginary character can suddenly emerge. I could have spent my life with this damn character, quite happily . . .

Perhaps Burgess's intimate identification with his minor poet-hero made him, in these novels in which he is the central character, the most humanly accessible and fully realized of all his characters.

Before the plot begins, Enderby is introduced to the reader by a chatty, busy body of a schoolteacher leading a group of disinterested children—the voices of posterity—to his bedside to survey him: "Mr. Enderby is not a *thing* to be prodded; he is a great poet sleeping." While the schoolteacher babbles on, Enderby sleeps and breaks wind: "PFFFRRRUMMMP." This is the opening "statement" of the novel. At once the high art of poetry is juxtaposed with the image of the rumpled forty-five year-old poet: "Mr. Enderby does not make a pretty sight when sleeping, even in total darkness." He becomes at once the object of comedy—how can this unsightly creature ever hope to create great art?"—

and the object of the reader's sympathies: would we like it
if the voice of posterity, like some disinterested mob of
reporters, tracked its dirt and disinterest into our bedrooms
while we slept? The schoolteacher remembers that Enderby
enjoys writing in the bathroom since "the poet is time's
cleanser and cathartiser." Solemnly, on this New Year's Eve,
she intones that despite the fact that Enderby seems lost to
the world in his "dyspeptic and flatulent sleep, he gives it
all meaning." Even his flatulence she compares pretentiously
to "the horns of Elfland." So much for poetic insight!

The schoolteacher, filled with her militant clichés and
dog-eared insights, concludes both *Enderby* and *Enderby's
End*. In the former, she leaves Enderby to his sleep in far-
off Tangier, a place of small, failed artists, where, she muses
wanly, "A man must contrive such happiness as he can. So
must we all. So must we all." In *Enderby's End* she comes
upon Enderby's corpse in his rented New York apartment—
he had just died of a third heart attack—but suggests that
perhaps he will continue to live in his poetry. On a more
affirmative and certainly less cliché-ridden note, she concludes, in the language of that great poet of sonnets, Gerard
Manley Hopkins, "Let him easter in us, be a day spring to
the dimness of us, be a crimson-cresseted east." No mere
object of derision and complacency now, he is reborn in the
immortality of his verse, however minor:

Another instalment of the human condition is beginning. Out of it:
he is well out of it, you say, Andrea? But no: He is in it, we are
all and always in it. Do you think that anyone can escape it merely
by—I will not utter the word: it is quite irrelevant. Out of it, indeed;
he is not out of it at all.

If by "it" Burgess referred to life, to art, and to the modern
world, then throughout the Enderby novels, Enderby is very
much a part of "it." He tries to keep to himself, to mind his
own business, and get on with writing poetry, but the world—
and often his own vanity—will not let him. He comes to
realize that "the state made no provisions for the punishment

of the perversion of art; indeed, it countenanced such perversion." He becomes involved with and hounded by all the "perversions" of modern culture, the "reality enforcers" of a pop culture he cannot abide. These include rock singers, high-fashion editors, and models, salesmen, religious zealots, homosexual poets, psychiatrists, drug pushers, mindless students, outraged wives, lecturers on the moon, television talk-show hosts, muggers, reactionary academics: the entire "cast" of contemporary culture assaults him. The misunderstandings, the manic episodes, the almost situation-comedy adventures of the plot threaten constantly to engulf him. As one critic suggests, "the confrontation of Enderby with the world signifies the clash of a genuine sensibility and a spurious one, of modest truth and sensational sham."[19]

In Book One—*Inside Mr. Enderby* (1963)—F. X. Enderby lives in a guesthouse along the south coast of England. He is trying to write a long, epic poem entitled "The Pet Beast." Using the Cretan myth about the minotaur in the labyrinth, he's trying to write an allegory about sin and guilt, fusing the myth with the Christian story. The Cretan labyrinth he compares to "the human condition, beauty and knowledge built round a core of sin," and he seeks a fusion with the Christian idea of resurrection and deliverance from such sin. The writing goes slowly on New Year's Day, the day on which the novel opens.

Enderby also ruminates about his family. His mother died at his birth. His father, a wholesale tobacconist, remarried a wealthy woman, the stepmother whom he (Enderby) loathes. She represents the archetypal bitch, "graceless and coarse," complete with loathsome personal habits, such as picking her teeth. She was a Catholic, "her religion a mere fear of thunder," complete with "relics and emblems and hagiographs used as lightning-conductors." She "had killed woman for him," once and for all. One time, when Enderby was seventeen, she became frightened during a summer thunderstorm and jumped into bed with him, bad breath and all. He fled to the lavatory, where he was sick, and locked himself in, reading until dawn. That lavatory became his sanctuary, as she—and all the slovenly female qualities attributed to her—became his nemesis. Because of her, he struggled free from Catholicism and became a poet to construct his own myths and visions to live by: "It was a mother he had always wanted, not a stepmother, and he had made that mother himself in his bedroom, made her out of the past, history, myth, the craft of verse." That horrible stepmother "had made his life a misery; he would give no other woman that privilege." The craft of his verse would avoid the gross reality of his stepmother's halitosis and bad habits.

Unfortunately, such dedication to art as craft also results in Enderby's unwillingness or inability to love anyone. He remains ultimately impotent, a minor poet, whose muse recognizes that "something went wrong early."

The modern world breaks in upon Enderby's solitary musings. In a letter, Enderby learns that Sir George Goodby, a supporter of poetry, wishes to present him with the annual Poetry Prize, a gold medal and fifty guineas, at a special luncheon in London. Although Enderby looks upon London as big and hostile, he decides at last to make the journey. Vanity breaks down the closed doors of his threadbare and mildly Edenic existence. He borrows a suit from 'Arry, the head cook at a local restaurant, in exchange for writing a series of love poems to 'Arry's girl friend, Thelma. Mrs. Meldrum, Enderby's querulous landlady, objects to Enderby's sloppiness and announces that she will raise his rent on the eve of his departure to London.

The luncheon proves to be a disaster. Goodby hurls platitudes about poetry to the numbed guests. Enderby, drunk, refuses the money and the medal, cries, breaks up the luncheon, and prepares to depart. Before he makes his disgraceful exit, he meets Rawcliffe, a small, mustached man, who looks like Kipling. Rawcliffe announces, "I'm in all the anthologies," and Enderby tells him about "The Pet Beast."

In the hotel where the luncheon has been held, a woman approaches Enderby. She announces herself as the Features Editress of *Fem*, a fashionable woman's magazine, and wants him to write poems for the magazine at two guineas a poem. She'll send him her full proposal. Enderby wanders about London, finds Rawcliffe's lyric poem in some poetry anthologies in a bookstore, gets drunk, fights in a pub and clambers onto a train. The woman from *Fem* finds him there, realizes he's on the wrong train, and directs him to the right one, after giving him some tea to sober him up a bit.

When he gets back to his room, he cannot find his key. Since it's still night, he goes upstairs to the apartment that Jack the salesman shares with a woman and asks to be allowed to sleep on her couch. She agrees. In the morning the milkman catches him coming down the stairs, the postman springs open the lock to his apartment, and a letter from Mrs. Meldrum declares that the rent rises next month.

Enderby decides it's time to move on. A parcel of past issues of *Fem* and a contract arrives, but he ignores them. Jack the salesman wants to fight with Enderby for sleeping with his woman. He declares war on "you fornicating poet," but Enderby won't let him into his apartment. Enderby goes to say goodbye to 'Arry and writes one more poem for Thelma. He returns to find Jack after him and clouts Jack with his loose toilet seat. As Enderby begins to pack to leave, a fellow named Walpole suddenly appears on the scene. He's a curious mixture of religious fundamentalism and Marxist zealotry who believes in a militant "theophanic socialism," and begs Enderby to fall to his knees and pray to give up writing his filthy poetry—"On your knees, Comrade Enderby!"—he pleads and reveals his true identity as the unpoetic Thelma's husband! At this bizarre moment the woman from *Fem* arrives and announces to Enderby, "I'm taking you home."

Vesta Bainbridge is the woman from *Fem*. She dresses in the latest high fashions, exudes money and power, commands with authority—"She had in her something of the thin-lipped Calvinist"—and poses like a model in *Vogue*. She was once wed to Pete Bainbridge, a racing-car driver, who was killed in the Monte Carlo Rally. She declares later on, "I've been entrusted with the care of a great poet." The representative of all the lacquered, elegant suavity and presence of the modern world that Enderby lacks, naturally, Vesta marries him. Enderby accepts the poet's post at *Fem*, writing under the pseudonym, Faith Fortitude. The two of them jet to Rome on their honeymoon. She falls ill. In the hotel bar Enderby meets a drunken Rawcliffe, who admits that the poetic muse has abandoned him and that he, now fifty-two, hasn't written anything since he was twenty-seven. Like a voice of doom, he warns Enderby about the desertion of the muse, especially from lyric poets. He mentions bitterly that Vesta has married Enderby only to share the glory in the biographies after his death.

Vesta arranges a bus journey out of Rome into the countryside. Enderby sullenly acquiesces. The purpose of the journey remains a mystery, until suddenly Enderby and thousands of other would-be pilgrims come upon the Pope's country villa. Vesta demands that he kneel. Enderby refuses and flees. A thunderstorm envelopes the countryside. He and Vesta, missing the last bus, must spend the night in a small hotel. Since the marriage has not yet been consummated, this would be the perfect time. Enderby, however, fails to rise to the occasion. He suddenly realizes that Vesta reminds him of his stepmother—the Catholicism, the fear of thunder, the authority, the need to possess him. Even the name reminds him of the vestal virgins. She is no more than a gleaming modern counterpart to that old "archetypal bitch."

When Enderby and Vesta return to Rome, Rawcliffe invites them to a film premiere, the film based on the screenplay he has written and entitled "L'Animal Binato." At the premiere Enderby is shocked. Rawcliffe has stolen the entire plot of his own "The Pet Beast." Betrayed, he visibly flinches when Vesta demands a full Catholic wedding in Rome. That night he sneaks stealthily out of the hotel

room and catches the first plane out of the Eternal City,
alone at last.

Back in England Enderby goes to see Dr. Preston
Hawkes for a physical checkup. He's well, but he's writing
no more poems. He feels listless, despondent, and asks
Hawkes what he thinks the purpose of life is. Hawkes
trumpets simplistically, "The purpose of life is the living of
it. Life itself is the end of life. Life is here and now and what
you can get out of it." This comforts Enderby not at all.
Hawkes thinks he should see a psychiatrist, a Dr. Greenslade.
Enderby leaves the office and discovers that an English
version of Rawcliffe's plagiarized film is now showing in
England as "Son of the Beast from Outer Space." Since
deserting Vesta, he realizes that he has written nothing, and
he wanders back to his rented room to swallow a bottle of
aspirin.

He awakens in the office of Dr. Greenslade. The good
doctor sends him to Flitchley, a minimum security institution
for mental cases. While there, Dr. Wapenshaw "cures" him,
creating a new, well-adjusted person. The resurrected Enderby is even given a name, Piggy Hogg, the last name his
mother's maiden name. He is sent to a bartender training
course at a Midland Hotel, after he completes a stay at
Shorthope, an Agricultural Station, where he supervises a
gang with hoes: "Shouldering his hoe, chucking away his
fag-butt, he marched." The insides of Enderby have now
been replaced by the outsides of Hogg, the poet "restored"
to a useful function in a marching modern world.

In Book Two—*Enderby Outside* (1968)—we find Piggy
Hogg, inconsequent bartender, working at Piggy's Sty, a
fashionable bar in a fashionably modern London hotel. He
works with a man known as Spanish John, whose brother,
Billy Gomez, also runs a bar in Tangier (a piece of information
Hogg will need later on). While Hogg is serving drinks, the
muse suddenly returns in the presence of a "phantom girl,"
and he dashes off a sonnet. Poetry has returned.

Weeks later he is summoned by Dr. Wapenshaw to his

office. Wapenshaw shows him the proofs of a book he has
written about the successful, psychological conversion of
Enderby to Hogg, called *Rehabilitations*. He also hands Hogg
a journal, *Confrontation*, in which is prominently displayed
a new poem by Enderby. Wapenshaw rages, accusing En-
derby/Hogg of ruining his reputation as a psychiatrist.
Evidently another doctor has come upon the recently published sonnet and revealed it to Wapenshaw. The doctor
shouts at Hogg to leave, and Hogg fires back, "I'll write what
poetry I want to, thanks very much, and not you nor anybody
else will stop me."

Yod Crewsy and the Crewsy Fixers, a famous rock
group, decide to hold their celebration for a "new golden
disc" and Crewsy's elevation as a Fellow of the Royal Society
of Literature—he's recently published a book of poetry—at
Piggy's Sty. The waiters must all wear hairy wigs to resemble
the group. Hogg mixes a deadly cocktail, which he christens
"the crucifier," for the occasion, hating the group and
delighted at his own rejuvenated poetic powers. The Prime
Minister arrives to toast the financially successful group.
Vesta Bainbridge appears on the scene, now as Mrs. Des
Wittgenstein, successful manager of rock groups. Yod reads
one of his poems, and Enderby/Hogg recognizes it as one of
his own, left at Vesta's Gloucester Road apartment after he
had deserted her. At that moment Jed Foot, a seedy fellow
who's been drinking heavily and had left the Crewsy Fixers
before their phenomenal success, pulls out a gun, shoots
"Crewsy," drops the smoking weapon into Hogg's hands, and
flees. Everyone sees Hogg with the pistol. He rushes out,
takes an elevator to the hotel basement, grabs a cab to the
airport, discovers an open seat on a charter flight to Morocco,
remembers Billy Gomez's bar in Tangier, discovers an ad in
a Tangier brochure for what may or may not be Rawcliffe's
restaurant, and settles back in the plane to make good his
escape.

On board the plane, Enderby meets Miranda Boland,
a middle-aged lecturer. Her specialty is selenography, the

study of the moon. Rawcliffe will later tell him that the moon
has no power over poetry: "The day of the moon goddess is
done. The sun goddess takes over." It is the sun that rules
the best poetry, and in "rejecting the sun, you reject life."
Miranda proves to be another failed muse, a possessive,
"stepmotherish" woman. When the tour spends the night in
Seville, Spain, she and Enderby romp naked in the moonlight.
When it came to sex, however, the poetic insight overcomes
Enderby just at the moment of climax, and he pulls away to
write his verse. Needless to say, Miranda is furious. On the
flight from Seville to Morocco, she discovers in the paper
who Enderby is—a possible assassin; Crewsy is not yet
dead—and screams her revelation to the other passengers.
The tour director lets Enderby off the plane before anyone
else in Morocco, so that he can flee.

  With the help of a fast-talking, drug pusher, Easy
Walker, whom he meets in a square in Marrakesh, Enderby
gets a ride to Tangier. There he shares a room in a brothel
over a bar with three homosexuals: Ali Fathi, an Arabic
Muslim from Alexandria; Wahab, a Moor and a petty thief;
and the fat, gross Souris. Nightly he must listen to their
homosexual carryings-on. Nearby he discovers that, indeed,
Rawcliffe does own and operate a restaurant-bar, "El Acan-
tilado Verde."

  Tangier lends itself to cheap bars and literary exiles.
At Billy Gomez's place, Enderby discovers a rag-tag, drugged
and drunken group of would-be poets, stifling in their own
hot-house pretensions. He discovers in the lavatory (where
else?) Yod Crewsy's book of poems, containing six of
Enderby's sonnets and one of Wordsworth's, the ultimate
proof of plagiarism. Enderby, suspicious of Gomez, rushes
back to his room. In the middle of the night, he overhears
Napo, the owner of the brothel, talking to the police. They
are hot on his trail. Quickly he rushes out the back way and
leaps over the fence. Safe and hidden, he applies boot-polish
to his arms and face to disguise himself as a Moroccan and
takes up an existence as a beggar.

At last, he discovers Rawcliffe, the failed lyric poet,
who pilfered "The Pet Beast" and turned it into a successful
film in his restaurant. Enderby is hungry for revenge, but
Rawcliffe is already dying of cancer. There is no need for
Enderby to murder him now. Enderby oversees Rawcliffe's
last miserable days, surrounded by brandy to ease the pain,
morphine when the pain becomes too intolerable, and his
three live-in house boys, who indulge in homosexual por-
nography and sex. Rawcliffe decides to leave the restaurant
and all the money he's saved stuffed in his mattress to
Enderby. Enderby, touched, sorrowful, administering to
Rawcliffe's decomposing body and needs, "forgave his stepmother everything." He has come slowly to terms with real
death and decay, in the shadow of which, all human cruelty
and injustice appear the solemn frailities of children. Pla-
giarizer to the end, Rawcliffe dies, spouting the lines of
George Herbert as if they were his own. Easy Walker drops
his body into the sea, Rawcliffe's final wish, and Enderby
renames the restaurant, "La Belle Mer."

Loose ends of the plot come together. Yod Crewsy fails
to die; he awakens from a long coma and rises Lazaruslike
to an increased surge of popularity and success. Enderby
thinks Vesta staged his "resurrection." Miranda writes to
apologize for her behavior in Seville and informs him that a
Harold Pritchard, a junior English lecturer, has discovered
Crewsy's plagiarism and exposed it fully in the *Times Literary
Supplement*. Jed Foot, drunk at yet another fashionable party,
finally confesses.

One fine day a tanned and golden girl walks into "La
Belle Mer." She remains mysterious and nameless but speaks
lovingly and knowledgeably about poetry. Clearly she is the
poetic muse reincarnate. She advises Enderby to use Catholicism as a mythology, not as a religious belief: "Pluck
it bare of images, but don't ever believe in it again." She
suggests he rely on the East-West clash of cultures and
values here in Tangier to inspire his poetry: "You can get
something here. This is a junction . . . Africa and Europe.

Christianity and Islam. Past and future." The advice to a
writer such as Enderby/Burgess is clear. One evening she
decides to swim nude, then wants sex. Enderby refuses. "Just
like Mr. Prufrock," she quietly upbraids him, suggesting
Eliot's poetic voice of failed sexuality and cowardice. Enderby
leaves her with a kiss, "his share, his quota, what he was
worth." It is a modest talisman of love and possible truth,
but in the wake of all else—the sham, the pretension. the
casual recklessness of the modern world—it is more than
enough.

The poet, even the minor, timid poet seeking his
sanctuary in the lavatory, modesty triumphs over the crush
of contemporary culture around him by hanging on to his art.
However diminished, his is an authentic voice and vision.
He remains his own man:

There's no obligation to accept society or woman or religion or
anything else, not for anyone there isn't. And as for poetry, that's
a job for anarchs. Poetry's made by rebels and exiles and outsiders.
it's made by people on their own . . . it's they who make language
and make myths. Poets don't need anybody except themselves.

To psychiatrists "this obsession with poetry" may be nothing
more than "the name of a prolonged adolescence," but to
Enderby and Burgess, art, in George Goodby's cliché-ridden
phrase, can "transmute the dross of the everyday workaday
world into the sheerest gold." In a modern world which insists
upon "the building of a new human society under the sheriff's
steadfast bright star," art may be the last refuge of the
individual consciousness. In a modern world marked by the
experience of dissolution, a world in which "everybody [is]
beginning to be alone, a common tradition providing no
tuning-fork of reference and no way of telling the time,
because the common tradition has been dredged away,"
perhaps only art can provide a sense of order and celebration.
Enderby thinks so and pays for it.

In the short, swift end to Enderby's career—*The Clock-*

work Testament or Enderby's End (1975)—Burgess accomplishes two things. Once again he creates a plot based on the often hilarious and frequently tragic confrontations between Enderby and the modern world, and at the same time, attempts to summarize Enderby's beliefs about and attitudes toward art in general. Based loosely on Burgess's own adventures as a visiting professor at City College in New York during 1972–73, the novel traces Enderby's last day. He is living in February-cold New York as a visiting professor of Creative Writing at the University of Manhattan for a year. New York is the modern world writ large, "a city otherwise dirty, rude, violent, and full of foreigners and mad people" with its "disfigured streets full of decayed and disaffected and dogmerds."

Enderby has been brought to New York, because he suggested the idea for a successful film. "The Wreck of the Deutschland," based originally on a poem by Hopkins. Unfortunately, the movie, reminiscent perhaps of Kubrick's film *A Clockwork Orange*, overemphasizes the rape of a group of nuns by some Nazi storm-troopers and underemphasizes Enderby's original suggestions about love and death. He receives $750 for the screenplay, having offered the idea to some film moguls, who had dropped in at "La Belle Mer" in Tangier. Currently, Enderby is working on a long epic poem on St. Augustine and Pelagius, the same conflict between free will and Original Sin that has appeared in nearly all of Burgess's novels.

Enderby's first confrontation is with Linda Tietjens, one of the students in his creative writing class, who comes to his apartment ostensibly to interview him on tape, but really to go to bed with him and get an "A" in the course. Enderby, astounded, weeps, and she leaves. He heads out into the bright, wintry cold to teach his class on minor Elizabethan dramatists, and in the process, fabricates the life and accomplishments of one Gervase Whitelady (1569–91), like him "one of the unknown poets who never properly mastered their craft, spurned by the Muse." In his writing class, students attack him for being old-fashioned and reactionary, for valuing form in art over slogan and sensation. One black student hurls epithets at him, raging that he doesn't understand the "ethnic agony . . . you misleading reactionary evil bastard."

Enderby has been asked to discuss the film, "The Wreck of the Deutschland," on the Sperr Lansing television talk-show. On his way to the theatre, in a bar he meets Kevin O'Donnell, the actor who played the role of Hopkins in the film. O'Donnell insists that Hopkins sodomized his mother's father, and Enderby, long a Hopkins admirer, is appalled. Shaken, he makes his way to the studio to confront a smarmy, leering Lansing, a self-assured Prof. Balaglas, who argues for censorship of all art and the sacrifice of the individual self to the communal good, and Ermine Elderly, a dimwitted Hollywood starlet. Enderby rails against Balaglas's specious arguments and recites a bawdy poem on the air. The tape of the show is never shown, and the show dissolves into accusations and bitter confusion.

On his way home, Enderby enters "the Times Square subway hellmouth." Three muggers are attacking a woman on the subway. At once he removes the sword from the cane he has been carrying and swashbuckles himself to victory. The muggers flee. He stops in to see the film, sees no great harm in it, and suffers his second mild heart attack of the day. (The first had occurred shortly after Linda Tietjens left him that morning).

A final confrontation in the day's long trial occurs when he returns to his apartment. A woman breaks in with a gun, furious at him and his poetry for disrupting her marriage. It is never made clear exactly what her gripe is, but she insists that Enderby strip and urinate on his books. She fires at him three times to get him to fulfill her bidding. He throws a book at her, grabs her gun, strips her, and completes the entire sexual act at last: "Oh, this is all too American," Enderby said, "Sex and violence. What angel of regeneration sent you here?" Shortly afterwards, when the ravished woman lies asleep in Enderby's bed, Enderby dreams that he is witnessing the running argument between St. Augustine and Pelagius between Original Sin and man's inherent goodness, on a television film. The debate is not resolved. Enderby's third heart attack kills him.

In the novel, Burgess plays with many forms and styles. Large pieces of Enderby's poem are strewn throughout the book. The Speer/Lansing affair is presented as an unedited transcript, "recorded but not used." Sections of the screenplay of the Hopkins film appear. The clash at the end between St. Augustine and Pelagius appears as a screenplay, complete with directions and facial expressions. In juxtaposing screenplay with poem, Enderby hopes that people "would see the poem as superior art to the film." It doesn't quite work that way, however, since Burgess's prose remains so inventive and funny. In any case, the form of *Enderby's End* does mirror the chaos of modern culture and the madness of living in New York. The novel zigs and zags from screenplay to verse to transcript in the manner of a rapidly paced television show or multi-media event. Burgess's playful use of various forms reflects the crazed content of the contemporary age.

By now Burgess's ideas about art, free will, and Original Sin are fairly clear. In *Enderby's End* he has attempted to summarize these. Free will and evil are inherently intertwined: "If you get rid of evil you get rid of choice . . . You've got to have things to choose between, and that means good *and* evil. If you don't choose, you're not human any more. You're something else. Or you're dead." The Manichean conflict continues unappeased. Art remains neutral in the struggle, an act of order and celebration somewhere above the violent, aggressive circumstance of man's life. It's not art that sins, but man: "People always blame art, literature, drama for their own evil. Or other peoples. Art only imitates life. Evil's already there." Art remains "beauty, ultimate meaning, form for its own sake, self-subsisting," almost like God. And it is accomplished, not by conformists and corporate men, but by "autonomous man—the inner man, the homunculus, the possessing demon, the man defended by the literatures of freedom and dignity."

Burgess's triumph in the Enderby novels is to have created a character visibly wrestling with his own notions of art and life. We see him searching for the exact word to bring the poem to life. We share with him the semblance of the act of creation, experience the revelation of a certain image in his mind, which then sends out certain rhythms, lines, visions. Enderby serves no thesis, no structuralist order, no tenets of modernist faith. He emerges as his own well-rounded man, weak, courageous, timid, and obsessed. Of course "he is not out of it at all." Enderby lives.

6

••

The Late Novels

Burgess's fascination and obsession with certain forms, structures, and themes become apparent when you regard Burgess's fiction as a whole. There are the clashes between East and West, the Manichean interpenetration of good and evil, the futuristic fables about the individual in conflict with the collective will of the state, the use of such specific musical forms and myths as symphonies and Algonquin tales, and the continuing experiment with language, syntax, and diction. Each of these areas exists as almost a separate entity, as if each were a phase or period through which Burgess's art had passed. The early phase focuses on his novels of manners, the clash of cultures. The middle phase focuses on the novels of futuristic fables and experimental language. The later phase focuses on the use of such conscious structures as symphonies and old legends. Each phase, of course, interpenetrates the others; none is sufficient in itself or entirely free from the others. But there is a distinct group or "bloc" of novels which fits into each category. Burgess's constant interest in different novelistic forms and structures may account for this division.

In his two most recent novels, *Man of Nazareth* (1979) and *Earthly Powers* (1980), Burgess seems determined to confront fully his ultimate ideas about the nature of good and evil, the necessity of free will, the role of evil in the universe, the Manichean conflict of warring opposites that shows no sign of ever being resolved. In *Man of Nazareth* Burgess

retells the life of Christ from the point of view of a decidedly
rationalistic and skeptical translator of documents. In *Earthly
Powers* (published in Britain as *Instruments of Darkness*) a
cynical homosexual and second-rate novelist assails the
unshakable faith and optimism of a priest who becomes Pope.
In both novels the everyday world of human corruption,
greed, and lust outlasts its saviors and would-be prophets or
kills them outrightly. The continued existence of that sinful
human realm suggests that the Manichean Devil reigns
supreme and has triumphed over any Christian attempts to
unseat him.

Man of Nazareth (1979): "Man's life
may be little more than a game."

Azor, the narrator of *Man of Nazareth*, "a mere story-teller,"
translator of documents, writer of letters, and auditor of the
accounts of a wine merchant believes little in old legends
and superstitions. He prides himself on his clear-eyed,
rational approach to the world around him. A man of little
vision, he doubts such tales about Lazarus's rising from the
dead or the nature of Jesus's baptism by John the Baptist,
but curiously accepts the existence of strange creatures like
the archangel Gabriel without hesitation. He spots ambiguities
in Christ's message easily but is "unwilling to believe" many
of the stories that surround him.

His tale of the life of Christ approaches "the sober
chronicle of fact" and not "some great phantasmagoric poem."
Consequently, his prose reads like a financial ledger, like
some cursory, unevocative document. He recreates a secular
world as dull as the world of one of his financial audits. The
High Priest Caiaphas might wonder at the mystery of God's
love, "a love so intolerable, so lacerating to the lover," but
Azor can never appreciate, let alone conjure up to describe,
such passionate doubt or conviction. He epitomizes, as one
critic suggested in reference to the style of the novel, "an

empty urbanity, breezy colloquialism and the rhetoric of skepticism and comical play."[1]

Azor views life as a game. In his eyes it appears as a tepid and colorless diversion, a sport of some disinterested gods. Opposites may conflict, the conflict may be unresolved, and perhaps "our stability is a kind of happy but unpurposed emanation of a mild war." In any case "the unresolved conflict between good and evil" seems to negate the powerful force of either one of them. Azor believes that the skills required to play this game, whose prize is the kingdom of heaven, include "tolerance, forbearance and affection." But in his words, even love sounds facile and powerless. Christ's vision, reduced to "playing the game of forbearance and charity," becomes flaccid and superficial, a juiceless generalized statement in place of a passionate mystery.

The plot of *Man of Nazareth* is constructed along the lines of the gospel according to Luke. At the beginning the archangel Gabriel on the Sabbath of Solemn Rest strikes the aged Zacharias dumb and tells his wife Elizabeth that she will give birth to a son. That son becomes John the Baptist. Joseph, a humorless carpenter, marries a young woman named Mary. The rest follows the Biblical pattern, including the birth of the Christ child in Bethlehem, Herod's slaughter of the innocents, the flight into Egypt, John's baptism of Jesus, the forty days and nights in the wilderness, and Jesus's exorcizing evil spirits and healing the sick. Disciples are gathered, Jesus enters Jerusalem, Caiaphas and Pontius Pilate bicker and plot, and the crucifixion takes place on schedule.

Burgess's imaginative additions to the Biblical tale merit some comment. In his portrayal of Judas as a political idealist and innocent, "those who believed that the world could be changed for the better by changing its governors," he creates a valid and interesting character. Burgess's Judas thinks that Christ wants both an earthly kingship and a spiritual rule within it. He betrays Christ to the priests, because he thinks they will keep him safe until the appointed hour of his triumph. Judas operates in a carefully drawn political landscape, which Burgess describes well: the Zealots willing to overthrow Rome, Pontius Pilate hoping to remain neutral as the procurator of Judea, and the priests attempting to prove Christ's apparent blasphemy as actual treason in their successful effort to transfer the act and responsibility of Christ's death from their hands into the State's.

Burgess created other interesting incidents in his narrative. Christ marries a young girl named Sara at Cana. She has several miscarriages and then is crushed to death during a riot at the temple in Jerusalem on a festival day. Salome, Herod's lascivious stepdaughter, joins Mary Magdalene and Mary, Christ's mother, at the crucifixion. She repudiates Herod's ways and is drawn to Christ's teachings. Joseph the carpenter is sterile, because his testes were crushed in an accident long ago.

Christ's doctrine according to Burgess is more or less close to the mark. Christ preaches love: "I call love rather a craft a man or woman must learn as I, in my youth, learned the craft of carpentry. Love is the tool." A craft and a tool: components of the rational if dispassionate game of life as drawn up by Azor. Christ's message carries no political content but upholds the things within the spirit of love, as opposed to the things without, Caesar's trophies. Such a spirit repudiates old customs, habits, and traditions which are upheld and celebrated for their own sake. And both soul and flesh are God's, as opposed to the Manichean sect, which hovers within the novel, repudiates the flesh, and "assign[s] to matter an origin and a purpose wholly diabolical." There will be a Day of Judgment in the future, and evil exists to prompt the choices that indicate man's will is ultimately free. Such ceremonies as communion and the recognition of Christ's ultimate sacrifice spring from such doctrines.

Burgess attempted to create distinct personalities for each of the disciples. To each he gave certain identifiable characteristics. Bartholomew, for instance, appears studious, melancholy, contemplative; he heals the sick. James on the other hand wrestles, and at the age of twenty, displays a muscular physique and aggressive attitude. John, the disciple closest to Jesus, speaks in a loud voice, yet soothes his listeners in his delicate fashion. And Burgess's Christ is no ethereal esthete, no ephemeral saint. He's a strong muscular fellow, self-assured, unassailed by doubts, conscious of the fact that he is part of some preordained design, some "necessary sacrifice," if not entirely clear exactly what it signifies. Unfortunately these characters remain undeveloped. They are stick figures who display superficial characteristics, quickly sketched in by the writer. We never get any glimpses of them as real people with passionate and multifaceted personalities.

Azor's world remains almost wholly secular, a place of political corruption and manipulation. As recreated by him in his narration, it is simply not worth saving, not because it is so evil, but because it is so banal. Christ's vision is reduced to a series of lectures within this barren realm. Christ preaches, but there is no real connection between his convictions and the world he inhabits.

Burgess's Christ, or the Christ whom Azor describes, fails as a human character and remains unconvincing as an inspired prophet. He seems little more than a wooden puppet, spouting his beliefs, marking time, until the political plots and his own crucifixion catch up with him. Burgess sends him to his death without any real recognition on his part of what that death may signify. At the center of *Man of Nazareth* lurks precisely that: a mere man railroaded by some querulous fate into some uncertain destiny. He reveals no passion, no conviction, and no depth. The novel reflects the essential hollowness of this Christ, as the narrator plods through the necessary and legendary events until they come to their prescribed conclusion.

Earthly Powers (1980): "Like Ruined Pastry."

Earthly Powers begins with what Burgess refers to in the novel as "an arresting opening": "It was the afternoon of my

eighty-first birthday, and I was in bed with my catamite when
Ali announced that the archbishop had come to see me."
Thus we are introduced to Kenneth Marchal Toomey, aged
popular novelist and homosexual, living in Malta, in exile
from his native England. The Archbishop of Malta comes to
question him about his brother-in-law, Carlo Campanati.
Campanati, recently elevated to the papacy as Pope Gregory
XVII, has just died. Toomey supposedly witnessed a miracle
by Campanati in Chicago in the twenties, and the archbishop
is seeking Toomey's testimony for Carlo's possible elevation
to sainthood. After the archbishop's departure, Toomey
recalls a short story he wrote, entitled "Laying On of Hands,"
and he did describe the remarkable recovery of an unnamed
child, dying of tuberculosis after a priest had blessed him
and supposedly exorcized the disease. The story was based
on an incident Carlo Campanati initiated. The child miraculously lived.

Trying to remember the actual events, Toomey begins
to recall his entire life as an artist, a practicing homosexual,
and as a witness to and participant in the history of the
Campanati family. His extended memories form the bulk of
the novel.

Toomey describes much of the cultural history of the
twentieth century in his memoirs, beginning with his own
homosexual seduction on June 16, 1904 in Dublin—the day
made famous by Joyce's *Ulysses*—through the Paris of the
twenties, Hollywood in the thirties, Nazi Germany in the
thirties and forties, New York and Hollywood in the forties
and fifties, and life as an aged novelist in exile in Tangier
and Malta in the sixties and seventies. In Paris in the twenties
we catch glimpses of Joyce, Ezra Pound, Gertrude Stein, and
the noted sexologist, Havelock Ellis. In Hollywood we see
the glitter and cynicism of sex and celebrity. In Nazi
Germany, in Toomey's attempt to rescue a fellow novelist
from Hitler's regime, we attend a Berlin film festival, rife
with Goebbel's propaganda, and witness an attempted assassination of Heinrich Himmler. Along the way Toomey enjoys

sex with wooden-legged actors, Black Power converts, would-be poets, and rowdy sailors in some of Burgess's most colorful escapades. And in the postwar era we experience the luxury and ennui of prosperous New York, a symbol of a prosperous America; become involved in lecture tours and Toomey's growing celebrity; and are privy to the conclave of cardinals, who elevate Carlo Campanati to the Papacy.

For Burgess political ideologies entrap and stultify the human spirit and society:

Nazi Germany had succeeded in producing a new type of human being, one that had abdicated the rights and duties of freedom of moral choice, that was capable of putting the abstraction of a political system before the realities of human life, that could obey without question, that was able, under orders, to perpetrate the most ghastly enormities totally without remorse, whose satisfactions were referred or collective, whose creed was mystical and insusceptible of any rational reduction.

So much for the earthly powers of secular states and the modern collective sensibility! Human choice is reduced to "cruelty and sentimentality and nothing between the two." Toomey's memoirs in part document the growth of this modern vision.

Toomey begins his recollections with his confession to a priest at Christmas, 1916, of his homosexuality, which the priest condemns outrightly. Since there is no room in the Catholic Church for a man of his sexual persuasion, he declares himself an infidel and withdraws from organized religion. He writes popular plays, light comic farces in the manner of Noel Coward, and takes as a lover, Rodney Selkirk, an actor in one of his theatrical successes. On one fateful day he and Rodney are discovered in bed by Rodney's wife Linda and two policemen. Toomey decides to leave England to avoid the possibilities of a public scandal. In the famous influenza epidemic of 1917–18, both his lover Rodney and his mother die.

In Paris in the twenties Toomey meets Domenico Campanati, a struggling composer of serious music, and

Domenico's brother, Don Carlo Campanati, an ambitious priest. Both are members of the wealthy Campanati family of Milan. Both describe the financial success of their brother Raffaele, who is a wealthy importer of Milanese food living in Chicago. After the death of Toomey's mother and the remarriage of his father, Toomey's sister Hortense comes to live with him in Paris. She's a liberated, outspoken, practical sort, who almost immediately seduces Domenico, drawn to his good looks and his money. She and Domenico are wed at the Campanati estate outside Milan in the summer of 1919, and in 1924, the twins, John and Ann, are born.

Toomey's publishers suggest a trip to Malaya for him to write stories about the East. The East for him suggests ultimate mystery, but turns out, in fact, to harbor only death, revenge, spiteful British colonials, and endless disease. In Malaya he befriends Dr. Philip Shawcross, a lonely, sensitive man with whom Toomey experiences an immediate kinship. Theirs becomes a Platonic relationship, a deep friendship based on mutual respect and love but, thankfully for Toomey—who regrets his homosexuality and is forever afraid of public exposure—no sexual involvement. Shawcross dies from a possible Malayan curse administered by Mr. Mahalingam. Mahalingam believes that Shawcross had been responsible for his son's death. In any case, with Shawcross's untimely demise, Toomey is left lonely and isolated once again and continues his travels without enthusiasm.

It is in Chicago, after wandering from place to place, that Toomey comes upon Raffaele's sudden death. Gangsters have mutilated Raffaele during a fight for control of the marketplace in a city rife with bootleg whiskey and mobsters' violence. Carlo Campanati arrives, but it is too late. He hears of a child dying from tuberculosis at the same hospital where his brother Raffaele has been taken and "touched with his own spittle the child's forehead and sternum and shoulders." Miraculously the child recovers. As Carlo suggests, "The mystery of God's will is beyond us."

In the raucous, racy Hollywood of the thirties, Domenico

becomes a composer for the new talking films and Toomey becomes a screenwriter. Domenico, selfish, smug, and sexually voracious, decides to divorce Hortense, who has been living with their two children in New York. Carlo, now a monsignor, upbraids his thoughtless brother, and Domenico reveals the fact that Carlo was adopted. Carlo's mother, now, is truly the church.

The most exciting escapade in the novel involves Toomey's attempted rescue of the famous German writer, the 1935 Nobel prize winner, Jakob Strehler. Toomey has gone to Berlin to pick up some book royalties and attend a film festival. He's appalled by the Nazi machine, by Goebbels' racist tirades, and realizes that demonic legions are slowly taking over Germany and the world. He casts a terrified eye at the rise to power of men like Hitler, Mussolini, and Stalin. In Berlin, Concetta Campanati, the mother of the Campanati clan attempts to shoot Heinrich Himmler. She's dying of cancer and has been helping Jews escape from Germany. On impulse, Toomey at the moment of the attempted assassination pushes Himmler out of the way of Concetta's bullet, and the police turn on her and shoot her down. Afterward Toomey's rescue of Himmler appalls him, and his rescue of Strehler suggests a way of evening the score.

Strehler has sent his son Heinz to Toomey in London to get him out of Nazi Austria. Heinz turns out to be a thief, a homosexual, a troublemaker, and a drunk. Toomey wants to be rid of him and plots to rescue the father, so that father and son can be reunited, and he will no longer be responsible for Heinz's behavior. Toomey journeys to Austria, but Strehler refuses to leave. Instead the local police arrest Toomey as a spy, because he's carrying a camera with him and because England and France have just declared war on Germany a few days before Toomey is discovered in Strehler's country cabin. Strehler, led away by the police, vanishes, another statistic of the concentration camps, no doubt, because of his Jewish background. Nazi officers force Toomey to deliver a two-minute interview on German radio. He proclaims his

antiwar sentiments and his negative feelings about England's
prime minister Neville Chamberlain in exchange for his
release. Officers from Scotland Yard's Special Branch, however, interview him back in London and consider his actions
to be if not treasonous at least dubious. His passport is taken
away, he's restricted to England, and he is publicly upbraided
and condemned in a newspaper article for not condemning
the Nazis when he had the chance.

In New York after the Second World War Hortense
takes a black woman, a former nightclub singer named
Dorothy Pembroke, as her live-in lover and companion. Both
of them introduce Dorothy's brother Ralph to Toomey, who
takes him on as a secretary/lover. Ralph becomes involved
in the African nation of Rukwa, changes his name to Kasam
Ekuri as he proclaims the ideological certainties of Black
Power, works in the Rukwan government for awhile, and
eventually, as an academic, retreats to the safety of the Black
Studies department at Columbia University. Toomey, celebrity, noted lecturer, and bon vivant tours universities, judges
films at the Cannes film festival, and publicly defends a
friend's volume of homosexual love poetry, *The Love Songs
of J. Christ*. At the trial the book is finally judged to be
obscene, but Toomey proclaims his own homosexuality and
shocks the literary world.

Other family members pursue their separate careers.
John, Hortense's son and Toomey's nephew, establishes
himself as a professor of linguistic anthropology and travels
with his wife Laura to Rukwa to study a certain African tribe
there. In Rukwa he and Laura are murdered, ostensibly
slaughtered by terrorists in the emerging civil war in that
country. Meanwhile, Carlo Campanati has worked his way
up from Bishop of Moneta, where he had taken a strong anti-
Nazi position in his sermons and actions, to Archbishop of
Milan, where he's become involved with workers' rights and
their Communist sympathies. Finally in October, 1958,
Campanati is elected Pope and chooses the name Gregory
XVII. He initiates the Vatican Council to reform the church.

Meanwhile Eve, the daughter of Ann Campanati (Hortense's daughter) and her husband, Michael Breslow, a professor of comparative literature, flee from the soulless wealth of materialistic modern America to a religious commune out in the desert of California. The commune is run by God Manning, a demonic faith healer, who brainwashes his flock and rules his private sanctuary like some pagan king. Toomey arrives at the militaristic commune to rescue Eve, but she refuses to leave, and he's forced to abandon his plans. Shortly thereafter, a Congressman investigates Manning, goes to the commune, and is shot and killed along with members of his party. Manning commands his followers to swallow cyanide pellets, escapes from their death agonies, but is finally captured and imprisoned. Manning's career and personality are clearly based on Jim Jones, and his commune reminds the reader of the disastrous Jonesville massacre in 1978 in Guyana.

Toomey ends his memoirs with the Pope's death and brings us back to the present day. He returns to England to live a quiet life with sister Hortense in a small country village, and they both enjoy attending clandestine Latin Masses, since outlawed by the recommendations of the Vatican Council.

Burgess's novel concludes with two revelations which throw the rest of the plot into high relief. Toomey learns that John and Laura, killed in Rukwa, were killed not by terrorists but by Africans participating in the reformed Communion service of the Catholic Church. One of John's associates, who has managed to escape, tells his tale to Toomey: "Some of them took this flesh and blood business a bit too literally . . . They don't see about changing it to bread and wine . . . your nephew and his wife were used as what are known as the accidents of the Sacrament of the Holy Eucharist." Carlo's reforms to "bring the faith closer to the people" have resulted in the sacrificial murders of his own nephew and his nephew's wife.

The second revelation involves a book entitled *Medic*,

which has been written by the doctor who attended the
tubercular child who miraculously recovered back in Chicago
in the twenties. Geoffrey Entright, Toomey's latest secretary/
lover, discovers the book on a trip to Chicago and sends it
to Toomey. The child's name was Godfrey Manning, and the
doctor exclaims, "Godfrey Manning it seemed to me was a
good name, bringing God and Man together." Manning of
course turned out to be the demonic faith healer who is
responsible for Eve's suicide. "The body of Christ administered as a cyanide tablet. Nearly two thousand slaughtered
in the name of the Lord," gasps Toomey. The great, all-
loving, reform-minded Pope has miraculously saved the
devil's child.

Throughout *Earthly Powers* Burgess pits the cynical,
pessimistic Toomey against the reform-minded, optimistic
Carlo. The two men constantly quarrel over the nature of
good and evil, the necessity of man's free will, and the
mysterious outlines of God's design in a modern universe
seemingly intent on denying any possibility of goodness or
redemption.

Pope Gregory XVII is clearly meant to be based on
Burgess's ideas about Pope John XXIII. Both men believed
in man's ultimate goodness, or at least this is what Burgess
feels was the result of much of Pope John's teachings and
public avowals. Pope Gregory is another believer in the
Pelagian heresy: man's essential goodness overshadows the
"Augustinian doctrine of his natural depravity." As a consequence, evil is a force external to man's basic goodness
and dignity: "He never had any doubt about the externality
of evil, and this is what made him so formidable . . . evil
is not in us but in the Powers of Darkness that harry us."
Therefore "evil is wholly external, entirely a diabolic mo-
nopoly. Evil is exorcizable." Carlo built his priestly career
on the successful exorcisms of evil spirits, pitting his strong
and unyielding will against those demonic forces. As a
shrewd, overweight gambler and glutton, Carlo has enjoyed
life's sensual pleasures—all but the sins of the flesh—but

his belief in external evil and the saving power of a reformed Catholic Church, based on some quasi-Marxist, quasi-Christian ecumenical philosophy, is unshakeable.

Kenneth Toomey, that "pederastic purveyor of shopgirl vomit," given to a literature of "easy thrills, crude chronology, and comfortingly flaccid language," and one of Burgess's most interesting and mercurial characters, sees himself as immoral, anarchic, agnostic, and faithless. Piety for him is impossible: "Writers of fiction . . . can never be really devout or pious. We lie for a living." Suggestively based on the lives of Noel Coward and Somerset Maugham Toomey regards himself as excluded from the faithful because of his irrepressible homosexuality. Guilt consumes him; "The worms of various kinds of guilt—at my sexual aberrancy, mediocre money-making prose, failure of faith," eat away at his consciousness: "My destiny is to live in a state of desire both church and state condemn and to grow sourly rich in the purveying of a debased commodity." He feels himself pilloried between two Gods, "the God of my nature and the God of orthodox morality." In his moral confusion, he alternatively sees himself as having made a choice, "a healthy act of wicked free will" in his homosexual carryings on, or as having been unable to choose his fate: "It is not a thing a man would want to choose. Not in a world like this, which looks with horror on it." An overwrought sentimentality, however, undermines his moral seriousness, for words such as "home," "duty," and "faith," when uttered, cause him to weep uncontrollably. A nostalgic sentimentality underlies his cynical rationalism.

Toomey's experiences lead him to believe that evil inhabits the human soul: "Man had not been tainted from without by the prince of the power of the air. The evil was all in him and he was beyond hope of redemption . . . Man was not God's creation, that was certain. God alone knew from what suppurating primordial dungheap man had arisen." God created evil, so that man could have the free will to choose, and life itself reflects the wartorn battlefield of that

choice: "The sole reality was the electricity of opposition
. . . You were doomed to take sides." In the long run,
Toomey decides, "life is a mystery and God probably does
not exist." Burgess's Manichean battlelines between the Pope
and the homosexual purveyor of popular fiction are clearly
drawn.

Since Toomey narrates his own memoirs, the world of
Earthly Powers is clearly his creation. He exclaims, "I can
do no more than transcribe memory," and since "all memories
are disordered," he can present things as he will. He
acknowledges that "I can't accept that a work of fiction should
be either immoral or moral. It should merely show the world
as it is and have no moral bias," and yet he admits to
admiring "the dialectic of fiction" in which "the evil is as
cogent as the good." All is relative in his world, a point of
view which necesarily undermines Carlo's spiritual concerns.
Toomey adds that "feelings are always a most difficult thing
to convey," adhering to his detached and rationalistic view
of the world, and yet we know exactly what he feels about
ultimate truths and beliefs.

Toomey's style is light, swift, and clipped. He writes
cleverly about food, sex, literary and political fashions,
clothes, manners and all kinds of minutiae that come his
way. Perhaps this is because of his homosexual persuasion,
for he describes a homosexual's language as "brittle yet
sometimes excruciatingly precise." Life becomes a series of
little ceremonies, of exquisite gestures and postures, of
campy affectations and delights. These brittle occasions, in
which the details of a dinner or the descriptions of a dress
often overwhelm the more subtle distinctions between characters and personalities, conjure up finally an unrelenting
picture of loneliness, ennui, and despair. Feelings are
reduced to sentiments; love becomes a mere gesture, a
carefully ironic pose. Toomey's reminiscences about living
in the twentieth century capture many facets of that century,
but at times, in long pallid stretches of insignificant detail,
he can become a bore.

However deft and precise, Toomey's style often appears superficial and inconsequential. At one point he whines, "What is the human memory playing at, that it can hold such inanities and forget great lines by Goethe?" What, indeed! At another point Toomey, flying above the Swiss Alps, looks down upon them and describes them as "ruined pastry." It's a clever image but an extremely superficial one. Such an image deflates the mountains themselves. No sense of majesty or power inhabits that image of them. Toomey describes only an immediate glimpse of the surfaces of the world he looks out upon. And it is a world deprived of any inherent force or glory. He flattens the world around him and reduces it to clever patter.

Toomey describes Joyce's art as one that recreates "naked factualities of time and place (the better to fix some extraordinary, to use Jim Joyce's term, epiphany)." There are few epiphanies in Toomey's world, simply because his descriptions are not naked enough. He goes for the arch one-liner, the sardonic and comical *bon mot*. Such a style can become ponderous and perilous in a novel which is as long and involved as *Earthly Powers*.

Toomey's is a totally secularized world. No spirits inhabit it. No unexplained or mysterious forces work through it. His own life appears splintered and disconnected, an almost random series of episodes and clever conversations with no overarching thread or point. Circumstances generate coincidences. Chance collisions of people and places pop up here and there. Death, disease, sexual passion, and ultimate betrayal stalk his flat landscape, and there seems to be no possible release from it whatsoever.

In Toomey's world, the world of *Earthly Powers*, Carlo's spiritual concerns emerge as long-winded sermons, undramatic lectures, lumps of theoretical and abstract musings. Carlo's case is lost before it even begins. He's reduced to the cant and rant of a willful priest, whom Toomey can in no way believe in. The Pope becomes a straw man, a pompous purveyor of religious ideas that the world of the novel undercuts at every turn. Despite his girth and his garrulous convictions, Carlo is a disembodied ghost in a world which recognizes only the reality of a white wine or a stuffed pheasant, never the reality of the spirit.

Toomey experiences no shock of recognition. His view of the world remains unchanged. Carlo's reforms have killed his nephew, his nephew's wife, and his grand-niece. Carlo himself miraculously saved the child who grew up to be God Manning. The world is evil. The spirit existing in it produces only evil. Man's free will allows him to choose evil again and again in a modern world corrupted by secular ideologies, sexual perversion, and superficial pleasures.

Burgess's world in *Earthly Powers*, as experienced and described by Kenneth Toomey, remains a world of surfaces and momentary distractions. It lacks ultimate significance. It remains pointless and disconnected, while Carlo's long and tedious conversations and pronouncements try desperately to prove that it might be otherwise. Perhaps the discrepancy between Toomey's secular feelings and quasi-spiritual thoughts may be Burgess's own. And if the spiritual does not operate in the material world, why spend so much time on the proposition in the first place? The novel's imbalance—Carlo plays a mere echo to Toomey's fully realized bitchery and gloom—unbalances Burgess's vision: the sides in this Manichean struggle are decidedly unequal. The Devil occupies this land of snide asides and sexual hijinx. God is dead, so why even talk about him? Yet here is no ultimate nightmare realm—perhaps the true Burgess landscape—as terrifyingly recreated as it was in *A Clockwork Orange*. In *Earthly Powers*—"this bulky . . . novel," a description Toomey applies to his own final fictional work— "one hears the cackling of the goose more often than the unlocking of the cygnic throat." The cackling—brittle, funny, bitter—goes on too long, but it does produce one of Burgess's most inventive novels and a heady apotheosis of his themes and obsessions.

7

•••

The Game of Art

Burgess has often spoken about life's being a game:

God had no necessity to create the world . . . He must have created it to amuse himself, not out of necessity, because the ludic element has nothing to do with necessity. It's just an extra. This I accept. The important things in life are games, are ludic . . . I mean, nature gets on with her own or of sustaining us, but as for the rest of the things we do, it must be ludic.[1]

In *1985* he reiterates his point: "The practice of love is, we may say, ludic: it has to be approached like a game." Man's humanity and creativity lie in the fact that "he's remarkably ingenious."

Burgess's sense of the game pervades his fiction. To play games, exploit myths, structure realistic novels around all kinds of war games, musical patterns, fables, and legends, is to create one's own independence, experience one's delight in his imagination. Language itself becomes a game, emanating as it does mysteriously from the unconscious shape of the imagination and mind: to grapple with it, stretch and explore it, is to grapple with the mind's ability to create. The choice of a particular structure, a form, assists the writer in coming to grips with his themes. The function of playing the game is to see how far it will carry you into some genuine revelation of insight.

Both game and myth partake of ritual and ceremony, forms of experience that lay very close to Burgess's lapsed-

Catholic, modernistic heart. Thus the sense of the writer as mythmaker and game player—the artist as conscious conjuror—pervades his vision. In his interviews he repeats again and again his interest in art as pure form:

What I want to make is not novels so much as prose structures . . . no moral, perhaps, no real plot even—in which the laws of probability can be suspended and in which you end up with a structure; something which you weigh in your hand and look at as you look at a Tiffany jewel, which gives pleasure as an artifact.[2]

So I oscillate between a hankering after pure form and a realization that literature is probably valuable because it *says things*.[3]

What Burgess's novels seem to say repeatedly is what Enderby in the Enderby novels proclaims, that guilt is "creation's true dynamo." Burgess has always maintained that "guilt's a good thing," equating it almost wholly with the nature of the human condition: "It's when you get rid of this very human quality of guilt that you lose a great deal of humanity." One critic has perceptively suggested how great a toll these feelings of ineradicable guilt may have taken:

Successful author though he is, he seems unhappy, the troubled lapsed Catholic, a man who has found a manner of mingled humour and cynicism to cover a near-despair for himself and for society. He regrets very much that he started writing novels only in his late thirties, but, more noteworthy, talk keeps returning to the slow death of his first wife from cirrhosis.[4]

Guilt, loneliness, isolation, and corruption stalk the landscapes of Burgess's novels. History embodies them all: politics, sex, and human betrayal reveal these qualities over and over again. The comic form of these novels, however, is quite another thing.

Burgess once wrote, "I see myself as a creature of gloom and sobriety, but my books reflect a sort of clown."[5] He is, for the most part, a comic and satiric writer, or as he himself has put it, "a comic writer, malgre moi."[6] He views the modern world as a chaotic, ambiguous place, fallen away—

like himself?—from the solid, moral virtures and values of
the past, and yet the sheer exuberance and delight, both in
his style and in his crazy-guilt plots, comes through. Burgess
has admitted:

I was surprised when the novel, the first novel I wrote, was regarded
as a funny novel. It came as quite a shock . . . it was in fact comic;
and I've *never* deliberately sat down since to write a funny novel,
but if I think of working on a plot seriously, comedy breaks in. I
exploit coincidence and exaggeration and that sort of thing.[7]

Burgess's plots have a tendency to twitch and gyrate, absurd
episodes tumbling one upon the other. They're roller-coaster
rides, filled with coincidence, mistaken identities, and
labyrinthine journeys. These coincidences, parallel situations, and outrageous circumstances become cyclical, repetitive, and are often suddenly transformed, suggesting the
possibility that all is not lost, that situations and even guilt
itself can be redeemed or at least partially transcended. In
a few pages a new circumstance, another coincidence, a shift
in perspective will occur, and the realm of guilt and isolation
may be miraculously overcome. Comedy, however bleak,
relies on such cycles and transformations.

At the center of these outrageous, almost ramshackle
tales lies one harried soul, struggling for some way out, trying
to seek some accommodation with ultimate meaning and
personal belief. Burgess's description of Saul Bellow's maturer
work may best describe his own: "The delineation of a
complex dissatisfied personality, a heaving centre with a
periphery glittering with near-hallucinatory detail. Man seeking self-definition is plot enough."[8] In Burgess's case the
rollicking plot often overshadows the personality of the man
at the center. The main character registers dissatisfaction,
but only in rare instances—such as Enderby, Alex, and
Toomey, and to a lesser degree Burgess's Napoleon and
Shakespeare—does he reveal any deep human complexities.
His character is often sacrificed to the comic coincidences
and gerrymandered structure of the plot. Certainly such a

theme can be treated tragically, but all of Burgess's authorial inventions—his style, his plots, his structures—provide the necessary distance to treat them, and his characters, comically.

Burgess's comedy raises some difficult questions. Often there seems to be a separation in his work between his intellectual grasp of a theme or idea and his emotional response to that theme or idea. Perhaps Burgess's sixteen years as a teacher may account for this, the sacrificing of character and honest emotion to theme and a specific thesis. Many of the novels delight and instruct, but they often fail to capture the heart of the matter. One recognizes the lines and shapes of his elaborate designs and structures, but they often seem superficial and thin as if he'd drawn the lines of his vision but failed to color it in. This is not necessarily true of comedy in general, but it does seem to be true of Burgess's comedies in particular.

Burgess may have used these mythic and comic devices as an attempt to overcome his own deep-seated feelings of guilt. To avoid what seems to be his most obsessive subject, to surround it with artifice and game, may account for the split between his verbal wit, his "throw-away" plots, his whirl of coincidence and design, and the very real Manichean concern about the nature of reality and moral choice. It's as if Burgess chose these particular forms for his novels to take the sting of guilt out of their content, to defuse the forces of guilt and isolation which seem to consume his characters. Their actions, then, become gestures in a game, self-consious postures in a comic whirligig of modern angst and alienation.

The price, however, in such an approach is that such other emotions as love, joy, and terror are also defused. The landscape flattens, and truth becomes not a passionate conviction dredged up from the soul of full-bodied characters, but a windy lecture in a world where nobody else is listening. Perhaps the force of guilt has crushed the fragile bloom of love in Burgess's view. And in order to assuage such ferocious and dark feelings, ritual has replaced real emotion. The urge to cleanse oneself in an act of contrition and deliverance has surpassed the need to create the emotional and passionate fullness of love, grief, and other human feelings.

When the artist, the mythmaker, the poet, and the word-player become the focus of a novel—when love and language become inseparable—Burgess's art triumphs. His best characters are men like himself—Enderby, the poet, and even Alex, the droog, who in a brutal futuristic world, still likes to "shine artistic." And Napoleon and Shakespeare come alive with their vast visions of humanity and expert enjoyment of language, gamesmanship, sexual appetite, and irrepressible spirits. Even some of the lesser characters, such as Denis Hillier and J. W. Denham and Kenneth Toomey, share his delight in language and concern about moral values in the contemporary world. When the single dogged consciousness of the artist occupies Burgess's energies in a novel, the vision of restorative, redemptive powers of art and language blossom fully, no matter how brutal the world which surrounds it continues to be.

In the portrayal of each of these characters, Burgess does not by-pass human frailty, disease, and guilt; in each, he confronts these fully, suggesting the very real possibility of redemption and fulfillment—especially in art and in his own Manichean "faith"—that may grow out of the very human soil in which they are planted. This is his triumph. In playing serious but comic games, in devising new myths or replaying old ones, in constantly celebrating the continuous display of man's imagination and creativity through word and deed, Burgess views the artist as a man capable of constructing his own salvation. It doesn't always work. In his best novels, however, he convinces us it can.

Notes

1. THE CATHOLIC EXILE

1. Anthony Burgess, interview with the author in Monaco, July 7 and 11, 1978. Subsequent quotations, unless otherwise indicated, are from the interview.
2. John Archer Jackson, *The Irish in Britain* (London: Routledge and Kegan Paul, 1963), p. 39; cited below as Jackson.
3. Jackson, p. 113.
4. Jackson, p. 146.
5. L. P. Curtis, Jr., *Anglo-Saxons and Celts: A Study of Anti-Irish Prejudice in Victorian England* (Bridgeport: University of Bridgeport, 1968), p. 44; cited below as Curtis.
6. Quoted by Curtis, p. 77.
7. This is the general thesis of Philip Mason, *Prospero's Magic: Some Thoughts on Class and Race* (London: Oxford University Press, 1962); cited below as Mason.
8. Mason, p. 123.
9. Anthony Burgess, *ReJoyce* (New York: Norton, 1965), p. 56; cited below as *ReJoyce*.
10. *ReJoyce*, p. 83.
11. Interview with Anthony Burgess, *The Paris Review Interviews: Writers at Work (Fourth Series)*, ed. by George Plimpton and introduced by Wilfrid Sheed (New York: Penguin, 1977), p. 345; cited below as *Paris*.
12. Anthony Burgess, "Manicheans," *Times Literary Supplement*, no. 3340 (March 3, 1966), p. 153.
13. *Paris*, p. 346.
14. Charles T. Bunting, "An Interview in New York with Anthony Burgess," *Studies in the Novel* (Spring, 1973), p. 521; cited below as Bunting.
15. Bunting, p. 524.

16. Anthony Burgess, quoted by Lila Chalpin, "Anthony Burgess's Gallows Humor in Dystopia," *Texas Quarterly* (1973), p. 84.

17. Anthony Burgess, quoted by Walter Sullivan, "Death Without Tears: Anthony Burgess and the Dissolution of the West," *The Hollins Critic* (April, 1969), p. 10.

18. *Paris*, p. 347.

19. *Paris*, p. 354.

20. Anthony Burgess, Introduction to *A Vision of Battlements* (New York: Norton, 1965), pp. 7–8: cited below as *Vision*.

21. *Vision*, p. 8.

22. *ReJoyce*, p. 27.

23. The new values of contemporary times are explained and defined as "technique information," "participatoriness," "transitoriness," and "self-indulgence" by Daniel Snowman, *Britain and America: An Interpretation of Their Culture, 1945–1975* (New York: New York University Press, 1977).

24. Paul Boytinck, *Anthony Burgess: A Bibliography* (London: Norwood Editions, 1977), p. 69.

2. THE CLASH OF EAST AND WEST

1. Anthony Burgess, "Epilogue: Conflict and Confluence" in *Urgent Copy: Literary Studies* (New York: Norton, 1968), p. 270; cited below as "Conflict."

2. "Conflict," pp. 268–69.

3. "Conflict," p. 272.

4. "Conflict," p. 270.

5. "Conflict," p. 270.

6. Anthony Burgess, review of *The Honorable Schoolboy* by John Le Carré, *New York Times Book Review* (Sept. 25, 1977), p. 45.

7. Thomas Churchill, "An Interview with Anthony Burgess," *Malahat Review*, XVII (1971), p. 119; cited below as Churchill.

8. "Conflict," p. 269.

9. Anthony Burgess, Introduction to *A Vision of Battlements* (New York: Norton, 1965), p. 8.

10. Churchill, p. 119.

11. Robert K. Morris, *The Consolation of Ambiguity* (Columbia: University of Missouri Press, 1971).

12. Anthony Burgess, interview with the author in Monaco, July 7 and 11, 1978. Subsequent quotations, unless otherwise indicated, are from this interview.

13. William H. Pritchard, "The Novels of Anthony Burgess," *The Massachusetts Review* (1966), p. 539.

3.   A MANICHEAN DUOVERSE

1. Anthony Burgess, interview with the author in Monaco, July 7 and 11, 1978. Subsequent quotations, unless otherwise indicated, are from this interview.

2. Charles T. Bunting, "An Interview in New York with Anthony Burgess," *Studies in the Novel* (Spring, 1973), p. 520; cited below as Bunting.

3. Interview with Anthony Burgess, *The Paris Review Interviews: Writers at Work (Fourth Series)*, ed. by George Plimpton and introduced by Wilfrid Sheed (New York: Penguin, 1977), p. 347; cited below as *Paris*.

4. Duncan Greenlees, *The Gospel of the Prophet Mani* (Adyar, Medras, India: The Theosophical Publishing House, 1956), p. vii; cited below as Greenlees.

5. Greenlees, p. clxxxvi.

6. George Widengren, *Mani and Manichaeism* (London: Weidenfeld and Nicolson, 1965), p. 62; cited below as Widengren.

7. Steven Runciman, *The Medieval Manichee* (Cambridge, England: Cambridge University Press, 1960), p. 179.

8. Discussed by Widengren.

9. *Paris*, p. 352.

10. Anthony Burgess, "Epilogue: Conflict and Confluence" in *Urgent Copy: Literary Studies* (New York: Norton, 1968), p. 272.

11. William P. Fitzpatrick, "Black Marketeers and Manichees: Anthony Burgess' Cold War Novels," *West Virginia University Philological Papers* (1974), p. 85; cited below as Fitzpatrick.

12. Fitzpatrick, p. 90.

13. In his short article, "No. 51: Burgess's *The Wanting Seed*," *The Explicator* (March, 1973), John Cullinan shows that Burgess's description of the sea at the end of the novel is in fact a literal prose translation from the last two stanzas of Paul

Valéry's poem, "Le Cimetiere Marin." The poem, which celebrates "the intimate relation between life and death" and "Valéry's affirmation of the sea as life force," clearly parallels Burgess's belief in "a necessary fecundity which the state's harsh policy violates."

14. Lila Chalpin, "Anthony Burgess's Gallows Humor in Dystopia," *Texas Quarterly* (1973), 16:83.

15. "According to Burgess himself, 'The title of the book comes from an old London expression—which I first heard from a very old Cockney in 1945: "He's as queer as a clockwork orange" (queer meaning mad, not faggish). I liked the phrase because of its yoking of tradition and surrealism, and I determined some day to use it. It has rather specialized meanings for me. I worked in Malaya, where *orang* means a human being, and this connotation is attached to the word, as well as more obvious anagrams, like organ and organise (an *orange* is, a man is, but the State wants the living organ to be turned into a mechanical emanation of itself)." Anthony Burgess, "Juice From a Clockwork Orange," *Rolling Stone*, No. 110 (June 8, 1972), p. 52–53, as quoted in Ken Anderson, "A Note on *A Clockwork Orange*," *Notes on Contemporary Literature*, 2 (1972), p. 6.

16. Thomas Churchill, "An Interview With Anthony Burgess," *Malahat Review*, XVII (1971), p. 110; hereafter cited as Churchill.

17. "The narrative invention was magical, the characters were bizarre and exciting, the ideas were brilliantly developed, and, equally important, the story was of a size and density that could be adapted to film without simplifying it or stripping it to the bone." Stanley Kubrick as quoted in Norman Kagan, *The Cinema of Stanley Kubrick* (New York: Grove Press, 1972), p. 167; hereafter cited as Kagan.

18. Churchill, p. 109.

19. This example of Alex's artistic consciousness and style is perceptively discussed in Richard P. Fulkerson, "Teaching *A Clockwork Orange*," *CEA Critic*, XXXVII (1974).

20. Churchill, p. 110.

21. Bunting, p. 511.

22. Anthony Burgess, "Letter from England," *The Hudson Review*, XX (1967), p. 458, as quoted in John J. Stinson, "Anthony

Burgess: Novelist on the Margin," *Journal of Popular Culture*,
VII (1973), p. 150.

23. William H. Pritchard, "The Novels of Anthony Burgess,"
Massachusetts Review, VII (1966), p. 534.

24. Basil Gilbert, "Kubrick's Marmalade: The Art of Violence,"
Meanjiin Quarterly, XXXIII (1974), p. 161.

25. Kagan, p. 167

26. *Paris*, p. 338.

27. Bunting, p. 525.

28. Bunting, p. 525.

4. THE MYTHIC METHOD

1. Anthony Burgess, interview with the author in Monaco, July
7 and 11, 1978. Subsequent quotations, unless otherwise
indicated, are from this interview.

2. Anthony Burgess, *Ernest Hemingway and His World* (New
York: Charles Scribner's Sons, 1978), pp. 56–57.

3. Anthony Burgess, *ReJoyce* (New York: Norton, 1968), p. 87;
cited below as *ReJoyce*.

4. Charles T. Bunting, "An Interview in New York with Anthony
Burgess," *Studies in the Novel* (Spring, 1973), p. 510; cited
below as Bunting.

5. *ReJoyce*, p. 87.

6. Anthony Burgess, "Ulysses: How Well Has It Worn?" in
Urgent Copy (New York: Norton, 1968), p. 83.

7. Guy Davenport, "Post-Modern and After," *The Hudson Review*
(Spring, 1978), p. 236.

8. *ReJoyce*, p. 47.

9. Anthony Burgess, "What is a Novel?" in *The Novel Now* (New
York: Norton, 1967), p. 15.

10. Interview with Anthony Burgess, *The Paris Review Interviews:
Writers at Work (Fourth Series)*, ed. by George Plimpton and
introduced by Wilfred Sheed (New York: Penguin, 1977), p.
354; cited below as *Paris*.

11. *ReJoyce*, p. 166.

12. Northrop Frye, cited by Brian Murdock, "The Overpopulated
Wasteland: Myth in Anthony Burgess' *The Wanting Seed*."
Revue des Langues Vivantes, v. 39 (1973), p. 216.

13. Anthony Burgess, *The Doctor Is Sick* (London: Heinemann, 1960), p. 50.
14. Anthony Burgess, "If Oedipus has read his Levi-Strauss," in *Urgent Copy* (New York: Norton, 1968), p. 258; cited below as "Oedipus."
15. "Oedipus," p. 258.
16. "Oedipus," p. 259.
17. Thomas Churchill, "An Interview with Anthony Burgess," *Malahat Review*, XVII (1971), p. 126.
18. Anatole Broyard's review of *Vladimir Nabokov: A Tribute* (New York; Morrow, 1980), ed. by Peter Quennell, *The New York Times*, April 15, 1980, C15.
19. John J. Stinson, "*Nothing Like the Sun:* The Faces in Bella Cohen's Mirror," *Journal of Modern Literature* (1976), p. 146.
20. Jonathan Raban, "What Shall We Do About Anthony Burgess," *Encounter* (Autumn, 1974), p. 86.
21. Malcolm Page, "Anthony Burgess: The Author as Performer," *West Coast Review* (1970), p. 23.
22. *ReJoyce*, p. 166.
23. Bunting, p. 505.
24. *Paris*, p. 334.
25. *Paris*, p. 344.
26. For an excellent close reading of *Napoleon Symphony*, see John Mowat, "Joyce's Contemporary: A Study of Anthony Burgess' *Napoleon Symphony*," *Contemporary Literature* (Spring, 1978), p. 180–95.

5. THE RITUALS OF LANGUAGE

1. Anthony Burgess's review of *Joyce's Voices* by Hugh Kenner, "Bloom and Friends," *The New York Times Book Review* (December 10, 1978), p. 14; cited below as *Times*.
2. Anthony Burgess, interview with the author in Monaco, July 7 and 11, 1978. Subsequent quotations, unless otherwise indicated, are from this interview.
3. *Times*, p. 14.
4. Anthony Burgess, *Shakespeare* (New York: Knopf, 1970), p. 43; cited below as *Shakespeare*.
5. Interview with Anthony Burgess, *The Paris Review Interviews:*

Writers at Work (Fourth Series), ed. by George Plimpton and introduced by Wilfred Sheed (New York: Penguin, 1977), p. 355; cited below as *Paris*.

6. Anthony Burgess, *ReJoyce* (New York: Norton, 1968), p. 21; cited below as *ReJoyce*.

7. *ReJoyce*, p. 50.

8. Ibid.

9. Anthony Burgess, "The Postwar American Novel: A View from the Periphery," in *Urgent Copy* (New York: Norton, 1968), p. 129.

10. Anthony Burgess, *The Eve of St. Venus* (New York: Norton, 1979), p. 2.

11. Ibid.

12. John Cullinan, "Anthony Burgess' 'The Muse: A Sort of SF Story,'" *Studies in Short Fiction* (1972), p. 216.

13. *Paris*, p. 340.

14. *Shakespeare*, p. 11.

15. Robert E. Wood, "Sexuality and the Muse in Anthony Burgess's Enderby Novels and *Nothing Like the Sun*," unpublished paper, Georgia Institute of Technology.

16. Bruce M. Firestone, "Love's Labor's Lost: Sex and Art in Two Novels by Anthony Burgess" *Iowa Review* (summer, 1977), p. 51.

17. *Shakespeare*, p. 43.

18. William P. Fitzpatrick, "The Sworn Enemy of Pop: Burgess' Mr. Enderby," *The Bulletin of the West Virginia Association of College English Teachers*, v. 1 (Spring, 1974), p. 29; cited below as Fitzpatrick.

19. Fitzpatrick, p. 28.

6. THE LATE NOVELS

1. Benjamin DeMott, review of *Man of Nazareth* by Anthony Burgess, *The New York Times Book Review*, April 15, 1979, p. 20.

7. THE GAME OF ART

1. Anthony Burgess, interview with the author in Monaco, July 7 and 11, 1978. Subsequent quotations, unless otherwise indicated, are from this interview.

2. Charles T. Bunting, "An Interview in New York with Anthony Burgess," *Studies in the Novel* (Spring, 1973), p. 513.

3. Interview with Anthony Burgess, *The Paris Review Interviews: Writers at Work (Fourth Series)*, ed. by George Plimpton introduced by Wilfrid Sheed (New York: Penguin, 1977), p. 348; cited below as *Paris*.

4. Malcolm Page, "Anthony Burgess: The Author as Performer" *West Coast Review* (1970), p. 21.

5. Anthony Burgess, "Epilogue: Conflict and Confluence" in *Urgent Copy: Literary Studies* (New York: Norton, 1968), p. 369; cited below as *Urgent Copy*.

6. *Paris*, p. 357.

7. Thomas Churchill, "An Interview with Anthony Burgess" *Malahat Review*, XVII (1971), p. 107.

8. Anthony Burgess, "The Jew as American" in *Urgent Copy: Literary Studies* (New York: Norton, 1968), p. 135.

Bibliography

1.   WORKS BY ANTHONY BURGESS

Time for a Tiger. London: Heinemann, 1956.

The Enemy in the Blanket. London: Heinemann, 1958.

Beds in the East. London: Heinemann, 1959.

The Doctor Is Sick. London: Heinemann, 1960.

The Right to an Answer. London: Heinemann, 1960.

Devil of a State. London: Heinemann, 1961.

One Hand Clapping. London: P. Davies, 1961 (as Joseph Kell).

The Worm and the Ring. London: Heinemann, 1961.

A Clockwork Orange. London: Heinemann, 1962.

The Wanting Seed. London: Heinemann, 1962.

Honey for the Bears. London: Heinemann, 1963.

Inside Mr. Enderby. London: Heinemann, 1963 (as Joseph Kell).

The Eve of St. Venus. London: Sidgwick and Jackson,
      Language Made Plain. London: Faber, 1965.

Nothing Like the Sun. London: Heinemann, 1964.

Here Comes Everybody. London: Faber, 1965.

A Vision of Battlements. London: Sidgwick and Jackson, 1965.

ReJoyce. New York: Ballantine Books, 1965.

The Long Day Wanes. New York: Norton, 1965. Contains the three
      Malayan novels.

Tremor of Intent. London: Heinemann, 1966.

The Novel Now. London: Faber and Faber, 1967.

Urgent Copy: Literary Studies. London: Cape, 1968.

Enderby Outside. London: Heinemann, 1968.

Enderby. New York: Norton, 1968. Contains *Inside Mr. Enderby*
      and *Enderby Outside*.

Shakespeare. London: Cape, 1970.

MF. London: Cape, 1971.

Joysprick: An Introduction to the Language of James Joyce. London: Deutsch, 1973.

Napoleon Symphony. London: Cape, 1974.

The Clockwork Testament or Enderby's End. New York: Knopf, 1975.

Moses: A Narrative. New York: Stonehill, 1976.

Beard's Roman Women. New York: McGraw-Hill, 1976.

Abba Abba. Boston: Little, Brown, 1977.

1982. London: Heinemann, 1978; New York: Little, Brown, 1978.

Ernest Hemingway and His World. New York: Charles Scribner's Sons, 1978.

Man of Nazareth. New York: McGraw-Hill, 1979.

Earthly Powers. New York: Simon and Schuster, 1980.

2.   WORKS ABOUT ANTHONY BURGESS

Aggeler, Geoffrey, *Anthony Burgess: The Artist as Novelist*. University, ALA.: University of Alabama Press, 1979.

———, "Between God and Notgod: Anthony Burgess' *Tremor of Intent*." *Malahat Review* 17: 90–102, 1971.

———, "The Comic Art of Anthony Burgess." *Arizona Quarterly* 25: 234–51, 1969.

———, "Enderby Immolatus: Burgess' *The Clockwork Testament*." *Malahat Review* 44: 22–24, 29–46, 1977.

———, "A Ghostly Entertainment: *Beard's Roman Women*." *Modern British Literature* 2: 169–75, 1977.

———, "Incest and the Artist: Anthony Burgess's *MF* as Summation." *Modern Fiction Studies* 18: 529–43, 1972–73.

———, "Mr. Enderby and Mr. Burgess," *Malahat Review* 10: 104–10, 1969.

———, "Pelagius and Augustine in the Novels of Anthony Burgess." *English Studies* 55: 43–55, 1974.

———, "A Prophetic Acrostic in Anthony Burgess's *Nothing Like the Sun*." *Notes and Queries* 21: 136, 1974.

———, "A Wagnerian Affirmation: Anthony Burgess's *The Worm and the Ring*." *Western Humanities Review* 27: 401–10, 1973.

Anderson, Ken, "A Note on *A Clockwork Orange*." *Notes on Contemporary Literature* 2: 2–7, 1972.

Bradley, Edward M. "Hand-Touching in the *Oedipus Tyrannus*" (adaptation by Burgess). *par rapport* 2: 3–8, 1979.

Brophy, Elizabeth, "*A Clockwork Orange:* English and Nadsat." *Notes On Contemporary Literature* 2: 4–6, 1972.

Bunting, Charles T., "An Interview in New York with Anthony Burgess." *Studies in the Novel* 5: 504–29, 1973.

Carson, Julie, "Pronominalization in *A Clockwork Orange*." *Papers on Language and Literature* 12: 200–205, 1976.

Chalpin, Lila, "Anthony Burgess's Gallows Humor in Dystopia." *Texas Quarterly* 16: 73–84, 1973.

Churchill, Thomas, "An Interview with Anthony Burgess." *Malahat Review* 17: 103–27, 1971.

Connelly, Wayne C., "Optimism in Burgess's *A Clockwork Orange*." *Extrapolation* 14: 25–29, 1972.

Cullinan, John, "Anthony Burgess' *A Clockwork Orange:* Two Versions." *English Language Notes* 9: 287–92, 1972.

———, "Anthony Burgess's 'The Muse: A Sort of SF Story.'" *Studies in Short Fiction* 9: 213–20, 1972.

———, "Burgess' *The Wanting Seed*." *Explicator*, 31: Item 51, 1973.

———, "An Interview with Anthony Burgess." In *Writers at Work: The Paris Review Interviews*, ed. by George Plimpton and introduced by Wilfrid Sheed. (New York: The Viking Press, 1976), pp. 323–59.

Davis, Earle, "'Laugh Now—Think Later!' The Genius of Anthony Burgess." *Kansas Magazine*, 7–12, 1968.

DeVitis, A. A., *Anthony Burgess* (New York: Twayne, 1972).

Dimeo, Steven, "The Ticking of an Orange." *Riverside Quarterly* 5: 318–21, 1973.

Elsaesser, Thomas, "Screen Violence: Emotional Structure and Ideological Function in 'A Clockwork Orange.'" In *Approaches to Popular Culture*, ed. by C. W. E. Bigsby. London: Edward Arnold, 1976, pp. 171–200.

Evans, Robert O., "Nadsat: The Argot and Its Implications in Anthony Burgess' *A Clockwork Orange*." *Journal of Modern Literature* 1: 406–10, 1971.

———, "The Nouveau Roman, Russian Dystopias, and Anthony Burgess." *Studies in the Literary Imagination* 6: 27–37, 1973.

Fiore, Peter A., "Milton and Kubrick: Eden's Apple or a Clockwork Orange." *CEA Critic* 35: 14–17, 1973.

Firestone, Bruce M., "Love's Labor's Lost: Sex and Art in Two Novels by Anthony Burgess." *Iowa Review* 8: 46–52, 1977.

Fitzpatrick, William P., "Black Marketeers and Manichees: Anthony Burgess' Cold War Novels." *West Virginia University Philological Papers* 21: 78–91, 1974.

———, "The Sworn Enemy of Pop: Burgess' Mr. Enderby." *The Bulletin of the West Virginia Association of College English Teachers* 1: 28–37, 1974.

Friedman, Melvin J., "Anthony Burgess and James Joyce: A Literary Confrontation." *Literary Criticism* 9: 71–83, 1971.

Fulkerson, Richard P., "Teaching *A Clockwork Orange*." *CEA Critic* 37: 8–10, 1974.

Gilbert, Basil, "Kubrick's Marmalade: The Art of Violence." *Meanjin Quarterly* 33: 157–62, 1974.

Isaacs, Neil D., "Unstuck in Time: *Clockwork Orange* and *Slaughterhouse-Five*." *Literature-Film Quarterly* 1: 122–31, 1973.

Johnson, Joseph, J., "Anthony Burgess, *MF*." In *Literary Annual* (New York: Salem Press, 1972), pp. 223–25.

Kateb, George, "Politics and Modernity: The Strategies of Desperation." *New Literary History* 3: 93–111, 1971.

Kennard, Jean, "*MF*: A Separable Meaning." *Riverside Quarterly* 6: 200–206, 1975.

Kennedy, Alan, comments on *A Clockwork Orange* in *The Protean Self: Dramatic Action in Contemporary Fiction*. (New York: Columbia University Press, 1974), pp. 21–23.

LeClair, Thomas, "Essential Opposition: The Novels of Anthony Burgess." *Critique: Studies in Modern Fiction* 12: 77–94, 1971.

Mathews, Richard, *The Clockwork Universe of Anthony Burgess*. (San Bernardino, CA: The Borgo Press, 1978).

McCracken, Samuel, "Novel Into Film; Novelist into Critic: *A Clockwork Orange* . . . Again." *Antioch Review* 32: 427–36, 1973.

Morris, Robert K., *The Consolations of Ambiguity: An Essay on the Novels of Anthony Burgess*. (Columbia: University of Missouri Press, 1971).

Mowat, John, "Joyce's Contemporary: A Study of Anthony Burgess' *Napoleon Symphony*." *Contemporary Literature* 19: 180–95, 1978.

Murdoch, Brian, "The Overpopulated Wasteland: Myth in Anthony

Burgess' *The Wanting Seed*." *Revue des Langues Vivantes* 39: 203–17, 1973.

Murray, William M., "Anthony Burgess on Apocalypse." *Iowa Review* 8: 37–45, 1977.

Page, Malcolm, "Anthony Burgess: The Author as Performer." *West Coast Review* 4: 21–24, 1970.

Pritchard, William H., "Burgess vs. Scholes." *Novel* 2: 164–67, 1969.

———, "The Novels of Anthony Burgess." *The Massachusetts Review* 7: 525–39, 1966.

———, "The Burgess Memorandum." *Partisan Review*, 319–23, Spring 1967.

Rabin, Jonathan, "What Shall We Do About Anthony Burgess?" *Encounter* 43: 83–88, 1974.

Rabinovitz, Rubin, "Mechanism vs. Organism: Anthony Burgess' *A Clockwork Orange*." *Modern Fiction Studies* 24: 538–41, 1978–79.

———, "Ethical Values in Anthony Burgess's *A Clockwork Orange*." *Studies in the Novel* 11: 43–50, 1979.

Reilly, Lemuel, "An Interview with Anthony Burgess." *Delaware Literary Review* 2: 48–55, 1973.

Saunders, Trevor J., "Plato's Clockwork Orange." *The Durham University Journal* 68: 113–17, 1976.

Sheldon, Leslie E. "Newspeak and Nadsat: The Disintegration of Language in *1984* and *A Clockwork Orange*." *Studies in Contemporary Satire: A Creative and Critical Journal* 6: 7–13, 1979.

Stinson, John J., "Anthony Burgess: Novelist on the Margin." *Journal of Popular Culture* 7: 136–51, 1973.

———, "The Manichee World of Anthony Burgess." *Renascence* 26: 38–47, 1973.

———, "*Nothing Like the Sun:* The Faces in Bella Cohen's Mirror." *Journal of Modern Literature* 5: 131–47, 1976.

———, "Waugh and Anthony Burgess: Some Notes Toward an Assessment of Influence and Affinities." *Evelyn Waugh Newsletter* 10: 11–12, 1976.

Sullivan, Walter, "Death Without Tears: Anthony Burgess and the Dissolution of the West." *The Hollins Critic* 6: 1–11, 1969.

Wilder, Thornton, Anthony Burgess, Arthur Miller, and Richard Wilbur. "Authors on Translators." *Translation* 2: 5–8, 1974.

Wood, Robert E., "Sexuality and the Muse in Anthony Burgess's Enderby Novels and *Nothing Like the Sun.*" Unpublished paper, Georgia Institute of Technology, Atlanta, Georgia.

Doctoral Dissertations on Burgess's Works:

Arnold, Voiza Olson, "Narrative Structure and the Readers Theatre Staging of *Nothing Like the Sun* by Anthony Burgess." University of Illinois, 1975.

Brown, Rexford G., "Conflict and Confluence: The Art of Anthony Burgess." University of Iowa, 1972.

Cullinan, John Thomas, "Anthony Burgess' Novels: A Critical Introduction." Columbia University, 1972.

Holte, Carlton Thomas, "Taming the Rock: Myth, Model and Metaphor in the Novels of Anthony Burgess." University of California (Davis), 1978.

Mablekos, Carole Marbes, "The Artist as Hero in the Novels of Joyce Cary, Laurence Durrell, and Anthony Burgess." Purdue University, 1974.

Moran, Kathryn L., "Utopias, Subtopias, Dystopias in the Novels of Anthony Burgess." Notre Dame, 1974.

Siciliano, Sam Joseph, "The Fictional Universe in Four Science Fiction Novels: Anthony Burgess's *A Clockwork Orange*, Ursula Le Guin's *The Word for World Is Forest*, Walter Miller's *A Canticle for Leibowitz*, and Roger Zelazny's *Creatures of Light and Darkness.*" University of Iowa, 1975.

Steffen, Nancy Lynn, "Burgess' World of Words." Brandeis University, 1978.

Stinson, John J., "The Uses of the Grotesque and Other Modes of Distortion: Philosophy and Implication in the Novels of Iris Murdoch, William Golding, Anthony Burgess, and J. P. Donleavy." New York University, 1971.

Wagner, Kenyon Lewis, "Anthony Burgess' Mythopoeic Imagination: A Study of Selected Novels (1956–1968)." Texas Tech University, 1974.

For a comprehensive bibliography of works by Anthony Burgess, see Paul Boytinck's "Anthony Burgess: A Bibliography," Norwood Editions, Second Edition, 1977. Also see Beverly R. David's

"Anthony Burgess: A Checklist (1956–1971)," *Twentieth Century Literature* 19: 181–88, 1973; and Carlton Holte's "Additions to Anthony Burgess: A Checklist (1956–1971), *Twentieth Century Literature* 20: 44–52, 1974.

Index

MODERN LITERATURE SERIES

In the same series (continued from page ii)